Library of
Davidson College

A Touch of Rhetoric
Ezra Pound's Malatesta Cantos

Studies in Modern Literature, No. 2

A. Walton Litz, General Series Editor
Professor of English
Princeton University

George Bornstein
Consulting Editor for Titles on Ezra Pound
Professor of English
University of Michigan

Other Titles in This Series

No. 1 *Faulkner's Uses of the Classics* — Joan M. Serafin

No. 3 *Wallace Stevens and Company: The Harmonium Years, 1913-1923* — Glen G. MacLeod

No. 7 *William Carlos Williams: A Poet in the American Theatre* — David A. Fedo

No. 9 *A Thought to be Rehearsed: Aphorism in Wallace Stevens's Poetry* — Beverly Coyle

No. 10 *Inverted Volumes Improperly Arranged: James Joyce and His Trieste Library* — Michael Patrick Gillespie

No. 12 *A Guide to the Prose Fiction of W.B. Yeats* — William H. O'Donnell

No. 21 *Kindled in the Flame: The Apocalyptic Scene in D.H. Lawrence* — Sarah Urang

A Touch of Rhetoric
Ezra Pound's Malatesta Cantos

by
Peter D'Epiro

UMI RESEARCH PRESS
Ann Arbor, Michigan

The Cantos of Ezra Pound. Copyright © 1934, 1937, 1940, 1948, 1950, 1956, 1959, 1962, 1963, 1965, 1966, 1968, 1970, 1971 by Ezra Pound. Copyright © 1969, 1972 by the Estate of Ezra Pound.

Pound/Joyce. Copyright © 1967 by Ezra Pound.

Guide to Kulchur. Copyright © 1970 by Ezra Pound. All Rights Reserved.

The Spirit of Romance. Copyright © 1968 by Ezra Pound.

ABC of Reading. Copyright 1934 by Ezra Pound.

Selected Letters, 1907-1941. Copyright © 1950 by Ezra Pound.

Literary Essays. Copyright 1918, 1920, 1935 by Ezra Pound.

Personae. Copyright 1926 by Ezra Pound.

Selected Prose, 1909-1965. Copyright © 1973 by the Estate of Ezra Pound.

Collected Early Poems. Copyright © 1976 by the Trustees of the Ezra Pound Literary Property Trust.

Gaudier-Brzeska. Copyright © 1970 by Ezra Pound. All Rights Reserved.

A Lume Spento and Other Early Poems. Copyright © 1967 by Ezra Pound. All Rights Reserved.

Previously unpublished material by Ezra Pound, Copyright © 1981 by the Trustees of the Ezra Pound Literary Property Trust. Published by permission of New Directions, agents.

All of the above reprinted by permission of New Directions Publishing Corporation.

Jefferson and/or Mussolini. Copyright 1935, 1936 by Ezra Pound; © renewed 1963 by Ezra Pound. Reprinted by permission of Liveright Publishing Corporation.

Copyright © 1983, 1981
Peter Francis D'Epiro
All rights reserved

Produced and distributed by
UMI Research Press
an imprint of
University Microfilms International
Ann Arbor, Michigan 48106

Library of Congress Cataloging in Publication Data

D'Epiro, Peter.
  A touch of rhetoric.

  (Studies in modern literature ; no. 2)
  Revision of thesis (Ph.D.)—Yale University, 1981.
  Bibliography: p.
  Includes index.
  1. Pound, Ezra, 1885-1972. Cantos. 2. Pound, Ezra, 1885-1972. Cantos—Criticism, Textual. 3. Malatesta, Sigismondo Pandolfo, signore di Rimini, 1417-1468, in fiction, drama, poetry, etc. 4. Outsiders in literature. I. Title. II. Series.

PS3531.O82C2844 1983   811'.52   83-5729
ISBN 0-8357-1404-7

For Dante D'Epiro
O fronda mia in che io compiacemmi
pur aspettando . . .

Frontispiece. Tempio Malatestiano, Rimini
Alinari/Editorial Photocolor Archives

Contents

Preface *ix*

List of Abbreviations *xi*

Introduction *xiii*

1 The Malatesta Manuscripts: Beginnings to the Watson Typescript *1*
    Itinerary of Pound's Work on the Malatesta Cantos
    The Malatesta Manuscripts: Pound's Reading Notes
    The Early Drafts before the Watson Typescript

2 From the Watson Typescript to the Final Version *33*

3 The Deflated Epic Style of the Malatesta Cantos *61*

4 The Malatesta Mystique in the Works of Ezra Pound *85*
    The Figure of the "Outsider" in Pound's Early Work
    Propertius and Mauberley: Major Visions of the Poet as Outsider
    The *Cantos*: From Outsider to Factive Personality . . . and Back Again

Appendix A: Major Textual Variants in the Published Versions of the Malatesta Cantos *115*

Appendix B: Some Sources for the Malatesta Cantos *119*

Appendix C: Pound and Eliot at Verona: A Passage from the Watson Typescript *123*

Appendix D: Allusions to the Malatesta Cantos in the *Cantos* of Ezra Pound *125 viii* *Contents*

Notes *131*

Selected Bibliography *151*

Index *155*

Preface

This study of the Malatesta Cantos is the first extended treatment of a poetic sequence whose main character remains one of Ezra Pound's most controversial heroes. In the course of working on the sources of these cantos, on the notes and drafts that led up to them, and on the significance of the "Malatesta-figure" in the Poundian canon, I came to understand why the poetic representation of this *condottiere* and temple-builder demanded that a new style be introduced into the *Cantos*—and why various tags from the Malatesta group keep recurring in Pound's poem, decades after the composition of Cantos 8–11. I have chosen to present my findings by discussing four main aspects of these cantos: their historical and historiographical background, the process of their composition, their stylistic and thematic implications, and their relationship with the rest of Pound's work. This procedure has enabled me to focus intensively on the Malatesta Cantos without, however, losing sight of Pound's total achievement, of which they form a small but important part.

The core of this book was a doctoral dissertation submitted to Yale University in March 1981. Since then, a number of articles have appeared (by Harper, D. Bornstein, and Kimpel and Eaves) that attest to a growing interest in the Malatesta Cantos—especially in their transmutation of historical materials into poetry. In addition, Daniel Bornstein is currently editing Broglio's *Cronaca*—an important source of these cantos—and I hear from Chicago that another book on the Malatesta sequence is in its early stages. And although the Romans would probably not "have called that an augury" (10/47), it's been heartening to me that the Pound journal, *Paideuma*, graces all of its back covers with the reproduction of a Sigismondo medallion. (When I had the pleasure of meeting Olga Rudge in 1980, she instructed me, with a twinkle in her eyes, to examine the medallion carefully, because "there's something wrong with it." Indeed, the medallionist had left out the first *s* from "Malatestis"—and inserted a pitifully tiny one at the last moment.)

I here wish to express my gratitude to Professor Louis L. Martz, who suggested that I work on the Malatesta Cantos and who directed me to the wealth of Poundian materials in Yale's Beinecke Library. His knowledge, patience, interest, and encouragement served as constant incentives to my getting "all of it down on paper" (11/51). I am grateful to Professor Walton Litz of Princeton University and Professor George Bornstein of the University of Michigan for including my book in this series. I thank Mary de Rachewiltz for her efforts in acquiring for the Beinecke a photocopy of Broglio's *Cronaca*. I wish to thank the New Directions Publishing Corporation for permission to quote from the published and unpublished writings of Ezra Pound. I am grateful to the Center for Study of Ezra Pound and His Contemporaries, Collection of American Literature, Beinecke Rare Book and Manuscript Library, Yale University, and to David E. Schoonover, the curator of the collection, for permission to quote from Pound's unpublished letters and manuscripts. I appreciate the help of Dr. James Sibley Watson, Jr., who provided me with copies of five of Pound's unpublished letters, and I thank Dr. Donald Gallup for suggesting that I contact Dr. Watson. Professor Christine Froula, one of the readers of my dissertation, wrote a report that provided me with a number of insights for revision. Lawrence Rainey set me thinking about some problems of chronology in Chapter 1, and Richard Jackson helped me polish a translation in Appendix B. Stephen Jones and the staff at the Beinecke are to be commended for their assistance in tracking down an assortment of materials.

Without the Italian I learned from my parents I should have found it quite difficult to wade through Pound's voluminous sources. I am extremely grateful to them for a lifetime's encouragement to read and write, to study and learn. And my love and appreciation go to Theresa Ann DeMattie, "the noblest Roman of them all" (or at least of those I've actually *met*).

New Haven
January 22, 1983

List of Abbreviations

The following abbreviations are used to refer to the works of Ezra Pound:

ABC:	*ABC of Reading*, New Directions Paperbook, 1960
ALS:	*A Lume Spento and Other Early Poems*, New Directions, 1965
CEP:	*Collected Early Poems*, ed. Michael King, New Directions, 1976
GK:	*Guide to Kulchur*, New Directions Paperbook, 1970
J/M:	*Jefferson and/or Mussolini*, Liveright Paperbook, 1970
LE:	*Literary Essays*, ed. T. S. Eliot, New Directions Paperbook, 1968
PERSONAE:	*Personae: The Collected Shorter Poems*, New Directions, 1971
P/J:	*Pound/Joyce: The Letters of Ezra Pound to James Joyce*, ed. Forrest Read, New Directions Paperbook, 1967
SL:	*Selected Letters, 1907–1941*, ed. D. D. Paige, New Directions Paperbook, 1971
SP:	*Selected Prose, 1909–1965*, ed. William Cookson, New Directions, 1973
SR:	*The Spirit of Romance*, New Directions Paperbook, 1968

Quotations from the *Cantos* are from the 1972 New Directions edition. Excerpts from the Malatesta Cantos are cited by canto number, page, and line number: 9.36.22; all other quotations from the *Cantos* are cited by canto number and page: 74/436.

Quotations from the unpublished notes and drafts for the Malatesta Cantos are cited by the number of the *Cantos* folder in the Pound Archive at Yale's Beinecke Library: #42, p. 10.

Quotations from the unpublished letters of Ezra Pound are cited by the letter number in the Paige Collection of Pound's letters at Yale's Beinecke Library: *Paige*, #628.

Introduction

> . . . si on ne comprend pas une oeuvre seulement par la lecture de cette oeuvre et rien que de cette oeuvre, on ne la comprendra jamais; même avec toute la masse de documents, de citations, de détails biologiques ou biographiques que vous voudrez.[1]

Sigismondo Pandolfo Malatesta, lord of Rimini in the fifteenth century, emerges as the dominant figure in the early *Cantos* of Ezra Pound. Not only is he the first individual in the poem to preside over a series of cantos (8–11)—a series, moreover, that straddles the central portion of the first installment of Pound's long poem, *A Draft of XVI Cantos* (1925)—but he is also the hero of a sequence that marks an important shift in style, from the epic stateliness of the earlier cantos to a predominantly colloquial diction and tone. In addition, Malatesta is the supreme embodiment of a recurrent type in Pound's verse—that of the outcast or "outsider" who is nevertheless "worth all the successes of his age."[2]

Ezra Pound has not told us how he first came to be interested in Sigismondo Malatesta. It may have been the result of his seeing the Tempio Malatestiano in Rimini or of his general research in the history of the Italian Renaissance. Perhaps Pound's curiosity had been whetted by the negative appraisal of Symonds:

> Sigismondo Pandolfo Malatesta . . . might be selected as a true type of the princes who united a romantic zeal for culture with the vices of barbarians . . . . This Malatesta killed three wives in succession, and committed outrages on his children. . . . As *condottiere*, he displayed all the duplicities, cruelties, sacrileges, and tortuous policies to which the most accomplished villain of the age could have aspired;[3]

or by that of Burckhardt:

> Unscrupulousness, impiety, military skill, and high culture have been seldom so combined in one individual as in Sigismondo Malatesta. . . . But the accumulated crimes of such a family must at last outweigh all talent, however great, and drag the tyrant into the abyss . . . .

> The verdict of history . . . convicts him of murder, rape, adultery, incest, sacrilege, perjury, and treason, committed not once, but often.[4]

Interested from an early age in individuals of genius who inhabited the peripheries of conventional morality, Pound might well have decided to look into the case of a man whose deeds could still make eminent historians squirm four centuries after the fact.

But what were the facts? Pound's perusal of the relevant documents led him to conclude that Malatesta's enemies had fabricated enormous lies out of flimsy evidence:

> The lump lot [of ecclesiastical accusations] given over
> To that kid-slapping fanatic il cardinale di San Pietro in Vincoli
> To find him guilty, of the lump lot
> As he duly did, calling rumour, and Messire Federico d'Urbino
> And other equally unimpeachable witnesses.
> (10.45.23–27)[5]

In a recent study, the first extended history of the Malatesta dynasty to be written since the nineteenth century, P. J. Jones begins his chapter on Sigismondo with the following observations:

> Sigismondo Malatesta is one of history's reprobates, a man burdened for centuries with the character of moral outcast. . . .
> Modern opinion is more circumspect. It is now understood that Sigismondo Malatesta . . . owes much of his evil reputation to hostile testimony. . . . The worst allegations against him were all transmitted to posterity by one authority: . . . Pius II, whose interests as ruler . . . envenomed him against the Malatesta, and whose published anathemas and, still more, his widely read historical *Commentaries,* represented Sigismondo with medieval gusto and indiscriminacy as a monster guilty of every possible public and private outrage. Many of these charges can be dismissed at once as the conventional invective of *curia* and church. Others, among the most grave, convicting him of the murder of his first two wives, Ginevra d'Este and Polissena Sforza, and of killing and dishonouring the corpse of a German noblewoman, were either inaccurate, improbable, or the offspring of malicious rumour.[6]

Even if some of the accusations against Malatesta were true, there was nevertheless more than one way to interpret them. D'Annunzio, for example, was to adopt an approach vastly different from that of Symonds and Burckhardt. In the "Commiato" (or envoi) to his tragedy *Francesca da Rimini* (1902), D'Annunzio pays rapturous tribute to the memory of Malatesta and his "divine Isotta," to the "new cult" of Grecian mysteries inaugurated by the building of the Tempio, and to the heroic resolve that led to Sigismondo's attempt on the life of Pope Paul II.[7]

Though it is difficult to say how Pound first became interested in Malatesta (was it because five of Sigismondo's ancestors figure in the *Inferno?*),[8] it is nevertheless undeniable that Pound steeped himself in the life and times of his newly found hero with an ardor and thoroughness that are all the more astonishing in view of the fact that his veritable "orgy" of research resulted in a mere twenty-five pages of printed text. Surely, had Pound wished to parade his erudition, he might well have composed a *Sigismundiad* equal in length to the entire *Cantos*, for in the course of a year (April 1922-April 1923) Pound managed to visit at least a dozen cities and towns in search of primary and secondary sources, compile a bibliography of scores of books and articles relating to Malatesta and his times, and amass many hundreds of pages of notes and drafts for these cantos, now housed in the Pound Archive at Yale's Beinecke Library.

But who was Sigismondo Pandolfo Malatesta? Those of Pound's contemporaries who could read Italian or French might have learned about him from the scholarly works of Tonini, Soranzo, and Yriarte.[9] We have already called attention to some relevant passages in the works of Symonds, Burckhardt, and D'Annunzio. Students of Italian Renaissance architecture would probably have learned something about Sigismondo during the course of their research on the Tempio Malatestiano, the cathedral of Rimini. On a more popular level was Edward Hutton's historical novel, *Sigismondo Pandolfo Malatesta, Lord of Rimini* (1906). Nevertheless, as Hugh Kenner indicates, "by the time (1923) the Malatesta Cantos were written their subject had been erased from literate consciousness. Pound nowhere tells his reader who Sigismundo is: his mind lingered in a time when people knew. R. P. Blackmur in 1934 thought the subject most recondite."[10] And so it has remained. What follows is a brief outline of the life and times of this Poundian hero.

Sigismondo Malatesta (1417–1468) was a great-great-grandson of Malatesta da Verrucchio (the "Mastin" or Mastiff of 8.32.26), who in 1295 had established himself as lord of Rimini. By the time of Sigismondo the family had carved out for itself a small principality in the vicinity of Rimini, including the cities of Fano, Cesena, and Pesaro. Because Romagna formed part of the Papal States, the Malatesti were technically vicars of the Pope and thus were required to pay a *census* (dues or rents) to Rome each year.

Sigismondo was one of three brothers: the eldest, Galeotto Roberto (born 1411) became a member of the Franciscan Order two years before his premature death in 1432, having dedicated himself to the contemplative life (8.33.5); the youngest of the three, Domenico (born 1418), called Malatesta Novello (Pound's "Novvy": 10.47.1; 11.49.26), became ruler of Cesena, finding himself, at times, fighting against Sigismondo, because of the continuous shifting of alliances that characterized this period of Italian history.

After the death in September 1429 of Carlo Malatesta, uncle and guardian of the three boys, Pope Martin V sought to confiscate the Malatesta domains because of non-payment of the *census* for the preceding three years (8.33.4), but in March 1430 a pact was arranged that confirmed the brothers in their major holdings while depriving them of many of their towns and castles in the March of Ancona.

Sigismondo's active career began in May 1431 when, upon the outbreak of an insurrection in Rimini, "he got out to Cesena / And brought back the levies" (8.33.7-8), but, by the time he returned, order had already been restored. Later in the same year there was an outbreak in Fano. Sigismondo slipped out of the city by night, swam the Foglia (8.33.9), and assembled a force of 300 infantry that managed to put an end to the uprising, though he almost lost his life during a riot in the piazza of Fano on November 3 (8.33.6; 9.34.14–15).

When Galeotto Roberto died in October 1432, he passed on to Sigismondo (aged fifteen) the lordship of Rimini, the principal city of the Malatesta domains. In the early part of 1433 Sigismondo married Ginevra d'Este, the daughter of Niccolò d'Este and Parisina Malatesta (who figure in later cantos and whose tragedy of incest and death is briefly alluded to in 8.32.29–30). When Ginevra died in 1440, there was "an unfounded suspicion of poisoning,"[11] which Pius II, Sigismondo's fiercest enemy, was later to include among his published accusations.

From 1433 to 1443 Sigismondo was involved in numerous campaigns, hiring himself out as *condottiere* to the various princes and communes of Italy. Jones reminds us that "his principality was small and his revenues slight. To win mercenary pay was therefore a necessity" (p. 178). During most of this early part of his career Sigismondo found himself allied with Francesco Sforza, the foremost *condottiere* of his day, whose skill and cunning eventually resulted in his seizure of the duchy of Milan, though he was but a "peasant's son" (8.31.9). Sigismondo's second wife was Sforza's daughter, Polissena, who was wed to Malatesta in April 1442, two months after the birth, by Vannetta Toschi, of his illegitimate son, Roberto (11.48.12,30; 11.50.7). In November 1443 Sigismondo helped to rout the papal forces at Monteluro, scoring an important victory for Sforza, who nevertheless remained unenthusiastic about supporting Sigismondo's designs on Pesaro (9.34.27–28). It was at this point that Malatesta first strained his relations with Sforza by demanding from him the *rocca* of Sinigaglia and by failing to assist him with his campaign in the Marches, because of his preoccupation with Pesaro.

In 1441 this town had come under the control of Galeazzo Malatesta, a cousin of Sigismondo and "a man totally unfitted for government" (Jones, p. 186). Sigismondo made an attempt to seize it from him late in 1443, but now, toward the end of 1444, the offended Sforza and the indignant Galeazzo (Pound's "Galeaz") came together at the instigation of Federigo da Montefeltro, lord of Urbino, and arranged a secret treaty by which Galeazzo should sell Pesaro to Francesco Sforza (who installed his brother, Alessandro, in the seigniory) and Fossombrone to Federigo, inveterate foe of Sigismondo (9.34.29–9.35.13). It was the sale of Pesaro that finally succeeded in embittering Sigismondo's mind against Sforza, and in confirming him in his hatred of Federigo or "Feddy." Henceforth, Malatesta's dominions were cut in two (9.35.10)—Pesaro lies on the Adriatic coast between Rimini and Fano—and the city of Fano itself was ringed round by the

Introduction xvii

hostile cities of Pesaro, Fossombrone, and Urbino. In retaliation, Sigismondo led the troops of Milan, Naples, and Pope Eugenius IV against the March of Ancona (where Sforza was attempting to carve a state for himself), and within a few months succeeded in conquering the entire province: "and we drove them out of the Marches" (9.35.13).

Close upon the heels of the Pesaro affair followed the trouble with Aragon: "And the King o' Ragona, Alphonse le roy d'Aragon, / was the next nail in our coffin" (9.35.14–15). In the summer of 1447 Sigismondo had signed on with Alfonso V of Aragon (and, since 1443, King of Naples), who was now pressing his claim to Milan, having been named heir by the Milanese duke, Filippo Maria Visconti. The papacy supported Alfonso, but the republics of Florence and Venice were determined to prevent the monarch from extending his rule to the north of Italy. Alfonso had paid Sigismondo 25,000 ducats to raise an army and march north, but when Malatesta pressed the king for further payments, Alfonso demurred and treated Sigismondo's envoys disrespectfully. In the meantime, the Florentine ambassador, Gianozzo Manetti, had come to Rimini "bearing gifts," and Malatesta, angered by Alfonso's conduct, switched his allegiance to Florence on December 10, 1447, but not before calling together the council at which Roberto Valturio, the engineer and military strategist, advocated keeping what remained of Alfonso's money: "as well for a sheep as a lamb." Alfonso would be enraged at Malatesta's betrayal anyway, so why not keep the money and "go the whole hog"?—as we would say (9.35.16–23). Even Sigismondo's bitterest enemy, Pius II, was to say afterward that this shift of alliance "saved the Florentine state."[12] Jones comments as follows: "Legally Sigismondo's defection may have been correct. It may also have conformed to *condottiere* practice. It was, none the less, politically mistaken. . . . More than any other single action it contributed to his ultimate downfall. . . . The offence he had now given a powerful king could be the ruin of a princeling like himself" (p. 199).

In June of 1449, with Sigismondo fighting for the Venetians, Polissena Sforza, his second wife, died (9.35.25). A rumor arose that she had been strangled by her husband, or at his orders; in reality, she seems to have succumbed to the plague. In any event, Pius II later treated the incident with all the impartiality of a sworn enemy, and thus this second charge of uxoricide has come down to our own day (10.44.22; 10.45.14). In a similar vein, Malatesta was accused of the rape and murder of "that German-Burgundian female" (9.36.27), a noblewoman assaulted and killed while passing through Verona on her way to Rome in the Jubilee year of 1450. "Once again it is impossible to pronounce finally on Sigismondo's guilt. But once again an equivocal accusation was adopted by Pius II" (Jones, p. 203).

In this same year, Francesco Sforza entered Milan, overthrowing the feeble republic that had been established after the death of Visconti, and proclaimed himself the new Duke. Wishing to rid himself of Sigismondo (whom the Venetians had sent against him), Sforza urged Federigo d'Urbino to approach Malatesta and *xviii   Introduction*

promise him aid in wrenching Pesaro from Alessandro Sforza. Sigismondo swallowed the bait and compelled the Venetians to grant him a leave, but when he arrived at Pesaro he discovered that Sforza had sent defensive troops to the city and that Federigo never had any intention of helping him (9.35.32–9.36.4; 9.36.30–9.37.6). The Venetians decided that they had had enough of Sigismondo: in addition to the "German-Burgundian" affair and the "six months vacation" for the futile attempt on Pesaro, they were still angry with Malatesta for having stolen marble from the walls of S. Apollinare in Classe "for the beautifying of the *tempio*" (9.36.5–26). As a result, Sigismondo "lost his job with the Venetians" (9.37.6).

It is the Tempio Malatestiano (the church of San Francesco, the present cathedral of Rimini) for which Sigismondo is chiefly remembered today, and for which Pound enthroned him at the core of his first book of Cantos. In 1447, Malatesta began remodeling the original thirteenth-century Gothic church into a "temple of fame" celebrating, among other things, his love for his mistress (later his third wife) Isotta degli Atti, the grand passion of his life. The Tempio was also to serve as the final resting place of Sigismondo, Isotta, and the humanists of Rimini's court, such as Roberto Valturio (author of *De re militari*) and the poets Giusto de' Conti and Basinio Basini (author of *Isottaeus* and the *Hesperis*, the latter in praise of Sigismondo's military exploits).[13]

Leon Battista Alberti designed the Renaissance "shell" that was built around the Gothic edifice—"the filigree hiding the gothic" (9.41.13)—and Matteo da Pasti served as architect for the interior of the structure. The Tempio was left unfinished both inside and out[14]—the great dome projected by Alberti was never built—but its interior was nevertheless "so full of pagan works" (9.41.10) and so devoid of Christian motifs that, according to Pius II, "it seemed less a temple of Christians than one of heathen devil-worshippers."[15] Adorning the six principal chapels of the Tempio are the elegant bas-reliefs of Agostino di Duccio (and perhaps of da Pasti), representing the classical deities, the allegorical figures of the liberal arts, the signs of the zodiac, and mirthful *putti*, frolicking in water and playing musical instruments. In the Santuario, or Chapel of the Relics, Piero della Francesca painted Sigismondo kneeling before his patron saint, while everywhere in the church the monogram of Sigismondo ($) may be seen, along with representations of Malatesta's two emblems: the rose and the elephant (the "aliofants" of 9.40.22,24).[16]

The Tempio was dear to Pound for many reasons: for its "clean and beneficent Christianity" (*GK*, p. 301)—that is, for its neo-pagan spirit—, for its glorification of earthly love, for its "make it new" aspect, for its remarkable workmanship, and for its being the *idée fixe* of a turbulent, passionate, and cultured man. Indeed, Sigismondo as builder was only slightly more interesting to Pound than Sigismondo as "Renaissance man": *condottiere*, poet (8.30.17-22), scholar, lover, inventor (9.37.11–14), and—perhaps most of all—assiduous patron of the arts:

"From the patron's angle, Giusto de Conti and Bassinio were the best poets of their day. . . . They stretched their legs under the same table that had received Pier della Francesca, Pisanello, Giovan Bellini, Battista Alberti, Mino da Fiesole; and the young Bassinio, at least, profited, presumably in head as well as in stomach."[17]

Pound's emphasis on enlightened patronage antedates his interest in Malatesta by many years. In 1915, for example, Pound had written to John Quinn: "My whole drive is that if a patron buys from an artist who needs money (needs money to buy tools, time and food), the patron then makes himself equal to the artist: he is building art into the world; he creates."[18] But by the time he started working on the Malatesta Cantos, Pound had actually attempted to put his ideas on patronage into practice. The result was "Bel Esprit"—a fund that would use the subsidies of individual guarantors to free the energies of certain pre-selected artists, enabling them to devote themselves to their craft on a full-time basis. Pound's first nominee was T. S. Eliot, whose job at Lloyd's Bank was preventing him from writing.

In Pound's prospectus for "Bel Esprit," he claims that "Aristocracy is gone, its function was to select," and that the "Only thing we can give the artist is leisure to work in. Only way we can get work from him is to assure him this leisure."[19] This sounds a great deal like Malatesta's offer to the *"Maestro di pentore"*:

> I want to arrange with him to give him so much per year
> And to assure him that he will get the sum agreed on.
> . . . .
> And for this I mean to make due provision,
> So that he can work as he likes,
> Or waste his time as he likes
> . . . .
>   never lacking provision.
>   (8.29.7–8,16–18,21)

In any event, Eliot balked at the scheme, and that was the end of "Bel Esprit."[20]

But let us return to our sketch of Malatesta's career. In 1452, Sigismondo entered the service of the Florentines, who were being attacked by the Aragonese (8.29.25–8.30.10). Shortly after reducing Vada (9.37.11–12), Malatesta, along with many other *condottieri*,[21] found himself unemployed because of the treaty of Lodi (1454), which had pledged the major powers of Italy to twenty-five years of peace. He was constrained to take a small job as Captain–General for the Sienese, who were fighting against Aldobrandino Orsini, Count of Pitigliano, comfortably ensconced at Sorano, while Sigismondo's besieging army was "dying of cold" (10.42.1) during the harsh winter of 1454. Without consulting the Sienese, Malatesta arranged a truce with Orsini. His angry employers set out to arrest him for treason, convinced of his ambitious designs on the seigniory of Siena. They failed to entrap him, but managed to seize his correspondence ("the post-bag");

Sigismondo had meanwhile fled to Romagna by making his way through Florentine territory (9.37.15–9.41.3; 10.42.1–10.43.5).

In 1456, Malatesta married his mistress, Isotta degli Atti. The shouting match with his inveterate foe, Federigo d'Urbino, occurred the next year (10.43.9–17), shortly after which Federigo and Giacomo Piccinino invaded Romagna. Pope Calixtus III, friendly to the Malatesti, and King Alfonso of Aragon both died in 1458 (10.46.12). Because the latter had also been King of Naples, a war of succession now broke out between his bastard son Ferrante (Ferdinando) and René d'Anjou, the rival claimant. The new pope, Pius II, supported the Aragonese, but Malatesta eventually threw in his lot with the Angevins (10.46.9–10).

At the Crusade Congress of Mantua (1459), Sigismondo was constrained to accept Pius II's arbitration of his feud with the House of Aragon (whose captains, Piccinino and Federigo, were devastating Romagna). Ill-contented with the harsh terms dictated by Pius, Malatesta made an agreement with the Angevins in the fall of 1460—an action that amounted to declaring war on the papacy. Jones remarks that "in Pius II he had chosen an adversary bitter, obdurate and pertinacious, who for the next three years, unmoved by the remonstrances of the other Italian powers, was to pursue him with blind and absorbing rancour."[22]

In December of 1460 Sigismondo and Malatesta Novello were excommunicated. On January 16, 1461, Pius convoked a public consistory on this fifteenth-century "difficult individual," Sigismondo Malatesta, "calling rumour, and Messire Federico d'Urbino / and other equally unimpeachable witnesses," such as Alessandro Sforza, to testify. But the main event was an unimaginably vitriolic diatribe against Malatesta, accusing him of almost every conceivable crime, delivered by the pope's creature, the Sienese *advocatus fisci*, Andreas Benzi (10.44.11–10.45.27). After commending the speech as an *"Orationem / Elegantissimam et ornatissimam"* (10.45.18–19), Pius ordered Nicholas of Cusa, "il cardinale di San Pietro in Vincoli" (10.45.24), to investigate these charges and, if they proved true, to prepare a formal indictment against Malatesta. The pious cardinal came to the conclusion, nine months later, that *all* the accusations were sound, and thus, on April 27, 1462, Sigismondo was burned in effigy in a few different locations in Rome (10.43.28–10.44.10; 10.45.28–10.46.2). The original sentence had called for Malatesta to be burned at the stake, but since Sigismondo had very wisely not appeared in person to answer the charges, Pius vented his anger on a "rare magnificent effigy costing 8 florins 48 bol" (10.45.29), and proceeded, in the bull *Discipula veritatis*, to re-excommunicate Malatesta, to place him under interdict, and to deprive him (at least on paper) of all his territories.[23]

In the meantime, however, Sigismondo had soundly defeated the papal troops at the battle of Nidastore (July 2, 1461), recounted in 10.47.4–11.48.26. The triumph was shortlived: "we got it next August" (11.48.29). The papal army, commanded by Federigo d'Urbino, trounced Malatesta's troops near Sinigaglia on August 12–13, 1462. Sigismondo hastened to Taranto, seeking help from the leaders of the Angevin faction, but found them "busted and weeping into their beards" (11.48.31–11.49.3).

In April 1463 Malatesta Novello sold Cervia and its salt industry to the Venetians in order to guarantee their intercession on behalf of the Malatesti; this monopoly had been the family's main source of income (11.49.24–25). When Novello surrendered to the Church on August 26, he was allowed to retain control of Cesena until his death—at which time it would revert to the papacy, as it did in 1465 (11.49.26). On September 25, 1463, Sigismondo's son, Roberto, was forced to surrender Fano to Federigo d'Urbino (11.48.30).

Rimini itself was spared by its strong fortifications and by an outbreak of the plague, both of which prevented Federigo from depriving Sigismondo of his last major holding (11.49.4–12). Pius craved nothing less than total destruction of Malatesta but, fearing the opposition of the Venetians (who wanted to keep papal power out of Rimini)[24] and needing their support for his long-projected crusade against the Turks, he allowed Sigismondo to sue for peace in October 1463. The terms stipulated that Malatesta could retain only Rimini and its immediate environs—and only for his own lifetime.[25] All in all, "dey got de mos' bloody rottenes' peace on us" (11.49.13–23).[26] The main beneficiaries of Malatesta's despoilment were the Pope's general, Federigo d'Urbino, who received more than fifty towns and castles, and Antonio Piccolomini—the Pope's nephew—who was awarded Sinigaglia and Mondavio. Most of the remaining lands went to the papacy.[27]

In June 1464 Malatesta departed for the Morea, in command of the Venetian troops sent out to fight the Turks. The expedition was a failure (11.50.15–20), and Malatesta returned to Rimini in April 1466, his only spoils consisting of the mortal remains of Gemisthus Plethon, which he buried in one of the Tempio's sarcophagi.

In the meantime the new pope, Paul II, was meditating an exchange of territories: Cesena and Cervia (or Foligno and Spoleto) for Rimini. When Malatesta learned of this in the fall of 1466, he was so enraged at the pope's temerity that he rode to the Holy City with intentions of murdering him. But Paul suspected Sigismondo's motives for requesting an audience and surrounded himself with seven stalwart cardinals before receiving him (11.51.16–25). When Malatesta realized that his plan had been thwarted, he fell to his knees and begged forgiveness. On his part, Paul denied the projected exchange and took Malatesta into his service, under the paltry conditions outlined in 11.51.9–15. When Platina[28] was asked about his conversations with Sigismondo, he replied in the words memorialized in Canto 11:

> *de litteris et de armis, praestantibusque ingeniis,*
> Both of ancient times and our own; books, arms,
> And of men of unusual genius,
> Both of ancient times and our own, in short the usual subjects
> Of conversation between intelligent men.
> (11.51.4–8)

Sigismondo died in Rimini, at the age of fifty-one, on October 9, 1468, having named Isotta and her son Sallustio as heirs (the "Malatesta de Malatestis" of 9.39.14–33). In Fano, Pope Paul donated to the city the former Malatesta palaces, *"palatium seu curiam* OLIM *de Malatestis"* (11.50.12), and, by the year 1501, Cesare Borgia had ousted Sigismondo's grandson, Pandolfo, from the seigniory of Rimini, the Sforza from Pesaro, the Montefeltri from Urbino, the Manfredi from Faenza, etc. At the very end of *A Draft of XXX Cantos*, we are shown the printer Soncinus bringing out in Fano (also under Cesare's control) an edition of Petrarch's *Rime*, the text taken "from a codex once of the Lords Malatesta" (30/148–49). The echo of "OLIM *de Malatestis"* reminds us that, in spite of Soncinus's craftsmanship, a monolithic tyranny, propped up by the Church, has stultified Romagna's former artistic initiative:

> and no history, no anything from 1507–1807
> under the papal sway.[29]

In marked contrast to this later period of papal rule had been "the thoroughness of Rimini's civilization in 1460." Pound goes on to say (some fifteen years after he wrote the Malatesta Cantos):

> If you consider the Malatesta and Sigismundo in particular, a failure, he was at all events a failure worth all the successes of his age. He had in Rimini, Pisanello, Pier della Francesca. Rimini still has "the best Bellini in Italy." If the Tempio is a jumble and junk shop, it nevertheless registers a concept. There is no other single man's effort equally registered.[30]

Donald Davie provides an excellent gloss on this passage when he uses a phrase of Erwin Panofsky's to claim that "Malatesta was the sort of patron who 'swallowed up the world that surrounded him until his whole environment had been absorbed by his own self.' That is the achievement which Pound celebrates."[31]

Several critics have claimed that Pound has painted a distorted portrait of his hero. George Dekker, for example, believes that the reader of the Malatesta Cantos

> . . . ought to bear in mind that Pound's version of Sigismondo leaves out whatever Pound considers "irrelevant" or "probably invented by Sigismondo's enemies." This is not to say that Pound is dishonest; but he is obsessed with the idea that history has everywhere been falsified by the ruling interests, and that the honest investigator must always read between the lines.[32]

But the exhaustive research of Giovanni Soranzo, at the turn of the century, as well as the recent labors of P. J. Jones, have demonstrated that, at least in this particular case, "the honest investigator must . . . read between the lines." Indeed, Machiavelli had come to the same conclusion as these twentieth-century scholars when he asserted, in his succinct way, that "the Pope made war in Romagna against the Malatesta, because he wanted to wrest Rimini and Cesena from them."[33]

Karl Shapiro has observed that "to my knowledge, I have never seen a discarded poem that excelled the final form. On the other hand, no final poem can ever tell as much about the intention of the poet or about the poetic psyche as those worksheets which he almost systematically destroys."[34] Pound, however, not only refrained from destroying his worksheets for the Malatesta Cantos, but indeed seems to have taken special care for their preservation, storing them all in a large black cardboard box. These papers, now housed in the Pound Archive at Yale's Beinecke Library, have been distributed among thirty folders whose contents range in bulk from 2 to 186 sheets. The materials consist of bibliographies, reading notes, lengthy transcriptions from various documents, manuscript drafts, typescripts, revised and unrevised carbons, miscellaneous items, and a few printed texts (mostly Italian journals). These Malatesta papers, amounting to well over 700 pages, now comprise Folders #40-67 and #69-70 of the *Cantos* folders at Beinecke.[35]

The first two chapters of this book will examine these worksheets closely, not only for their intrinsic interest, but also because of the light they shed on Pound's methods of composition and on his use of historical materials as sources for poetry. The last two chapters will focus on the published version of the Malatesta Cantos—their style, tone, significance, and the crucial role they assume in the portrayal of a certain type of recurrent figure in Pound's verse. I hope that this first full-length study of the genesis, evolution, and import of the Malatesta Cantos will help to answer many of the perplexing questions of exegesis and interpretation raised by the sequence, and that it will also alert readers of the *Cantos* to the "Malatesta paradigm" that lies behind much of Pound's work—that of the heroic rebel whose tenacious capacity for insight and achievement leads inexorably to his defeat by the forces of orthodoxy.

Mary de Rachewiltz remembers the active assistance provided by her father while she was engaged in translating the Malatesta Cantos into Italian during the war years of 1941–43.[36] Her typescripts (with Pound's revisions) and Pound's own Italian versions are also at Beinecke, but I have omitted them from my discussion because they more readily fall within the province of a work that would focus on Pound's theory and practice of translation. As it is, this book might very well have grown to twice its present length—but that would have involved ignoring the Confucian dictum that

> in
> discourse
> what matters is
> to get it across e poi basta.
>
> (79/486)

1

The Malatesta Manuscripts: Beginnings to the Watson Typescript

Itinerary of Pound's Work on the Malatesta Cantos

In December of 1920 Pound put an end to his dozen years of residence in London by transferring himself to Paris, settling eventually at 70 *bis* rue Notre Dame des Champs. His disillusionment with London and his hopes for Paris may be gleaned from his "*Dial* Letter" for February 1922, in which he already seems to be caught up in his dream of Malatesta's Rimini, demanding that "our envy must be for a period when the individual city (Italian mostly) tried to outdo its neighbor in the degree and intensity of its civilization, to be the vortex for the most living individuals. *Gli uomini vivono in pochi.*"[1] It is thus very probable that Pound had decided to write about Malatesta before he set out for an extended vacation in Italy (March 27-July 1, 1922); indeed, his interest in the "Vorticist *condottiere*" may have led him to some of the places he visited. By April 5 he was in Siena,[2] where he may have seen, in the Archives, the letters written to Sigismondo during a five-month period in 1454, confiscated by the Sienese in the "post-bag" incident (9.37.15–9.41.1). Between April 13 and May 3 he visited, among other places, Ancona, Rimini, and Ravenna (*Paige*, #611-13)—all of which figure in the Malatesta Cantos. He seems to have been in Venice during most of May and June, and at some point toward the end of this period he stopped off in Milan (*Paige*, #612–13; 616).

On June 20, 1922, Pound informed John Quinn that he had "blocked in four cantos"—four cantos, that is, after "Canto 8" (with some changes, the present Canto 2), which had appeared in the *Dial* the previous month.[3] Since the Malatesta canto here indirectly referred to would thus have been numbered "Canto 9," it seems that Pound already had at least a rough draft of the "Baldy Bacon," "Kung," and one of the "Hell" cantos (present Cantos 12–14), in addition to the Malatesta material. Pound returned to Paris on July 2, and, in the following month, wrote to his father that he now had "a rough draft of 9, 10, 11, 12, 13. IX may swell out into two" (*Paige*, #616, p.1). In an interesting letter to Quinn, dated

August 10, Pound goes on at some length about Malatesta and the canto he had inspired. He writes that he is in the process of doing some background reading on Sigismondo, but he doubts that it will improve the draft of his canto, because "all the *minor* points that might aid one in forming an historic rather than a fanciful idea of his character seem 'shrouded in mystery' or rather lies." Indeed, if he discovers that Malatesta was "TOO bloody quiet and orderly it will ruin the canto. Which needs a certain boisterousness and disorder to contrast with his constructive work." He tells Quinn of Malatesta's attempt on the life of Paul II and of Platina's description of his conversations with Sigismondo (11.50.30–11.51.25), and concludes that it was "a bloody good period, a town the size of Rimini, with Pier Francesca, Pisanello, Mino da Fiesoli, and Alberti as architect. The pick of the bunch, all working there at one time or another. . . ."[4]

We know that by August 20 Pound had not yet decided to write more than one Malatesta canto: "Have various materials for my Malatesta canto lying about"; nor was he sure by September 2: "Am plugging along on my Malatesta Canto, may run into two Cantos; the four to follow it are blocked in" (*Paige*, #619; #621). It is only by October 3 that the fissure has finally taken place: "I am plugging along on my Malatesta cantos; will take years and years at the present rate" (*Paige*, #623). Toward the end of the month, Pound granted himself some respite from the seemingly recalcitrant Malatesta material (*Paige*, #625), but not before he had given public expression to some of the concerns that had first attracted him to Sigismondo. In his "Paris Letter" to the *Dial*, composed in October and published in November of 1922 (pp. 549–54), he refers to "the talk '*de litteris, de armis, de praestantibus ingeniis*' which Platina considered natural between intelligent men," and he goes on to formulate his views of enlightened patronage à la Malatesta:

> It, the vortex, has, historically, come from free groups, or from groups formed about men who had reached a condition of more than freedom; and these men or groups have acted as consumers. Whatever they have constructed, they have also consumed. . . . It has been repeated often enough in these pages that 'the only thing you can give an artist is leisure' (i.e., food, shelter, et cetera, plus leisure) to work in.
>
> (*Paige*, #622, pp. 1–2)[5]

Next comes a direct allusion to Sigismondo:

> There was once a man in a small town who had Pisanello, Pier Francesco, and Mino da Fiesole all working for him at one time or another. They might have turned out bad jobs, but they didn't. They might have smashed up their work when they had finished, and he would have been out of pocket several months' board.
>
> (p.3)

Finally, he praises D'Annunzio (who, in his combination of deep culture, military heroism, neo-pagan spirit, and febrile eroticism, struck Pound as a Malatesta *redivivus*), in speaking of "some sort of vigour, some sort of assertion, some sort of courage, or at least of ebullience that throws a certain amount of remembered beauty into an unconquered consciousness" (pp. 5–6).[6]

Almost two months elapse without Pound's referring to his work, until on Christmas day of 1922 he writes: "Have got three of the Malatesta cantos into some sort of shape; attempt to avoid going away with huge mass of notes. Don't know how many more will be needed to deal with S.M.; several cantos blocked in to follow the Malatesta section" (*Paige*, #626). One of the few dated sheets among Pound's MSS bears the heading "Notes Dec 24," and it and the following sheet[7] consist of abbreviated references to various incidents in Malatesta's career— obviously part of Pound's "attempt to avoid going away with huge mass of notes."

The final week of 1922, however, must have been a period of intense work, for by January 4 Pound not only had a version of four Malatesta cantos (and a short coda, beginning "Canto 13"), but he also felt sufficiently satisfied with them to submit them to James Sibley Watson of the *Dial*, suggesting that they appear in the July number of the magazine.[8] This important early draft (the "Watson Typescript," discussed in Chapter 2) was sent off to Watson on January 5, the same day that Pound left Paris for Rapallo. In the portion of his letter dated January 4, Pound informs Watson that "I intend, or intended to continue research on the subject; but it very probably won't change much of the actual test" (p. 1), but, on re-reading the typescript the next day, just before putting it in the mail, he concedes that "there may be a few revisions," but adds that he believes "it will stay pretty much as it is, unless I find some disconcerting document during the next twelve weeks" (p. 3).

The anticipated "few revisions" eventually amounted to a rewriting of a substantial portion of these cantos, not because of finding "disconcerting" documents, but because of discovering materials that could amplify and variegate his account of Malatesta. Up to this point Pound had relied very heavily on Yriarte for most of the documents translated for or transcribed into his poem.[9] He had also used Clementini, Battaglini, a long, tri-partite article by Soranzo, and Pius II's *Commentaries*.[10] Soon after leaving Paris on January 5, however, he must have received a copy of Soranzo's book-length study of Pius's relations with Sigismondo, which was to become an important source of the Malatesta Cantos.[11] But more crucial for the evolution of these cantos was his perusal, in March 1923, of Gaspare Broglio's manuscript life of Sigismondo, housed at Rimini's Gambalunga Library. This chronicle, along with a number of letters and documents dug out of various Italian archives, enabled Pound to incorporate some additional first-hand accounts into his poem, thereby facilitating the excision of many weak, generalizing passages on Sigismondo's life and times.

On February 12, 1923, Pound and his wife, along with the Hemingways, started south from Rapallo (*SL*, p. 186). Among the towns they visited (Pisa, Siena, Grosseto, etc.) were Piombino and Orbetello, where Hemingway explained to Pound how Sigismondo's battles there would have been fought.[12] By February 17, Pound was in Rome, doing research in the Vatican Archives,[13] and he writes on the 24th: "I continue work in Vatican library. Have discovered that Soranzo still exists. Expect to do a little cross country plunge next week. . . . Results . . . scheduled for July *Dial*, unless something intervenes" (*Paige*, #628). On March 2, he informs his mother, in a letter written in limping Italian, that he and Dorothy have arrived in Florence from Rome, via Orvieto. He intends to examine the Florentine Archives and then proceed to Cesena (*Paige*, #629)—the town formerly under the control of Sigismondo's younger brother, Domenico Malatesta (Malatesta Novello), who had the Malatestine Library built there. Pound later referred to this library as "a unique monument to the culture of the best decades of the Renaissance,"[14] and it was there that he met Manlio Torquato Dazzi, the Malatestiana's librarian, who figures in several of Pound's works. On March 9, Pound registered at the Archivio di Stato in Modena, where he examined Malatesta's letters to the Este family.[15]

Toward the end of March 1923 Pound was in Rimini, examining, at the Gambalunga Library, Gaspare Broglio's unpublished chronicle of the life of Sigismondo.[16] Pound's MSS reveal his considerable debt to Broglio's text:

1. Pound transcribes from Broglio 179 the description (8.31.5–7) of "the twelve girls riding in order" during the reception at Rimini (1442) of the newly wed Francesco Sforza and Bianca Visconti (Folder #42, pp. 95, 135).

2. He transcribes from Broglio 191*r* the description (9.34.30–9.35.9) of "the wangle" and "the wiggling" involved in the sale of Pesaro (#42, p. 133).

3. Pound transcribes Broglio's account (p. 202*r,v*) of the events that form the background of 9.35.32–34 (#42, pp. 96–97); he also indicates (#42, p. 99) that he read in Broglio (p. 209*r,v*) the rest of the story of Sigismondo's "bite for Pesaro" in 1450 (9.36.1–4, 31–32; 9.37.1–5).

4. He learns about "the silk war" (9.37.8) from Broglio, as well as about Malatesta's planting of "the bombards" at Vada (9.37.11–12; Broglio, p. 220*r*; Folder #42, pp. 97–98).

5. Pound transcribes Broglio's account (pp. 272*v*-274*v*) of Sigismondo's speech of exhortation and of his victory over "the papishes" (10.47.4–11; 11.48.1–26; Folder #42, pp. 100, 136–39).

6. He finds the story of Malatesta's desperate visit to Tarentum (11.48.3l–11.49.3) in Broglio (p. 253), and the account of his expedition against the Turks in Morea (11.50.15–20) on pages 276–78 of the *Cronaca*; here he also reads (p. 280) about Pope Paul II (Folder #42, pp. 99, 177).

On March 24 Pound sent Watson a revised version of the Malatesta Cantos, quite probably incorporating the new material drawn from Broglio.[17] Pound was in Venice by March 30, where he wrote that he was "exhausted and glad the library is shut till Tuesday" (*Paige*, #633).[18] Here Pound seems to have examined the documents dealing with Doge Francesco Foscari's relations with Sigismondo. By

April 24, 1923, Pound was back in Paris (*Paige*, #634), his Malatesta Cantos very likely in their finished form.[19] From the evidence of the MSS we know that he must also have done research in Bologna, Ravenna, and Milan (#42, pp. 76, 191–92; #43, pp. 23–29, 36; #44, pp. 37–38, 40); it is less certain that he did research in Pesaro, Fano, and Ferrara (#42, pp. 103, 116; #44, p. 40).

Back in Paris, Pound was elated by William Bird's proposal to publish a book of *Cantos*: "S'Oiseau is preparing de looks edtn. of Malatesta at 25 dollars a shot; with still more valued edtn. at 50 bones. Strater at work on special capitals" (*Paige*, #636). Pound here seems to equate his prospective first book of Cantos (1–16) with his section on Malatesta—a synecdoche that indicates the centrality of Sigismondo in Pound's view of the *Cantos* at this point.

In the meantime, by April 23, Scofield Thayer had fired Pound from his position as Paris correspondent for the *Dial*. Thayer had been angered by Pound's "Paris Letter" for November 1922, in which (his mind on Sigismondo and "Bel Esprit") he lamented that "the individual patron is nearly extinct"—in the pages of the *Dial*, which cost its backers $84,000 a year and which had already instituted a $2,000 Dial Award.[20] Adding to Thayer's perturbation was Pound's insistence that Eliot be well paid for *The Waste Land*, which appeared in the same issue of the *Dial* as Pound's vexatious letter.

In early May 1923, a day or so after Pound had mailed off the final version of his Malatesta sequence to Watson (who admired the *Cantos*), he received "that ukase" from Thayer (who considered them "unbelievable rot").[21] Watson and Thayer could veto each other's selections for the *Dial*;[22] and Thayer's view of things had been clearly enunciated as far back as October 22, 1922:

> . . . I feel forced to refrain in the future from publishing such matter as the silly cantos of Ezra Pound and as the very disappointing "Waste Land" and I should like to secure for The Dial the work of such recognised American authors as Edith Wharton.[23]

Thus, toward the end of May, when Pound received a letter from Kenneth Burke, stating that Thayer wished "to inspect said Cantos," Pound concluded that "the intentions toward sabotage were fairly apparent, and questions of literary opinion ceased to be relevant."[24] He thereupon dispatched a curt note to Watson, asking him to return his Malatesta Cantos.[25] And indeed Pound's premonitions were well-founded, for Thayer was to tell Gilbert Seldes on June 6 that he hoped the *Dial* would reject the new cantos.[26]

T. S. Eliot had been requesting cantos for the *Criterion* since late 1922.[27] Now that Pound had been ruffled by Thayer, he submitted his typescript to his friend's journal, and in the *Criterion* for July 1923 appeared

MALATESTA CANTOS.
(CANTOS IX TO XII OF A LONG POEM),

which Pound shortly thereafter considered "rather an advance on anything I had done before."[28]

The *Criterion* text differs only in several minor respects from that of the 1972 New Directions edition, the most significant of these being the absence of the first five lines (8.28.1–5)—which, with the exception of the first line, were composed only after Pound had reshuffled the earlier parts of the *Cantos*—and the suppression of the epithet "s. o. b.," intended for Pius II (10.44.14). It seems that Richard Aldington, acting as editor in Eliot's absence, had deleted the expression in deference to Roman Catholic sensibilities; Pound thus applied the epithet to Aldington by return mail.[29] The rest of the differences are fairly unimportant: lineation (in general, the *Criterion* text makes use of longer lines than the New Directions version), spacing, positioning, punctuation, capitalization, a few spelling differences, and several minor divergences in phrasing (see Appendix A).

By late August 1923 Pound had finished the first sixteen cantos and had extensively revised the earlier parts of the poem. The old "Canto 8" became, with its opening lines rewritten, the present Canto 2. The old Cantos 1–3 were pruned of their Browningesque ruminations, reordered, and condensed into two cantos, making way for the inclusion of the old "8" between them. The Malatesta Cantos thus acquired their present numeration of 8–11 (*Paige*, #642, #643, #686).[30]

By May 24 Pound had submitted the final version of his first sixteen cantos to William Bird's Three Mountains Press in Paris. In the fall, Pound was searching for another "factive" historical personage around whom a sequence of cantos could be structured: "Must start on another *LONG* hunk of Canti, like the Sigismundo. . . . U.S. presidents do not present ALL the features required for the full mind. Am using a bit of Jefferson in the XX or thereabouts" (*Paige*, #698, Oct. 25, 1924). It is interesting to note that, more than a year after the publication of the Malatesta Cantos, Pound still considered Sigismondo the archetype for his next major character in the *Cantos*: "Am . . . ready for another long chunk; and trying to find some bhloomin historic character who can be used as illustration of intelligent constructivity. Private life being another requisite. S.M. amply possessed of both; but other figures being often fatally deficient" (*Paige*, #700, Nov. 1, 1924). By November 12 he seems to have settled on his choice: "Old T. Jefferson has some excellent passages" (*Paige*, #701).

Early in 1925 appeared *A Draft of XVI. Cantos / for the Beginning of a Poem of some Length*. Pound was delighted with the look of this impressive folio volume, assuring William Bird that it (like Isotta) "placuit occulis." In the same letter, he asks Bird: "Have you a spare page 31 (Canto IX)? . . . I shd. like to send that sheet to the ole archivista at Ravenna who made me the sketch of the oxcarts" (*SL*, p. 195). These are the "plaustra" of 9.36.23, used in Sigismondo's despoliation of S. Apollinare in Classe; the sketch (on which Henry Strater presumably based his illustration of the oxen bearing away the marble) has survived among Pound's MSS (Folder #53, p. 15v). On August 24 Pound proudly writes to Bird that a copy of the book "was placed in the Malatestiana at Cesena by my own honourable hands with fitting inscription. . . . I read Dazzi the Sidg., the Hell. . . ." (*SL*, p. 200). Pound's apparent preoccupation with Malatesta, at the expense of the rest of the subject matter of his *Cantos* thus far, is probably due to a number of causes. Not only had Pound invested a great deal of time and research in the composition of the Malatesta sequence, but he had also found in Sigismondo the first hero worthy to merit an in-depth examination in an extended block of cantos. He had apparently discovered a partial solution to the problem of writing a long, nonnarrative poem: instead of flitting about from subject to subject, mechanically devoting a canto or parts of a canto to each, Pound would henceforth vary his schema by fixing his attention, at suitable intervals, upon significant characters or, indeed, upon entire cultures, that would represent islands of relative stability and order (both thematically and structurally), surrounded by the flux and movement of the rest of the poem. From another point of view, we may remark that the Malatesta sequence originally straddled the central portion of *A Draft of XVI Cantos*—a centrality now obscured by the incorporation of the earlier grouping into *A Draft of XXX Cantos*, the first subdivision of the current New Directions text.

By way of concluding this sketch of the external history of the Malatesta Cantos, we may amuse ourselves with the story of two "inadvertent" suppressions of a blasphemous Latin distich that Pound had intended to insert into his Malatesta sequence. The scatological couplet, repeatedly encountered in Pound's MSS, runs as follows:

> Cacat Christus ac restat sedia Petri
> Cacat Christus, pontificis officium restat.[31]

On September 18, 1925, Pound writes to Bird:

> DON'T WORRY ABOUT Christus cacat. So long as it wuz involuntary. There ARE reasons for its omission. I mean why it is justuzwell OUT. It was not in Criterion, but on sep. slip of paper, with mark on Criterion pages that it wuz to go IN. Easily lost. Perhaps just as well that book shd. remain circulatable in countries that *don't* onnerstan English. Bit of Latin might get one suppressed everywhere BUT in the U.S. and Hengland, and that wd. be annoying.
> (*Paige*, #773, p. 1)

One can imagine how "easily lost" was that "sep. slip of paper" for the *Criterion*, when even the relatively innocuous "s. o. b." had been considered too harsh an epithet for a pope by Aldingtonian standards of decorum.

The Malatesta Manuscripts: Pound's Reading Notes

Pound's reading notes are preserved in the first seven folders that deal with the Malatesta material in the Pound Archive at Yale's Beinecke Library (40–46).

Interspersed among these notes are hundreds of bibliographical references and cross-references, as well as a number of short passages conceived as a result of jotting down some snippet of information. On one occasion, for example, Pound records the following meteorological data:

>   1442. hail
>   broke towers
>   & walls
>   3 Aug. . . .
>   sun (eclipsed
>   oscuro).[32]

He then jots down some unrelated facts, but his mind soon reverts to the ominous weather, and associating the destructive hail-storm with two other instances of nature's inclemency, he arrives at an early form of the lines that now open Canto 9:

>   one year the river rose
>   "   "   they fought in the snows
>   one year the hail
>   beat down the towers
>   & trees.
>
>   (#42, p. 2)

From his main sources (identified in notes 9, 10, 11, and 15), from various other texts, and from his archival research, Pound recorded a massive amount of factual information: the major events, of course, in Sigismondo's life; data pertaining to the various battles, alliances, treaties, births, deaths, sums disbursed, troops deployed, etc.; and numerous instances of jealousy or treachery on the part of Sigismondo's enemies. But besides this typically "historical" information on the military and political maneuverings of the time—which Pound gathers with the same assiduousness that has packed the *Cantos* with thousands of names, places, and dates—there are also many notes that deal with the "human" qualities of his major characters, as well as with the social (and even topographic) ambience of Renaissance Italy.

Pound's interest in the personal or private lives of his characters stems from the same conviction that prompted Plutarch to write that "the most glorious exploits do not always furnish us with the clearest discoveries of virtue and vice in men; sometimes a matter of less moment, an expression or a jest, informs us better of their characters and inclinations, than the most famous sieges, the greatest armaments, or the bloodiest battles whatsoever."[33] Accordingly, Pound is careful to note that, even after Sigismondo's final defeat, he nevertheless maintains an interest in the hardships of the poor:

>   Giohan Riccio
>   to pay peasant
>   for 2 horses   decent
>   I'll pay him   price
>   . . . .
>   Giuliano—dead
>   Kids to get
>   what's left[34]

In a similar vein, Pound transcribes from Clementini a seemingly trivial bit of information about Francesco Sforza's favorite pastime, "varie ricreazioni e particolarmente della pesca di cui godeva molto" (#42, p. 9)—but to prefer fishing to more aristocratic sports (Malatesta asks for "huntin' dogs" in 11.49.28) reveals Sforza as "the peasant's son" that he was (8.31.8–13). On one occasion (#42, p. 131), a scrap of personal information about Pius II, "stone in the bladder," is juxtaposed with a scrap of papal speech, "testibus idoneis" ("by means of suitable witnesses," that is, testifiers against Sigismondo), to produce the Latin pun on "appropriate testicles" that appears in Canto 10 (45.21–22): "(stone in his bladder / *testibus idoneis*)," this partially accounting for Pius's "pustulous temper" (10.46.21)—or should we say for his testiness?

Related to this interest in the ostensibly insignificant detail is Pound's solicitude in transcribing snippets of Latin and Italian (from letters, documents, records of conversations, etc.) that are meant to capture the authentic "linguistic flavor" of the times as well as to reveal the character of the speaker. Among Pound's notes we thus find a transcription (from Soranzo, *Pio II*, p. 26) of the threats exchanged between Federigo d'Urbino and Sigismondo, which may be translated: "I'll rip your guts out!" and "I'll tear your belly open!" (#42, p. 110; cf. 10.43.15–17). Pius II's reluctant admission that Malatesta's betrayal of King Alfonso had nevertheless saved the Florentine state ("rem eorum saluavit," #42, p. 125) is carefully earmarked for the *Cantos* (9.35.20), along with less ingratiating papal dicta—those, for instance, memorializing the confiscation of Fano (#40, p. 144; 11.50.12) or dealing with the curtailment, Lear-style, of Sigismondo's retinue (#42, p. 123; 11.51.13). But for Pound all these ecclesiastical pronouncements fade into insignificance compared with the Church's fierce invectives against Malatesta; in his notes there are no fewer than five separate transcriptions of the epithets hurled at Sigismondo by Pius II and Andreas Benzi, which now appear in the *Cantos* in the original Latin (10.44.19–24), in Soranzo's Italian (10.45.12–14), and in Pound's English (10.44.25–10.45.11).[35] Pound seems to have felt that nothing could go further toward extenuating Sigismondo's conduct than a generous selection from the vile-mouthed "oratory" of his enemies. The obverse side of this strategy consists of Pound's eagerness to record any facts or interpretations that would help to exculpate Malatesta: "strangled Polixena 'although no cause for death was found afterward.' S. on other side the peninsula" (#43, p. 6; cf. 9.35.25), and "Betrayed *Alf.* not out of *avarice* but of ambition" (#43, p. 9).

Pound's transcriptions from Broglio's *Cronaca* demonstrate the extent to which he was willing to grapple with what is, to an untrained modern eye, an almost illegible manuscript. In the following example we see Pound struggling to decipher this text, sometimes listing as many as four possible readings for one word or phrase:

> grād ment li antichi caveler
>   e valentj
> romanj davano grâ dissima
> fed a quisty /anuitij/
>   /amitj/
>   /ari/
>   /annutii/
> chiamatj agurij β la qual
> β te ne pigliano grâ conforto
>   pigliamo
> β ch essendo noj /dis o/   della
>   /dis aisi/
>   /dis cessy/
> progienia e sanguinita dello Ili^{mo}
> /philno/   scipione affricano nobile
> romano β *o loni*potente dio
> /naficto/   di mashationi
>   (#42, p. 138; from Broglio, p. 273*r*; cf. 10.47.6-8)

It is clear that, beyond the "message" encoded in this bewildering philological specimen, Pound was fascinated by the orthographical conventions of an early Renaissance manuscript such as this. Though he spares his reader anything so baffling as the above passage, he nevertheless incorporates into the Malatesta Cantos many of the linguistic peculiarities of his sources.[36] These sometimes lend an air of scholarly authenticity to the text, and sometimes of ceremonious silliness, as in "Ex^{so} D^{no} et D^{no} sin D^{no} Sigismundum Pandolfi Filium / Malatestis Capitan General." They all result, however, from the same obsession with the verbally exotic that caused Pound to jot down in his notes words and phrases like "*concret Allgemeine*," "Poliorcetes," "polumetis," "spingard," and "bombards" (noun).

In addition to the linguistic climate of Sigismondo's era, Pound also shows considerable interest in the pageantry, technology, and social amenities of the early Renaissance. In his notes for the scene with Bianca Visconti and Sforza in Canto 8, for example, Pound apparently has trouble visualizing exactly what type of horses "ubini" are,[37] then looks up the word and jots down "piccolo cavallo Scozzesse," and this leads him to guess triumphantly that they must have been "*Shetland*" (#41, pp. 19–20). Similarly, he struggles to determine the exact color of the sails of Sforza's fishing-boats:

> & the sails
> > banded with
> > > orange
>
> . . . .
> sails yellow
> > & rust-coloured.
> > > (#41, p. 22)

The same eye for detail is evident in the following note on the workings of the Malatesta salt industry at Cervia,

> salt heaps
> 2 metre high.
> covered with
> reeds—
> yellow—canna
> > paulustra.
> canna
> paviera
> herba
> palausta
> & even the
> little square
> tower at
> <u>Cesenatico</u>
> salt heaps
> & the pines,
> > (#45, p. 6)

which results in the imagistically poignant lines:

> And the salt heaps with the reed mats on them
> Gone long ago to the Venetians.
> > (11.49.24–25)

It is thus not surprising to find, among Pound's notes, three photographs of wax seals—two belonging to Malatesta Novello and one to Sigismondo's son, Sallustio (the "Malatesta de Malatestis" of 9.39.14–33)—that Pound had commissioned from a photography studio in Modena, probably during his visit in early March of 1923 (#45, pp. 1-2). Years later he used Sallustio's seal as the frontispiece to *Guide to Kulchur*, remarking that it is indicative of "the thoroughness of Rimini's civilization in 1460." He explains this statement—and also unconsciously sheds light on one of the major sources of his own poetic power—when he says that "I mean it was carried down and out into details" (*GK*, p. 159).

The Early Drafts before the Watson Typescript

Among Pound's MSS are a relatively small number of autograph drafts[38] that are, in general, unimportant for studying the evolution of the Malatesta Cantos because most of what they contain is duplicated elsewhere among the typescripts. In addition, the chaotic order of the MSS themselves renders futile any attempt to group the individual leaves into coherent units of composition. Simply as an example of the style of Pound's autograph drafts—and, more important, as an indication of how his early technique often differs from that of his final version—I transcribe a passage that was later "condensed" into the enigmatic line, "And what he said was all right there in Mantua" (10.46.20):

> & Pio came down to Mantua
> & Sig. said if you go to war
> with Turk,
> you'd better do the thing properly
> I wont talk about naval warfare
> as it is not my business—
> but for the land troops
> take italians.
> (#41, page after 24)

We now understand why what Sigismondo said at the Congress of Mantua was "all right." His suggestion about using Italian land troops (rather than those of other Christian nations) in the upcoming crusade against the Turks was considered sound advice. In the early draft, the episode is treated briefly but coherently; in the final version, the reader—unless he be an expert in fifteenth-century Italian history—is left completely in the dark.

Bound up with such helpfully explanatory passages, however, is the tendency toward a verbose, discursive technique among the MSS that Pound later filed away in a large envelope labeled "Drafts pre-Ital."—that is, the drafts composed prior to his Italian vacation of January 5 to April 24, 1923 (Folder #46). Pound had not yet discovered a style appropriate to his subject and, consequently, he talks a great deal about (or around) Sigismondo, but presents comparatively little:

> Led the fleet into Morea,
> prepared to murder a pope,
> Collected ten artists, among whom Pisanello,
> Alberti, Duccio, Pier Francesca,
> having some sense of life
> no morals, infinite heroism,
> and a respect for tradition.
> i.e. the grand geste, Caesar at the Rubicon,
> Buggared a bishop, a pure act of exuberance,
> broke all the commandments, a mere feat of punctillio

> adored graven images (possibly those of Alberti)
> and, in the language of Pius
> > "built a church
> noble but Impius,
> ....
> and therein raised to his concubine
> a magnificent pagan sepulchre, and inscription
> Unto the Goddess Isotta,
> > > sacro
> > alla Diva Isotta,
> > a much respected, /&/ longsuffering woman,
> with upper lip, a sense of humour, excellent glands,
> lacking the hyperthyroid of her paramour,
> but intelligent, and undoubtedly amused at the
> > difficulties of Ser Galeotto,
> excommunicated.[39]

Here Pound baldly lists some of Sigismondo's deeds, as if to cow the reader into submission before the obvious *virtù* of this Renaissance Übermensch, and he then proceeds to editorialize upon them—as if the deeds were really *not* sufficiently self-explanatory. Similarly, the attempt to portray Isotta by means of endocrinology results in pure bathos. We sense that the poet is interested in his subject, but we remain unsure about why *we* should share his enthusiasm. The following passage reveals the same wish to tell a self-contained story, but it also embodies two other aspects of the pre-Italy drafts: an excessive concentration on the minor characters—that is, on the motivations of Malatesta's enemies—and explicit criticism of Sigismondo's actions. (The subject is the sale of Pesaro by Galeazzo Malatesta to "Alex" Sforza, via the machinations of "brother Francesco" Sforza and Federigo d'Urbino):

> And then Galeaz, uncle, and scoundrel,
> wanting pay for his cattle, ole, toothless,
> > codardo, no sport,
> with the fox of Urbino trailing and taleing.
> That Alex wants to marry a girl of noble blood,
> > and lackland, needs a state of sorts,
> So brother Francesco risks it, his soft side,
> > and pays, oh damn it, pays, loses the marches,
> Driven from all but Pesaro, down and out,
> > but for the throw at Milan.
>
> > and Sigismund's seven wrong moves.
> > > (#46, 35th sheet)

We recognize the contours of a story—but Sigismondo's own interests in Pesaro recede into the background. Although Galeaz and Urbino are treated unfavorably, there is a bit too much poignancy in Alex's being "lackland"[40] and in Francesco's fraternal solicitude. These qualities of historical "objectivity" or plenitude may have been laudable in Pound's prose sources, but they blur the point of Malatesta's exemplary status in the *Cantos*. The remark about Sigismondo's "seven wrong moves" is another instance of Pound's not yet realizing that he was not composing a historical treatise, but a poem—a poem in which Malatesta's positive accomplishments must not be vitiated by the kinds of charges his enemies were quick to make ("buggared a bishop"—"exuberance" indeed!) or by the sympathetic qualities of his adversaries. And I say this, not with reference to an abstract schema for what semi-historical, "exemplary" narrative poems should be like, but with reference to the final version of the Malatesta Cantos themselves, in which an objective perspective has, for the most part, ceded to the interests of thematic coherence. There, we are not asked to wander in the mazes of moral ambiguity (how "right" was Sigismondo? and did his enemies have a case against him?), but to acquire a respect for the "factive personality," while realizing that its relentless pursuit of excellence (for Sigismondo, the Tempio) almost inevitably leads to personal catastrophe. Although Pound does not distort the facts that he uncovered in his research on Malatesta, it is well to remember that, in Bernstein's assessment of the *Cantos* as a whole,

> it is history itself that constitutes the essential fiction of the poem, and in Pound's epic that fiction must be allowed to speak as if it were history itself. This desperately precarious balancing act, in which the world's history is fictionalized, appropriated with all the thematic license and willful patterning of art, only so that it can re-emerge in the (fictional) text as "valid" history, constitutes Pound's basic solution to the problem of a modern verse epic.[41]

The following is a typical example of an early passage in which a crime attributed to Sigismondo (here, the rape and murder of a German noblewoman) looms too large:

```
And then on the way to rome,
        "Her hair like a rain of gold"
and scandal.
     he waited, say this, her return,
with every gentleness.
                /&/ death.
some say in Rimini, some in Verona, Fano,
    but all shout murder, by him, or a captain,
or /by/ someone or other,
                    save Broglio, who says nothing at all.
But a star crime, among all his crime/s/,
    the largest shudder,
some /say/ near Brescia, /& Ser/ Broglio nothing
                            /at all/.[42]
```

The one-line final version of this passage raises a problem that the reader is free to pursue or ignore, as he sees fit:

> And there was the row about that German-Burgundian female.
> (9.36.27)

The insensitivity of the narrator here speaks only to those who have inquired into Pound's sources; to all others, this oblique reference to the crime constitutes a minor puzzle that does not, however, distract them from the main issues of the poem. The reader who *does* look up the allusion is indeed perplexed by the narrator's abrupt dismissal of the murdered woman,[43] but this bewilderment presumably arises only when he has been teased into the kind of interest in Malatesta that Pound has sought to arouse all along.

If the iniquities ascribed to Sigismondo play too prominent a role in the pre-Italy drafts, so does Malatesta's greatest achievement—the building of the Tempio:

> Leaving at last the cherubs, Alberti's labour,
> Di Duccio's carving, Pisanello's, and Da Pasti,
> the stolen marbles, and Gemisthus' tomb.
>   Divae Ixottae Manes
>   . . . .
>   the fat rumped putti, and marble waters
> flow over marble feet, Primaverile, surely,
>
> For at a given moment the dumb stone took shape,
>   and of dead slabs, live figures rose,
>   treading the dolphins, lyra aegyptiorum,
>   lygdiorum cithera, scraping the viel strings,
>   thumping on tympana. Ferruci/'s/ leading children
>   circle/ing/ the well-head/s/, born aloft with palms,
>
>   Pan's-son-hath-built this place.
>   (#46, 27th sheet)

Pound must have realized that this kind of *ekphrasis* violated his dictum of not doing in one art what another art (here, sculpture) can do better.[44] In the final version, he utters in his own voice a few generalized (but very effective) lines describing the Tempio (9.41.12–16), while he nevertheless endows the edifice with a mediated ubiquity by allowing it to surface in many of the letters and documents woven into the text. We can imagine, however, with what reluctance Pound decided to excise lyrical paeans such as that reproduced above when, at one point, he had even drawn a parallel between Malatesta's creative audacity and his own:

> Chien de metier,
>   hopelessness of-writing an epic,
>   chien de metier,

> ~~hopelessness of building~~ a temple,
> in Romagna, in a land teeming with cattle thieves.
>
> (#46, 23rd sheet)

From an examination of Pound's earliest version of the "post-bag letters" (#47, pp. 68–78), it is evident that he had already decided to reproduce the semi-illiterate qualities of some of the originals (pp. 70–71), as well as the stilted pretentiousness of the letter from Malatesta's young son (p. 78). It is instructive to note that the only translated letter he eventually discarded *in toto* is one in which Isotta reveals herself to be very much the bourgeois mistress:

> Signor Mio . . .
>   I should be very much pleased if you wd. regularize
> our position
>   You have said, often enough, that you wanted to
>   I have only your letters, and if my last was not
> as agreeable, as it might have been,
>   You know why . . .
>   Yxotta da Rimini
>   (#47, p. 75)

One of the letters that Pound translates rather fully in his early notes, but from which he quotes only an enigmatic, unidentified snippet in his final text, is the letter from Malatesta's court poet, Trachulo— "Trachulo's damn'd epistle," as it is called in 10.42.9. Pound's original translation makes clear why Trachulo's letter to Malatesta corroborated the view of his Sienese employers that he was meditating some treacherous action against them:

> Illustrious Prince, and Excellent Lord in especial.
> . . . .
> Unfitting as it is that I shd. offer councils to Caesar.
> I wd. advise that you do all things convenient to gain
>   favour with the Sienese people,
> . . . .
> for if later they break into faction it wd. be but in
>   the order of things that the general
> should take over the seignory.
> . . . .
>   (#48, p. 10)

Pound omitted the details of this "epistle" because, as the Watson Typescript makes clear, the presentation of the post-bag letters is meant to simulate the alternately rapid or absorbed scanning of them on the part of Malatesta—the implication being that, when he comes to Trachulo's, the sycophantic clause, "Unfitting as it is that I should offer counsels to Hannibal" (9.40.2), causes him to throw the letter aside impatiently.⁴⁵ Thus, part of the evidence for Malatesta's disloyal designs, which the Sienese discovered upon seizing his post-bag, was based on a letter never even read by the recipient. (Cf. #56, p. 19, where it is "Trachulo's unread epistle.") This, at least, seems to have been Pound's intention; but the execution of that intent is marred by a technique that relies for its success on the reader's knowledge that the excerpt on 9.40.1-2 is from Trachulo's "epistle," and also that the unreproduced contents of that letter had urged Malatesta to seize power in Siena. All that can be said for such lapses is that Pound failed to keep in mind the enormous gap separating his own minute familiarity with these materials from the relative ignorance of his readers. As late as 1938 he still insisted that "no one has claimed that the Malatesta cantos are obscure" (*GK*, p. 194).⁴⁶

If the Malatesta Cantos sometimes do not furnish enough information, the early drafts for them often provide *too* much. This loquacity results in the absolute flatness of passages such as the following, in which irrelevant details spoil the singleness of effect attained in the final version. The early passage reads:

> And that day, or on some such sort of day
> The ambassador came before Cosimo,
>   dux fiorientiae, the same that built
> the great citadel in Siena,
>   and whose balls
> hang over every pawn shop in our day,
> And the ambassador said Drusilia Sforza
> is proposed as wife for the sapling, son of Piccinino,
>
> Whereat the face of Cosimo, wrinkled and amiable
> showed o̶n̶e̶ m̶o̶r̶e̶ minor wrinkle, approaching a smile,
>   /some/
>
> And Pontius Pilate said that the matter was not his
>   affair.
>   (#48, pp. 12–13)

Compare this with the sardonic humor of Canto 10, in which it is clear that the wise old fox, Cosimo, is fully aware that the troublesome Piccinino is being "set up" by Sforza ("old Wattle") and King Ferdinand:

> And that day Cosimo smiled,
> That is, the day they said:
>   "Drusiana is to marry Count Giacomo . . ."
> (Piccinino) *un sorriso malizioso*.
> Drusiana, another of Franco Sforza's;
> It would at least keep the row out of Tuscany.
> And he fell out of a window, Count Giacomo,
> Three days after his death, that was years later in Naples,
> For trusting Ferdinando of Naples,
> And old Wattle could do nothing about it.
>   (10.43.18–27)

The early drafts continually remind us how difficult it was for Pound to stick to his subject—the deeds of Malatesta—and to avoid excursions into areas not strictly related to his purposes. In the final version, for example, the two and a half lines on Guillaume (8.32.22–24) do not strike us as an intrusion, especially because Pound relates the troubadour's achievement to that of Malatesta—a first "renaissance" being compared with (or foreshadowing) a later one. But in an early draft, Pound gets lost in a labyrinth of Provençal lore by attempting to trace the thread of troubadour fortunes:

> Viel and ribibi,
>   I have told you
> How Guillaume of Poictiers came up out of spain
> riding, and his men with him, and over the saddlebows
> viel and ribibi, and the song of the Arabs with them
>
> And in that time Guillaume . . .
>   and after him Elinor,
> and En Richart,
>   and Simone di Montfort, and the burning of Mt Segur,
>
> and how en Richart was in Cypress
>   and the lady made captive.
> And Simone, fell under Tolosa.
> Whither Guido in due time,
>   and in Narbonne by the canal bank
>   Girart Riquier.
>
> / / to put things into some order)
>
>   upon which the new learning.
>   (#48, p. 33)

We can surmise Pound's intention here—to provide a "genealogy" from Guillaume to Cavalcanti and, implicitly, on to Malatesta; but how many separate stories are contained within these seventeen lines! And how far afield from Malatesta any one of them would take us.

A fairly typical specimen of Pound's Malatesta drafts is furnished by a typescript whose remoteness from the printed text points to an early stage of composition,[47] but whose opening with an allusion to the events of 1457 leads us to believe that it was meant to follow at least one other Malatesta canto. In any event, the most interesting aspect of these opening passages consists in their being narrated by Sigismondo's younger brother, Malatesta Novello (the only other brother being long dead by this time):

> . . . my brother at least seems honest
> Faerico
> and farigo writes, at any rate, like liar.
> very possibly
> my brother, of course you know him
> better than I do. . . .
> (#49, p. 7)

It is evident that Pound intended to narrate at least part of his story by means of Novello's correspondence with some unnamed contemporary. A few traces of this early intention survive into the printed text,[48] but the idea was soon abandoned in favor of an indeterminate narrator who seems to be one of Malatesta's subordinates. Pound's ultimate narrative strategy may thus owe something to Edward Hutton's historical novel on Malatesta, in which the events are narrated by a fictitious contemporary of Sigismondo named Pietro Sanseverino.[49] It is not certain that Pound knew this book, but the significance of the gesture is nevertheless clear: Pound wished to convey a sense of immediacy greater than that which a chronologically and culturally distanced narration could provide. This same urge prompted him to intersperse excerpts from contemporary documents throughout his text, as well as to retain or translate many of the quaint or archaic terms and modes of address he found therein. At the same time, Pound reserved the right to speak in his own voice occasionally, especially in the lyrical and elegiac parts of the poem. This multiple voice provided a suppler mode of narration than would have been possible with Novello's telling of the story, and it also enabled Pound to deal with the final events of Sigismondo's career—his brother having predeceased him by three years.

As in most of the early drafts, here too we notice a certain amount of criticism directed at Malatesta. In the passage narrated by Novello, for example, he applies Broglio's dictum to Sigismondo, "dove la potentia . . . ragione si cela,"[50] ("Where there's power, reason goes into hiding"), and he characterizes Malatesta as "given to promising overmuch" (#49, p. 7). The passage quoted earlier, about buggering a bishop, reappears in this draft, though now with the qualification, "unproven" (#49, p. 12). There is also an unpleasant screechiness in some of the passages in Pound's own voice, "Then replied Pio Secundo, speaking like the shits in our own day" (#49, p. 13), which he was later to tone down or to put into the mouth of his main narrator, at the same time removing many of his references to Malatesta's more questionable deeds.

Once again, as in the other early drafts, we notice here a pronounced attempt to define (rather reductively) the motives of Sigismondo's enemies, rather than an endeavor to let the facts and documents speak for themselves. Thus, Pius II's hypocrisy is made overt in this early version:

> . . . not saying "I want the land" but saying
> that Sigismund was an heretic, and a despiser of

> religion. (i.e. papal monopoly)
>
> as reported by himself . . .
> (#49, p. 13)

The apparent clemency of Venice toward the despoiled Malatesta is shown to be selfishly motivated, "And Venice says he has suffered sufficiently, / (Venice wanting supplies from Romagna)" (p. 15), and Malatesta's attempt on the life of Paul II is set in the context of the "trade" proposed by the Pontiff: "'Well, take Foligno and Spoleto' / Arimnium suits us, a leg for St Peter's chair" (p. 17).

A small detail included here, but omitted from the final text, deals with how Malatesta "finds Gemisthus' ashes" in Morea (#49, p. 16). This fact would have balanced the rather developed section on Gemisthus Plethon in Canto 8, which tells of the philosopher's visit to Florence in 1439 and suggests the influence that the neo-pagan cast of his conversations there might have exercised on the young Malatesta. To have retained the detail of Sigismondo's transferral of Gemisthus's ashes to the Tempio would have provided further justification (from the end of Malatesta's life) for the text's inclusion of an apparently extraneous episode that had occurred during his youth. It would also have added a sense of closure to the incident: the man who might have inspired the Tempio ends up reposing therein. On the other hand, the conclusion of this draft is distinctly inferior to Pound's final version, for it ends with the death of Malatesta rather than with the humorous contract presented at the end of Canto 11. In the printed text, our last impression of Malatesta is that of a defeated man retaining his sense of humor in spite of misfortune; his enemies have despoiled him of most of the external trappings of wealth and power, but they have not succeeded in crushing the man himself.

So far, I have been considering isolated passages from Pound's early drafts because of the anarchic state of the manuscripts themselves. Because Pound was working with anecdotal "tesserae" to be presented in no strictly chronological order, and because he rarely allows his individual typed sheets to flow over in meaning from one sheet to the next—preferring to "end-stop" his episodes—it is often impossible to determine questions of grouping, ordering, and successive layers of composition. Thus, on many occasions, a page numbered by Pound may fit equally comfortably into any number of drafts that are all missing that page. Rather than attempt a systematic (and necessarily arbitrary) grouping of all the MSS, I have preferred to quote and discuss passages illustrative of certain basic differences between Pound's drafts and his finished product, restricting questions of structure to only those drafts whose constituents can be grouped with some certainty.

It is fortunate that what appears to be Pound's first typed draft is among those whose components can be ascertained and ordered accurately.[51] It is by far the shorter of the only two versions that attempt to encompass the entire saga of Malatesta within a single canto, and thus it seems the obvious candidate for Pound's first draft, dating from perhaps as early as June 1922. (In discussing the draft I will retain Pound's enumeration of the sheets, 1–5.)

What is striking about the typescript is the central importance of T. S. Eliot to the narrative frame. This Malatesta canto—here (and only here) dedicated to "T.S.E."—opens with Pound's evocation of *The Waste Land*, "These fragments you have 'shelved',"[52] and proceeds to associate the literary fragments supposedly "shelved" by Eliot with the architectural fragments collected by Malatesta, "Sigismundo / had shelved / a broken arch, spoils of Ravenna," and, implicitly, with the fragments of a life that Pound had assembled concerning this historical character. But more important than this introductory gesture (quite appropriate in light of Pound's recent "maieutic" operation on *The Waste Land*) is the "coda" of this typescript—roughly one half the length of the whole—which deals primarily with two meetings between Pound and Eliot on the Continent, the first, in Provence, in the summer of 1919, the other, in Verona, "1920 or thereabouts" (78/481). Between the two parts of the narrative frame the account of Malatesta is presented, arising—like a sermon from a text—from Eliot's line about shoring fragments against one's ruin, and then in turn giving rise to Pound's re-creation of his meetings with Eliot and to somber ruminations on the transience of human relationships and the decline of great civilizations, both of these topics occasioned by the circumstances of his encounters with Eliot. The structure of this first draft thus resolves itself as follows:

1. An adaptation of a line from Eliot's text is used to introduce a historical personage, as well as to provide the *leitmotif* for Pound's own fragmentary handling of Malatesta.

2. Sigismondo's story is narrated, with special emphasis on his being constrained to "piece together" his Tempio.

3. Pound and Eliot are now presented against a backdrop of futile personal ambitions and amidst the detritus of crumbled civilizations—a setting that partially accounts for the attempt, on the part of both poets, to "shore" their fragments, namely, those incorporated into *The Waste Land* and the Malatesta canto.

The pattern is circular but intricate. Eliot's text gives rise to Pound's, which, in turn, leads to an autobiographical sketch that comments on the two texts while re-creating the gloomy emotional state that had helped to generate them in the first place. Nevertheless, Pound later abandoned this strategy: he became more interested in Malatesta in his own right and more reticent about presenting sensitive personal issues so explicitly. As a result, the meeting at Verona with Eliot (and with Bride Scratton, with whom Pound was romantically linked) diminishes in scope in the Malatesta Cantos, but continues to surface enigmatically in Pound's work for the next twenty years.[53]

But let us proceed to a closer examination of this first draft. After the initial gesture toward *The Waste Land* and its relation to Sigismondo, Pound launches into the genealogy of Malatesta, beginning with "Mastin Vecchio" and including Paolo and Francesca (cf. 8.32.26–28), but containing a glaring error: Pound asserts that Sigismondo was descended from Francesca's husband, "Lo Squercio" (Gianciotto), by his second marriage, whereas, in fact, he was descended from Gianciotto's youngest brother, Pandolfo. Pound also refers to Sigismondo's illegitimate birth—a detail omitted from the final version, as was the qualifying phrase "con voce di veleno" ("with rumors of poisoning") with regard to the deaths of Ginevra d'Este and Polissena Sforza (#50, p. 1). There follows a short passage on Isotta, asserting that the Tempio was reared specifically in her honor. Pound then registers Pius II's shock at the pagan cast of the images housed in the edifice, and he provides a brief description of some of the Tempio's sculptures and bas-reliefs.

After juxtaposing Guillaume Poictiers's achievement, "bringing his / jongleurs, and viel players out of Spain," with that of Sigismondo, "behind it all, the urge to refound the world" (#50, p. 2), Pound proceeds to offer an interesting rationalization for Malatesta's underhanded procurement of marble:

> Il tempio,—theft,
> oh well, you can replate Appollinaire in Classe
> with flat marble slabs, whenever the wish takes you
> no idea is needed . . . .
>   Fragments against his ruin.
>   (#50, p. 2)

Immediately afterwards, in a passage canceled by Pound, the theft of the marble is seen as the justifiable, desperate act of a man who is trying to create a perdurable monument before the extinction of his dynasty:

> The urge, life in a setting, and the word made stone.
> Against his ruin and the house's ruin fifty years later
> and no history, no anything from 1507–1807
>   under the papal sway.
>   (#50, p. 3)

The passage ends with Sigismondo's death:

> /These/ Fragments against his ruin,
>   at 54, his head in Isotta's
>   lap.
>   /Sono venuto a mal passo./

And so, after a mere two and a half typed pages, ends the story of Sigismondo. The second half of this draft is entirely concerned with autobiographical events that comment on Malatesta's story and, at the same time, acquire added resonance and depth from it. Pound sets the scene by the Roman arena at Verona, which has fallen prey to modern commercialism: "inside it, the footlights, the clowns, dancers / performing dogs" (#50, p. 3). Pound is with Eliot ("you, Thomas amics"), Bride Scratton ("Galla Placidia" and "Ti"), and, apparently, with an unidentified woman referred to as "the Roman." He then links this meeting with one that had occurred during the summer of 1919, when Pound and his wife had journeyed with Eliot to Excideuil. The Provençal milieu (combined with a remark Eliot had made on that occasion and with line 427 of *The Waste Land*) prompts Pound to associate Eliot with Dante's heaven-aspiring Arnaut, " 'e poi gli affina' for you,"[54] and himself with Bertran de Born as he appears in the *Inferno*: "Me swinging the burning head" (#50, p. 3).[55] It is at this point that Pound introduces the lines

> I have sat here a thousand years, /or/
>   forty-four thousand, to be more exact
>   /years/.
>   (#50, p. 3)

Sitting by the Roman arena, Pound pictures himself as a spectator in the arena of *all* human history, since the figure of 44,000 years points roughly to the time when Cro-Magnon man first appeared in Europe (the first truly human being, Pound implies, because of his being the first artist), responsible for the cave drawings that Eliot went off to see after his meeting in Provence with the Pounds. What this archetypal man has learned from his long contemplation of human history is that "Things run, and run to the worse" (#50, p. 3), a variation on the earlier lines from *Mauberley*:

> All things are a flowing,
> Sage Heracleitus says;
> But a tawdry cheapness
> Shall outlast our days.
>   (*PERSONAE*, p. 189)

• The emphasis then shifts to personal frustrations. Bride Scratton, or "Ti," is identified with "Galla's hypostasis," a reincarnation of Galla Placidia, the Roman empress whose mausoleum Pound had visited at Ravenna (just as Pound and Eliot are seen as avatars of Bertran and Arnaut). But the modern Galla

> . . . disintegrates
>   puts on Venetian clogs,
> digs into your [Eliot's] powdered past,
>   smells your soiled cuff lace,
>   /sniffs/

At which time I?
>	was lifting sedan chairs, preparing the
revolution,
(in a brown fustian coat).
>	paying the bill
.unpaid for the "banquet," by Veronese.
>	/&/ . . . never learning . . . .
>	(#50, p. 4)

The long-dead woman acquires an aura of magnificence from the artistry lavished upon her:

and she's buried in Ravenna,
lit by the alabaster panes,
yellow, sun yellow, in the gloom the gold
> gathers the light against it.
>	(#50, p. 4)

But the survival of scattered monuments of civilization (like Galla's mausoleum or the Tempio) only serves to emphasize the transience of human achievement:

Byzance,
/&/ the empires /gone/, slide to nothing here in the
>	marsh drift,
Caesarea, gone, roof deep in the marsh,
. . . .
Empires end in the marsh.
>	(#50, p. 5)

The draft ends with a lovely evocation of former artistic grandeurs—fragile now, and almost obliterated by the ravages of time:

>	on mosaic walls, the souls,
gonads in organdy, rose-flakes in the arid darkness,
a wing exists for a moment and goes out,
> flame intermittent,
an emerald lizard peers through the border grass,
>	(#50, p. 5)

a passage that reminds us of the ending of Canto 3:

Drear waste, the pigment flakes from the stone,
Or plaster flakes, Mantegna painted the wall.
Silk tatters, "Nec Spe Nec Metu."
>	(3/12)

Though eventually canceled from the Malatesta sequence, elements of this passage resurface later, in Canto 21, not long after Pound briefly recalls Placidia's mausoleum and the Roman arena at Verona:

>   . . . dry darkness
> Floating flame in the air, gonads in organdy,
> Dry flamelet, a petal borne in the wind.
>   (21/99)

"Gonads in organdy"—a phrase too well-turned to be discarded. The two nouns demonstrate an affinity in the realm of sound ("organdy" containing all the letters of "gonad") in spite of their vastly antithetical connotations. The coldly stark Greek scientific term is set against the lush French word, evocative of warm, richly furnished interiors—a "callida iunctura" not quite Horatian but certainly Poundian, the yoking together of apparently irreconcilable levels of diction into a satisfying, sometimes seemingly inevitable, unity. This technique, extensively employed in the Malatesta Cantos, hardly appears in the first draft. It was only after Pound had decided to reduce the autobiographical episode in the early drafts almost to non-existence and to amplify greatly the portrayal of Sigismondo himself—in short, it was only after Pound had discovered what his artistic priorities really were at this point—that he was able to evolve a radical of presentation suitable to narrating the deeds of a somewhat obscure, morally suspect Renaissance princeling.

The earliest draft (Folder #51) that bears even the remotest resemblance to what we now know as the Malatesta Cantos consists of a typescript, heavily corrected in hand, nine pages in length and interspersed with bibliographical references. It is evident that Pound had begun doing quite a bit of research on Malatesta, and his text reflects the first groping gestures toward a much more comprehensive view of Sigismondo than had been apparent in what I believe to be the earliest draft of all. The first thing we notice about this version (which, for the sake of convenience, I shall refer to as "Draft Two") is that the material dealing with Pound himself, Eliot, and "Ti" has been completely expunged.[56] Indeed, even the former opening line of the poem has been temporarily "shelved": "T̶h̶e̶s̶e̶ ̶f̶r̶a̶g̶m̶e̶n̶t̶s̶ ̶y̶o̶u̶ ̶h̶a̶v̶e̶ ̶s̶h̶e̶l̶v̶e̶d̶?" The emphasis is entirely on Sigismondo, though the technique of fragmented presentation is much more obvious (and much less successful) than in Pound's final text. The draft opens with a snippet from the same letter of Malatesta to Giovanni de' Medici that is now found in Canto 8.[57] Then there appears the answer made by the captain of the watch at Ancona: "'Yes, Messire Sigismund, but we want this town for ourselves'" (#51, p. 116)—totally unsupported by any context.[58] Only after a brief reference to Federigo d'Urbino and a return to the letter requesting a painter for the Tempio does Pound provide Sigismondo's statement to the captain of the guard, "'You have me like a hen in a coop'" (#51, p.

116), upon which he repeats the captain's rejoinder. Finally, there is a two-line reference to Drusiana Sforza's marriage to Piccinino and to the enigmatic smile that this bit of news elicits from Cosimo de' Medici.

Pound then launches into his description of the wedding visit to Rimini of Francesco Sforza and Bianca Visconti, which now constitutes 8.30.33–8.31.15. But apparently realizing that he has not yet presented Sigismondo in great enough depth to warrant the introduction of another major character, Pound feels his way toward the opening that he was eventually to adopt, scrapping his "fragmentary" introduction and replacing it (#51, p. 118) by a substantial extract from Malatesta's letter to Giovanni de' Medici, in which he requests the services of Piero della Francesca and shows himself to be the ideal patron:

> . . . he /may/ work as he likes
> /or waste his time/
> /as he like/.
> (#51, p. 118)

After he has thus provided a certain favorable context for our first view of Malatesta, Pound asks himself, in a handwritten note, "then fragments?"—meaning the snippets with which he had originally begun this draft.

At this stage, Pound introduces his translation of the document ratifying Sigismondo's *condotta* with the Florentines (presently 8.29.25–8.30.10) in almost exactly the same form as it appears in the final text, and he then struggles to extract some artistic form from a sprawling poem that Malatesta had written in honor of Isotta degli Atti. He begins translating:

> O spirits who /of/ olde were in this land,
> And each one shaken with love /& shaken/
> /under/
> /go with [?] lute [indec.]/
> /with her the [indec.]/
> be kind,
> send in upon her mind,
> the sweetness of the time,
> Should roses die, spring born,
> Ye heavenly stars and signs,
> ye tame beasts and ye wild,
> tame.

He continues with allusions to the stories of David and "Batzabe," Samson, Pyramus and Thisbe, Paris and Helen, Dido, Narcissus, Phyllis and Demophon, Leander, Phaedra, Tristan and "Isotta"—in short, he is beginning to be deluged by the flood of Ovidian, Biblical, and medieval love-lore that had found its way into Malatesta's poem. Pound then tries to produce a rhymed quatrain from his material,

> Beauteous majesty and worthy of rule
> /fair/ Helen's equal, needing no school
> nor parallel, what Helen or what Isotta
> > is thy peer.
> unique and needing no exemplaire,

which yields immediately to the concise paraphrase of these lines that he ultimately retained:

> /who hath not/
> /Helen for peer,/
> /Yseut, nor Batsabe/.
> > (#51, p. 122)

Sigismondo's rambling poem was eventually compressed into one of the most *cantabile* of Pound's own lyrics:

> "Ye spirits who of olde were in this land
> Each under Love, and shaken,
> Go with your lutes, awaken
> The summer within her mind,
> Who hath not Helen for peer
> > Yseut nor Batsabe."
> > > (8.30.17–22)

The draft ends with the extract from Malatesta's letter that, in almost the identical words, now constitutes 8.30.24-32.

It is obvious that this is a fragmentary draft: it ends too much "in the middle of things" to produce the impression of a satisfactory whole. But as yet there are no clear indications that Pound had decided to extend his Malatesta material beyond the limits of a single canto. It is only with the version that I shall refer to as "Draft Three" (#53, pp. 34–44) that Pound begins to sense that his growing fascination with Malatesta demands ampler treatment.

Draft Three begins with an eleven-line extract from Malatesta's letter requesting a painter. Pound then seems unsure exactly where to place his parody of the line from *The Waste Land*, very tentatively inserting it *after* Sigismondo's letter: "These fragments?" (#53, p. 34). Indeed, Pound's deletion of the word "These" seems to indicate that, instead of Eliot's line, he was contemplating moving the series of fragments that had opened Draft Two to this position in the poem. He then blocks in the passage beginning ". . . and because the aforesaid illustrious / Duke of Milan" (8.29.25–8.30.10), as well as Malatesta's lyric (the only difference from our text being "O spirits . . ." instead of "Ye spirits . . .") and the passage beginning "Venice has taken me on again" (8.30.26–32).

This is followed by an early version of the lines about Guillaume Poictiers, including a specific reference to Malatesta's renovating influence on his times: "And the next notch here" (#53, p. 36). Pound proceeds to associate some of the mythical lovers from Malatesta's poem with the Tempio itself, and he also repeats the line with which this draft begins: "If Pier Francesca will come. . . ." After a very inchoate version of the Bianca Visconti scene, Pound presents the captain's rejoinder to Sigismondo at Ancona, "Aye, Messire Sigismund, but we want this town for ourselves" (#53, p. 36). We notice that the fragment is still meaningless, without proper contextualization, but that at least it has separated itself, in Pound's plan, from the puzzling barrage of isolated fragments with which he had begun Draft Two—it has taken wing, so to speak, and alighted in its own part of the poem, from where it can continue to grow in definition and scope until it has acquired at least the minimal amount of self-sufficiency to justify its inclusion.

Indeed, this was part of the problem Pound faced in composing his account of Malatesta's life. How does one avoid a dull, plodding narrative technique associated with outworn literary modes? The answer seemed to lie in making use of brief, self-contained "tesserae" of information. But how were they to be ordered and juxtaposed into a meaningful "mosaic"—chronologically? thematically? antithetically? And how could each unit of the poem contain enough information to be comprehensible, but at the same time sharp and concise? In short, how does one tell a story without calling undue attention to the fact that one is telling a story? I shall discuss these problems of structure in the next two chapters, but it is well to be aware of these issues here, in the midst of examining Pound's early struggles with them.

Draft Three continues with the arrival in Florence (1439) of Gemisthus Plethon, the Greek Neo-Platonic philosopher. Here, Plethon's catalytic function with regard to the Tempio is made more explicit than in the final text:

> . . . Gemisthus, an old man talking the gods.
> /Came later/ Later Alberti that the painter should
> set hunger in men for building.
>
> And thus grew, thus sprang to flower,
> sea poppy, luteumve papaver.
> By the sea gate, /&/ the sun's gate.
> caught in the stone.
> a song caught in the stone.
> (#53, p. 36)[59]

Toward the end of the passage that follows (an early form of 8.32.1–16), Pound is also explicit about the other major source of inspiration for the Tempio:

> Raised a temple, unto the Diva Isotta.
> /"to the divine"/
> (#53, p. 37)

In Pound's final version, Sigismondo's major achievement is made to spring less from the intellectual proddings of Gemisthus and the emotional impetus of Isotta, than from Malatesta's own indefatigable vision and will—another instance of Pound's gradual highlighting of his hero.

In the same vein is Pound's excessive concentration, in this draft, on Sigismondo's family history, especially with the part of it dealing with Paolo and Francesca:

>   /&/   /there came then/ /down/
> Down from Verruchio, then, came Mastin the old
> And took Arimnium, and lived a hundred years;
> Lo Squercio killed his brother, Dante has told
> The tale; /And/ the dark clears,
> And the wind is still for a little, the dusk rolled
> A little to one side. Appears
> Francesca born [sic] upon the wind, and with her her lover
> "as doves born [sic] up and whirled upon the strife"
> that seemed for a moment still. The spirits hover
> And come to rest:
>   Francesca i tuoi martiri.
> A scabbard caught in the arras.
>
>   (#53, p. 39)

Dante has indeed "told the tale"—and told it much better than this. As irresistible as such an episode must have been for Pound the inveterate Dantist, he nevertheless came to realize that brevity is the soul of allusion:

> And Mastin had come to Verucchio,
>   and the sword, Paolo il Bello's,
>   caught in the arras
> . . . .
> And the wind is still for a little
> And the dusk rolled
>   to one side a little.
>
>   (8.32.26–28,33; 8.33.1–2)

Here, there is just enough of Dante's famous scene in Canto 5 of the *Inferno* to add historical and thematic depth to Malatesta's ill-fated life, while, at the same time, Pound avoids entering into a futile competition with Dante himself.

After dealing, in greater or lesser detail, with the execution of Parisina Malatesta, Pius II's charges against Sigismondo, the unpaid papal *census*, Ginevra d'Este, Polissena Sforza, and the sale of Pesaro, Pound breaks off his continuous narrative and begins merely to list the other characters and events that he intends to incorporate into his canto:

>   Sforza and Venice.
>   / / /
> Tempio.
>   and Alfonso.
> Pio . . . Sforza
>   Cosimo
>   Borso
>   ///   Sono venuto a mal passo
> Stick of the rocket.   Morea
>   Paul II
>   Mort.
>   Isotta. blue robe brushing the grass.
>
>   Verona.⁶⁰
>
> Nov [i.e., Novello]   Novello
>   Urbino
>   mail bag
>   Nov.
>   (#53, pp. 43–44)

It seems that Pound meant to interweave passages he had already composed into the body of this draft. His references to Malatesta Novello, for example, probably refer to episodes that Sigismondo's younger brother was originally meant to narrate. One such passage in Pound's early drafts begins: "My brother was twelve at the time . . ."; another begins with the words: "But Urbino was back of it all, always Urbino / my brother and brother in law" (Novello having married Federigo d'Urbino's sister); a third begins with: "and the next year in September my brother signed with the Venetians ('49) / but missed fire somehow, / perhaps a mere error, they said he was scared of Francesco" (#53, pp. 45–46). The last quotation also demonstrates the frequent criticism of Sigismondo that characterizes Pound's early drafts. Along the same lines, we find the following remarks attributed to Novello: "And he lost his head that year over / the german; . . . it did the house no sort of good"; about Sigismondo's betrayal of King Alfonso, Novello claims that there was "something / not quite in order," adding that Florence had offered Malatesta "ten thousand more"; even with the Pesaro affair, Novello indicates that Galeazzo had his reasons for despising Sigismondo: "Gismon always had plagued him, plagued him / out of his life / Pinching cattle, laughing when he heard of the raids" (#53, pp. 46, 47, 50).

In the process of working on Draft Three, Pound must have realized that his material had become too sprawling for a single canto, that the deeds of Sigismondo and his enemies had to be divided up into several cantos, according to some general scheme of organization and progression. He thus composed a number of drafts that attempted, for the first time, to apportion the events of Malatesta's career among individual cantos. Among these we find a draft of Canto IX that is subsequent to any of the drafts so far discussed (#54, pp. 98-105); drafts numbered Canto X (#58, pp. 106-11) and XI (#59, eight typed leaves, corrected in hand); unnumbered drafts that were eventually worked into the old Cantos XI and XII (#55); and a draft numbered "?XII" (#60). None of these will be discussed because they were all incorporated into the "Watson Typescript" (by far the most important of the early drafts), which will be examined in detail in the following chapter. Such differences as exist between the drafts listed above and the Watson Typescript are in general quite negligible, and thus I have thought it more rewarding to devote our attention to a version of the Malatesta Cantos that Pound had at one point considered ready for publication in the *Dial*, presided over by Scofield Thayer and James Sibley Watson, Jr.

2

From the Watson Typescript to the Final Version

> "Nothing can create the poem but toil."[1]

The so-called Watson Typescript, consisting of twenty-seven numbered sheets typed in Pound's violet ribbon, is an early version of the Malatesta Cantos ("9" to "12") that Pound submitted to James Sibley Watson of the *Dial* on January 5, 1923. The letter that accompanied the typescript is highly instructive in that it clearly expresses Pound's desire to be read with comprehension, thus dispelling any notions of deliberate obfuscation or calculated impenetrability. Scanning his work before sending it off to Watson, Pound observes: "It seems to read easily. That's something."[2] But in spite of this impression, he wonders if he has succeeded in making his materials accessible to the general reader:

> I shd. very much like to know, from you, who presumably have not mugged up the history of Romagna, whether I have made the *main* points of the story CRYSTAL CLEAR. . . .
> And DO if you have the patience. Write me a list of the events, that you gather from the story. Also any doubts or obscurities. Anyone here from whom I might get an honest opinion, has heard me talk about S.M. and therefore comes to the cantos with a damaged instead of a perfect ignorance: or some fortuitous, unfair interest in the subject, apart from that shoved at them by the page.
>
> (pp. 1, 3–4)

Pound's learning, if not profound, was extensive; his scholarship was multifaceted, if not rigorous; his curiosity was boundless, as was his capacity for enthusiasm. In the *Cantos*, he often overestimated the willingness to be instructed on the part of readers possessed of "a perfect ignorance." If this was naiveté, it was nevertheless akin to that which prompted Aristotle to preface his *Metaphysics* with the quixotic pronouncement: "All men by nature have a desire to know."

The Watson Typescript[3] begins with the evocation of *The Waste Land*, line 430, that opens the present version of the Malatesta Cantos, but it omits the next three lines, which were added at a very late stage of composition. This initial canto, "Canto 9," corresponds in its basic contours to the present Canto 8, sharing with the latter the following material:

1. Sigismondo's letter to Giovanni de' Medici;
2. The contract between Sigismondo and the Florentines, dated August 5, 1452;
3. Sigismondo's lyric (8.30.17–22);
4. An excerpt from Malatesta's letter to "Johanni di Cosimo" (8.30.24–32);
5. A reference to the troubadour Guillaume Poictiers;
6. A description of the newly-wed Francesco Sforza's visit to Rimini;
7. A reference to Gemisthus Plethon;
8. The anecdote of Sigismondo trapped between the gates of Ancona (8.31.26–34);
9. The catalogue of Malatesta's foes (8.32.1–21);
10. References to "Mastin" (founder of the Malatesta dynasty), Paolo and Francesca, and Parisina d'Este (8.32.26–8.33.2);
11. References to the unpaid dues (the papal *census* or rent) and to Sigismondo at the age of twelve (8.33.3–4).

It is readily apparent that Pound was to add very little new material to this canto. By a relatively early date he had fixed the general outlines of his introductory canto on Malatesta, having chosen materials that were calculated to produce a favorable first impression on the reader. Thus, we observe Sigismondo seeking an artist for his Tempio and promising to provide for him handsomely—even though he is currently engaged in the siege of Cremona. Similarly, his love-lyric to Isotta is sandwiched in between documents relating to his military career. We also notice that, although Malatesta's services are in great demand with the Florentines and the Venetians (and although the town of Ancona seems to be in mortal terror of his martial prowess), his own chief concern is the building of his Tempio, in spite of the hostility of his fellow princes, and especially of Francesco Sforza, whose main interests, by contrast, seem to be subterfuge and fishing: " 'La pesca, di cui godeva molto'" (p. 4). In addition, there is an attempt to put Sigismondo into historical perspective by associating him with Guillaume Poictiers, whose poetry initiated the "Provençal Renaissance":

> Say that Poictiers had it all in his saddlebags
> And the next notch here,
> The broken, unfinished temple, set by the
>   sea's edge.
>   (p. 4)

Pound goes on to associate his hero with Gemisthus Plethon (whose Neo-Platonism and "paganism"[4] helped to fire the Italian imagination with enthusiasm for Greek studies) and with Paolo and Francesca (whose passionate life and death are here used to invest the Malatesta clan with a tragic, Dantesque grandeur). Toward the end of the canto there is a brief flashback to the very beginning of Sigismondo's career, when his various troubles began.

The one major shortcoming of this canto, however, is the way it ends. Instead of merely listing some of the events from Sigismondo's early youth—as in our Canto 8 (33.3–9)—Pound closes "Watson 9" with a long Latin quotation from Pius II's *Commentaries*, dealing with the burning in effigy of Malatesta (presently 10.43.29–10.44.10). The reader is quite unprepared for this leap from Sigismondo's childhood to an event late in his career—an event, moreover, that has not grown out of anything narrated in the canto and that is not taken up immediately afterward in the next canto. Nothing but the briefest mention has been made of the Church's enmity toward Malatesta, yet, at the end of this introductory canto, Pius has already consigned him (at least symbolically) to the flames. Malatesta's troubles thus seem to arrive at a critical juncture before they have even begun, that is, before they have been amply presented to us.

In other respects, however, "Watson 9" is quite similar to our present Canto 8, though it lacks a few short passages and finishing touches that will be mentioned in my discussion of Pound's later drafts. It also differs in the tone of greater deference with which Sigismondo addresses Giovanni de' Medici. Compare

>   Concerning the money for my service
>   I shd. like you and yr. father to favour me,
>   And to draw these moneys in due form
>   And send them on to me as quickly as possible,
>   (p. 1)

with:

>   As for my service money,
>   Perhaps you and your father wd. draw it
>   And send it on to me as quickly as possible;
>   (8.28.24–26)

or

>   If you will be so good as to
>   tell him this
>   And to let me have his answer clearly . . . ,
>   (p. 2)

with:

> And let me have a clear answer.
> (8.29.11)

In general, the lines of this versified letter in "Watson 9" are longer and less clipped than in the final version, and there is less of a colloquial snap to them—"thrown away" (p. 2) rather than "chucked away" (8.28.31), for example.

With "Watson 10," serious problems of structure arise, both within the canto itself and in its relation to the other cantos of the draft. Indeed, Pound's confusion with regard to the ordering of his material is sometimes overtly transferred to his narrator in the hope of excusing the poet's own floundering:

> That Aeneas wanted the land;
> That Sforza. . . .
> Oh well, Francesco: I will show you
> That document later[5]
> ....
> And Borso—but of that, also, later,
> I will come to that later. . . .
> (p. 12)

An instance of this confusion occurs toward the beginning of "Watson 10." Immediately after a line on the death of Malatesta's first wife, Ginevra d'Este, Pound jumps to a brief exposition of the Pesaro affair, introducing the passage quite awkwardly: "but about Pesaro in '45." He proceeds as follows:

> His brother, i.e. old Sforza's brother Alessandro
> Wanted a wife (Costanza da Piergentile /da/ Verano,
>   olim)
> And had no place to keep her;
> And we drove them out of the marches,
> Urbino was in, on their side,
> It was their time to be under interdict,
>   And he began building the tempio,
> And then Polixena died. . . .
> (p. 8)

Besides the unfortunate allusion to Peter Pumpkin-Eater, the passage does not communicate the essential facts of the loss of Pesaro—that is, that the lord of the town, Galeazzo Malatesta, called "l'Inetto" ("The Inept"), sold the seigniory to Francesco Sforza, who put it in the hands of his brother, Alessandro. There is an anticipation of the passage in "Watson 9," where Pound writes

> . . . who /stole/ (Francesco stole) Pesaro in October
> (to convenience Alessandro his
> (Francesco's) brother,
> (p. 5)

and, further on,

> So that Galeazzo l'inetto made the deal
> "To get, at last, pay for his cattle,"
> And bitched the whole business. . . ,
> (p. 6)

but these two pieces of the same puzzle are separated by twelve lines of verse (concerned, for the most part, with other matters), and nowhere are we told that Galeazzo was lord of Pesaro.[6] Returning to the passage from "Watson 10," we also notice how ineffectually it trails off into a reference to the Tempio and how it gives the impression that Sigismondo went through two wives with astonishing rapidity.[7]

Pound's narration of Malatesta's problems with Alfonso of Aragon is handled even more awkwardly. It opens with the absolute flatness of "Then there was Aragon, that started in '47" (p. 8), which may be compared with the final version's

> And the King o' Ragona, Alphonse le roy d'Aragon,
> was the next nail in our coffin,
> (9.35.14–15)

where, in spite of the cliché, an ominous vividness has been brought to our first glimpse of Malatesta's powerful enemy. Immediately after its inauspicious opening line, "Watson 10" casts a one-line backward glance at the Pesaro affair, then proceeds with two more lines on Alfonso, only to interrupt itself with a four-line segment that manages to allude to "that row over the german," the Rocca Malatestiana, and the Tempio (p. 9). There follows a nine-line passage on Alfonso, in which the narrator, ostensibly Malatesta Novello, reminds the reader that his brother "*had* signed with Aragon," thus calling more attention than necessary to Sigismondo's treachery toward the Spanish king. After a two-line digression on Malatesta's technique for making "bombards," the passage on Alfonso draws to a confused close with a three-line rumination on the opportunities for making peace with Aragon that Malatesta did not seize, and a two-line irrelevancy on how Francesco Sforza "was always afraid of him, / Trying to keep him out of good jobs" (p. 9). It is clear that Pound was attempting to heighten suspense and produce the impression of a multifarious busyness by interspersing subordinate narratives within the frame of a larger one, but he had not yet realized that this can only be satisfactorily achieved by blurring the outlines of neither the encompassing frame nor the intercalated episodes.

An excellent illustration of this technique occurs in Pound's final version (9.35.26–9.37.6). The main point of this long passage is how Malatesta lost the favor of the Venetians by allowing himself to be distracted from his military duties by Sforza and Federigo d'Urbino, who tricked him into believing that they would help him regain Pesaro. The passage begins with the Venetians' annoyance over Sigismondo's failure to keep Sforza from crowning himself Duke of Milan. Sforza then confers with Urbino on the best method for discrediting Malatesta in the eyes of Venice. Urbino suggests holding out Pesaro as bait. Doge Foscari of Venice also promises to aid Sigismondo regain the town, but "Feddy offered it sooner" (9.36.4). In the meantime, Malatesta has already angered Venice by his spoliation of the church of S. Apollinare in Classe (beautifully and humorously told) and by the incident concerning the "German-Burgundian female." Finally, the passage is brought to a close by the narration of the inevitable outcome of Malatesta's trusting Federigo,

> And Feddy finally said "I am coming! . . .
> . . . to help Alessandro,"

(that is, the current lord of Pesaro), and by the coda toward which the entire passage has been moving: "And he'd lost his job with the Venetians" (9.37.6).

But aside from its internal weaknesses, "Watson 10" also evinces a faulty structural relationship toward the rest of the Malatesta sequence: much of what is contained in this second of the Malatesta Cantos belongs properly in the third—and vice versa. Once again (as in the "burning in effigy" incident tacked onto the end of "Watson 9"), the effect is one of anticlimax because of the relative neglect of suspense-building techniques. (Indeed, it is only in this canto, five pages after the Latin quotation describing the incident, that Pound finally deals with it in his own narrative.)[8] The main objection that may be raised against Pound's handling of his material in "Watson 10" is that he introduces prematurely Sigismondo's difficulties with Pius II (the real beginning of the end for Malatesta), while postponing until "Watson 11" the narration of the Sienese fiasco and the reproduction of the letters written to Sigismondo just before he was constrained to flee the wrath of the Sienese. Not only do these latter events precede the problems with the Church in terms of actual chronology, but they also lead up to them in a subtle way, obscured by Pound's extended hysteron proteron, as we may dub his infelicitous transposition of incidents.

Pound begins his story of the papacy's condemnation of Malatesta with a line that has benefitted from no previous elucidation within the sequence: "And there had been that affair near Siena." He goes on to relate this mysterious Sienese affair with the enmity of two Sienese prelates:

> So in the end that pot-scraping little runt Andreas Benzi
> da Siena

> Got up to spout out the bunkum
> That that monstrous swollen swelling son of a bitch
> > Papa Pio Secundo, Aeneas Silvius Picolomini
> > > da Siena
> Had written out in his best bears-greased slicked up
> > latinity.
>
> (p. 10)

Adjacent to this passage, we find Pound's handwritten note to the printer, instructing him to preserve the emphatic line-arrangement of the two "da Siena" phrases, which are meant to reinforce the inscrutable connection between Siena and the papacy's hatred of Malatesta.[9] It is only late in the next canto, "Watson 11," that we discover the nature of this connection: Sigismondo had hired himself out to Siena and was subsequently accused by the city of having betrayed it in his dealings with Count Pitigliano. Benzi and Pius, as prominent sons of Siena, would naturally have come to despise Sigismondo. In the final version of the *Cantos* all of this is relatively clear: Pound sketches in the background of the Sienese affair (9.37.15–25), proceeds to translate some of the letters to Malatesta that the Sienese confiscated from his hastily abandoned headquarters during late December of 1454, and returns (at the beginning of Canto 10) to Malatesta's dealings with Pitigliano and to his subsequent flight for his life, so that when we notice, soon afterward, the provenance "da Siena" of his ecclesiastical foes, we are in a position to appreciate this admittedly minor detail in the gathering flood of Sigismondo's misfortunes. But the final version also achieves a *crescendo* effect. First we see Malatesta treated ignominiously by the Sienese. This is powerful enough, but it pales in significance compared with the burning in effigy and the scurrilous venom of the papacy's charges against him, which bring him to the nadir of his career, just before his glorious last stand and ultimate defeat. In addition, Pound's final ordering allows us to peruse the delightful post-bag letters, full of homely details, familial warmth, and news of the Tempio, before we are confronted with documents of a very different nature:

> *Stupro, caede, adulter,*
> *homocidia, parricidia ac periurus,*
> *presbitericidia, audax, libidinosus,*
> wives, jew-girls, nuns, necrophiliast, *fornicarium ac sicarium,*
> *proditor, raptor, incestuosus, incendiarius, ac*
> *concubinarius.*
>
> (10.44.19–24)

In "Watson 10," by contrast, Sigismondo is condemned by the Church before we have seen enough of him to know what to make of the accusations. And when we finally see the domestic side of Malatesta in "Watson 11," our receptivity to it has already been skewed by our previous familiarity with the ecclesiastical invectives.

Though Pound ends "Watson 10" with three lines that are meant to prepare us for the letters in "11" (which open the canto), these verses nevertheless constitute an empty generalization about Sigismondo, such as is quite common in the early drafts:

> And Sigismundo that lost his soul?
> by activity
> But his character: /oh well, his character:/
> (p. 13)

They also seem to epitomize the major weakness of "10" and "11": we are shown Malatesta "losing his soul" (at least in the Church's view) before we know what kind of person he is. When the narrator realizes this, he decides, almost as an afterthought, to do what he should have done earlier—to present the domestic concerns of a character whom we have just seen attacked by fanatical persecutors.

An interesting aspect of "Watson 10" is the overt criticism of Sigismondo that is frequently put into the mouth of Malatesta Novello, Pound's ostensible narrator in this canto:

> And my brother missed fire some how,
> It was for the Venetians
> against Sforza, by Brianza,
> And he went over the Adda, and worried Francesco
> But without ever really attacking,
> And the old fox nipped into Milan,
> in February of '50.
> (p. 8)

When Pound realized that this kind of undercutting obscured the thematic design of his sequence, he cleverly transmuted his telling of the incident, impersonalizing it, obfuscating the facts, and making the Venetians (rather than his own brother) criticize Sigismondo's dawdling:

> And the Venetians sent down an ambassador
> And said "speak humanely,
> But tell him it's no time for raising his pay."
> And the Venetians sent down an ambassador
> with three pages of secret instructions
> To the effect: Did he think the campaign was a joy-ride?
> And old Wattle-wattle slipped into Milan.
> (9.35.26–32)

Perhaps even more obtrusively objectionable are Novello's occasional cloying paeans to Sigismondo,

> Oh, my brother, all things were forgiven thee,
> All things were forgiven thee, save thy gaiety,
> And that they could not forgive thee,
> (p. 11)

or his making excuses for his brother's behavior:

> "O maladecta avaritia!" but that passes,
> And perfidy, a thing of the times, that passes;
> And the beautiful putti, and the carved stones in
> the chiesa
> And the marble stolen in Classe,
> And remade into images . . . /?/
> (ibid.)

Here, Novello is admitting that Sigismondo is avaricious and perfidious (with reference to the betrayal of King Alfonso) as well as thievish (the marble), but that these traits are to be considered *sub specie aeternitatis*—the eternity, that is, of art, as embodied in the sculptured beauties of the Tempio. The moral is, of course, a plausible one, especially for a poem. But to formulate it so baldly is to imply that the reader is unable to infer.

"Watson 11" corresponds rather closely to our present 9.37.27–10.42.29, opening with the post-bag letters and closing with Filippo Strozzi's written comments to Zan Lottieri concerning Sigismondo's flight from the Sienese. By far the most interesting glimpse into Pound's strategies in the post-bag section is afforded by the version preserved in "Watson 11," where some of the letters are glossed by remarks put into the mouth of Sigismondo, who is imagined scanning his correspondence while we eavesdrop on him. Thus, after reading a few lines of the architect Matteo Nuti's letter (9.37.27–32), Malatesta emits an "ugh!" (p. 14), elicited, perhaps, by the redundance of "the nave that goes in / the middle of the church"—and this from an architect! Thus, the breaks in the letters that occur in our text are not attributable to the techniques of "collage," "Cubism," or fragmentation, but constitute the remnants of an originally realistic dramatic scene in which a character is overheard as he skims through a batch of mail, reading some letters in their entirety and a phrase here and there from others. This is made even more explicit by the next excerpt (our 9.37.33–9.38.1), in which Sigismondo, sorely tried by the writer's illiteracy, asks himself "who the devil!" (p. 14) and glances impatiently at the bottom of the page, only to discover that he has just been subjected to the thoughts of "Giovane of Master alwise" (Giovanni, son of Master Alvise)—one of the carpenters working on the Tempio. The third and last of these interjections occurs after Sigismondo reads the medallionist Matteo da Pasti's request for "the silver for the small medal" (p. 16) and says to himself "blast the silver."

If we now go through the letters to Malatesta, keeping in mind the three exclamations in "Watson 11," we find that, as obsessed as Sigismondo is with his Tempio, he nevertheless places his primary emphasis on familial matters:

1. He breaks off reading Matteo Nuti's letter, discussed above (9.37.27–32);
2. He breaks off reading Giovane of Master alwise's letter, also discussed above (9.37.33–9.38.6);
3. He reads only the salutation and the first two words ("Messire Battista") of a letter that obviously deals with the Tempio (9.38.7);
4. He glances at only four of the "items" in a contract for materials to be used on the Tempio—the original document (Yriarte, pp. 398–99) contains fourteen— and then, like any good businessman, seeks out "the bottom line": "danars 151" (9.38.8–12);
5. It is significant that the first letter he reads in full deals with Isotta's visit to a young woman with whom Sigismondo had been having an affair, and ends with a few comments on his children (9.38.13–26);
6. He picks out only two lines from a letter about the Tempio (9.38.27–28);
7. The second letter he reads in full deals with his young son and with a minor problem of insubordination on the part of "Georgio Rambottom" (Giorgio di Ranbutino) (9.38.29–9.39.9);
8. He glances back at the letter referred to in #6 above, picking out only two more lines (9.39.10–11);
9. He returns to Matteo Nuti's letter (#1 above) and reads only a few more words from it (9.39.12–13);
10. The third letter he reads in full is a charming exercise in precocious bureaucratese by his six-year-old son (9.39.14–33);
11. He reads only the bombastic opening clause of his court-poet Trachulo's "damn'd epistle" (9.40.1–2);
12. Finally, Sigismondo reads the full text of a letter from his secretary "Petrus Genariis," dealing with various aspects of work on the Tempio. It seems that, only after he has gone through his batch of letters and read the more personal ones, does he allow himself the leisure of reading in its entirety this one on the Tempio (9.40.3–35).

It thus appears that Pound's chief interest in the post-bag section was not to display Malatesta's unstinting interest in the Tempio, but to present him as a solicitous and devoted paterfamilias who did not allow his domestic affections to be stifled by even the most sublime architectural aspirations.

Farther on in "Watson 11" we find confirmation of the theory that we are meant to read Malatesta's letters "over his shoulder," when we discover that the original for "Trachulo's damn'd epistle" (10.42.9) was "Trachulo's unread epistle" (p. 19 of "Watson"; see also #11 above, and the discussion of this phrase in Chapter 1). This letter, it will be remembered, urged Sigismondo to betray the Sienese, his employers in the war against Count Pitigliano, and to aspire to the seigniory of the commune he was fighting for. As we have already seen, this is a classic case of Pound's not telling us enough. How are we supposed to guess that the "counsels to Hannibal" offered by Trachulo were treasonous ones, or indeed how do we even go about attributing that two-line excerpt to its rightful author? By an involved process of ratiocinative acrobatics, we might be able to deduce the authorship *and* the contents of the letter as follows. It seems that the thrust of Trachulo's "epistle" must be similar to that of Count Pitigliano's treasonous overtures to Malatesta, the substance of which is that Sigismondo should be ruling rather than serving Siena (see 10.42.1–9). In addition, the letter that begins "Unfitting as it is that I should offer counsels to Hannibal . . ." is the only letter in the post-bag section that is neither read in full (so that we should know its contents), nor related to the construction of the Tempio—"Hannibal" implying that the counsels are to be of a military or political nature. Of course, this is the kind of attention that poets often demand of their readers—but to elucidate one line of verse?

One of the missed opportunities that Pound recovered in his final text is the way in which he allows the narration in "Watson 11" to continue, uninterrupted by canto division, beyond the elegiac lines that now close Canto 9:

> And the old sarcophagi,
>   such as lie, smothered in grass, by San Vitale.

In "Watson" these lines are immediately followed by "And the poor devils dying of cold, outside Sorano . . .," which plunges us, without pause, into Malatesta's problems with an enraged Siena. In the New Directions version we are first informed of the military engagement that led the Sicnese to question Malatesta's behavior toward Pitigliano, invade his abandoned headquarters, and seize the letters he had left behind (9.37.15–26). Next, we are allowed to read some of the letters—albeit somewhat anachronistically—as Sigismondo had first read them. Finally, there is a short passage in which two of the major motifs of the letters (Isotta and the Tempio) receive lyrical treatment, and which ends by focusing on an ominous detail of the Tempio—the sarcophagi cut into its outer walls. On this note of uneasy calm the canto draws to a stately *decrescendo* close, from which, at the beginning of Canto 10, we are conveyed back to the mundane political entanglements that led to the seizure of the letters in the first place. Thus, we move from the world of action to the world of love and art, and then back to the world of action—the last of these opening a new canto and thereby implying that, however seductive the sphere of love and art may be, the world that Sigismondo must actually live in (and which will eventually destroy him) is one of being forced to flee from the wrath of a commune bent on reducing to submission

>   . . . a man with a ten acre lot,
>   Pitigliano . . . a lump of tufa.
>   (10.42.10–11)

Toward the end of "Watson 11" there is a vague two-line reference to a story that Pound does not tell:

> However, a luncheon invitation. Not accepted . . .
> Carmagnola had accepted one once.
>   (p. 20)

We are expected to know that the Venetians had arrested the great *condottiere* at a banquet and had subsequently tortured and executed him for treason (May 5, 1432)—and that now the Sienese are trying the same ploy with Malatesta. Pound's final version provides us with a built-in footnote, but also falls into an unintentional syntactic ambiguity:

> And he, Sigismundo, refused an invitation to lunch
>   In commemoration of Carmagnola
>   (vide Venice, between the two columns
>   where Carmagnola was executed).
>   (10.42.20–23)

Was the lunch in commemoration of Carmagnola? And was *that* why Malatesta declined the invitation? Or did Malatesta refuse to attend because he "remembered" Carmagnola's fate? What *is* clear is Pound's failure to mention, in either version, the fact that young Sigismondo had been betrothed to Carmagnola's daughter, whom he repudiated after the disgrace of her father's execution. He never returned the dowry.

"Watson 11" ends with the passage about Filippo Strozzi and Zan Lottieri that now forms 10.42.26–29. Pound's former arrangement of the present lines had allowed him to end the canto on a note of suspense with Strozzi's conjecture " 'I think they'll let him through at Campiglia' " (p. 20)—that is, that the Florentines would probably grant the fleeing Sigismondo safe passage through their territory on his way back to Rimini. Next to having brought the canto to a close with the lines about the sarcophagi, this is the best possible division of the material relating to the Sienese fiasco. The problem with it, however, is that it leads nowhere: "Watson 12" dismisses the rest of the tale (cf. 10.42.30–10.43.5) with the three words, "And so on" (p. 21)—not a very well-wrought opening for a new part of the poem. Pound then touches on some of the events from the end of Sigismondo's career, but without managing to convey the impression that Malatesta's ruin was a gradually accelerating process, gaining ever greater momentum from the growing number of dangerous foes he made. Instead, the Sienese fail in their attempt to murder him. So ends "Watson 11." But in the next canto Sigismondo is already prostrated and almost entirely despoiled by Pope Paul II. How did we get from there to here?

The answer is that in "Watson 12" Pound pays the price for the weak arrangement of his material in the two previous cantos. Since he had already told the story of Pius II's determination to ruin Malatesta in "10," there is no middle term left to link the Sienese affair with Sigismondo's final defeat at the hands of the new pope. If it is the enmity of the Church that ultimately ruins Malatesta (as, in Pound's view, it is), why order the events Pius, Siena, Paul, instead of Siena, Pius, Paul? Not only is the latter arrangement (ultimately adopted) true to chronology, but it also presents a series of increasingly grave humiliations for Sigismondo. This earlier mishandling of material, coupled with Pound's failure to narrate the story of Sigismondo's heroic last stand (see 10.47.4–11.48.26), produces an impression of jumbled anticlimax in "Watson 12," into which all the leftover pieces of the Malatesta puzzle are jammed willy-nilly.

Thus we are here told the story of the shouting-match between Sigismondo and Federigo d'Urbino (pp. 23–24), though Federigo hardly figures in the Watson Malatesta Cantos at all; we are informed that "Piccolomini," that is, Pius II, "wanted the land" (p. 24)—but long after we have actually seen the Pontiff's machinations to get it (pp. 10–13), indeed even after we have seen Malatesta attempting to murder Paul, the *next* pope; we are treated to the posthumous defenestration of Count Giacomo Piccinino (p. 24), only three lines before Pound brings his Malatesta material to an end in "Watson 12"—a time when his hero should loom a bit larger than he does; and we even meet our old friend

> Christus cacat ac restat sedia Petri
> Cacat Christus, pontificis officium restat.
> (p. 23)

The least unified of the Watson cantos, "12" offers a hodgepodge of interesting but mutually independent anecdotes.[10]

As in most of the early drafts, the Watson Typescript displays a tendency toward narrative elaboration rather than suppression of details and background events. Thus we find in "Watson 12" (and not in the final version) the reason for Malatesta's attempt on the life of Paul II:

> They had offered Foligno and Spoleto . . .
> on condition the guard of Arimnium
> be transferred to the vicar *papale*.
> (p. 22)

Knowing that the Pope had proposed a trade of Rimini for two little towns helps us to put Sigismondo's wrath in perspective. But sometimes Pound's attempts to provide a rounded, factually sound historical vignette result in an attenuation of poetic effect. In our Canto 11, Pound writes:

> And he said in his young youth:
> Vogliamo,
> *che le donne*, we will that they, *le donne*, go ornate,
> As be their pleasure, for the city's glory thereby.
> (11.50.26–29)

This is a moving little anecdote to record in a canto that deals with the ruin of Malatesta. It recalls the happier times of his youth, but also gives testimony to his appreciation of feminine beauty, his detestation of sartorial prudery, his respect for freedom of choice, and his recognition that splendidly attired women help bring "glory" to a community.[11] How fresh and far away that youthful world seems from the grim realities of Sigismondo's last years! The lines also appear in "Watson 12," but with an appendage that vitiates the emotional impact of the scene:

> When the Fanesi, that was,
> Wanted to cut short the trains,
> and might have ousted out the pearl-sellers and broiderers.
> (p. 21)

We now know more of the historical situation, but feel less moved by the vignette. It now seems that uppermost in Sigismondo's mind was the economic well-being of Fano: the repressive measures of the Fanesi would have had a disastrous impact on the business of the "pearl-sellers and broiderers." However wise on the part of a prince, this economic motive is less endearing to the reader than a purely aesthetic one. When a literary character is being treated elegiacally (as Malatesta is, for the most part, in both "Watson 12" and New Directions "11"), we respond more readily to signs of his emotional and aesthetic sensitivity than to his sagacious economic policies.

Our last glimpse of Malatesta's world in "Watson 12" is a rather disappointing one:

> But Venice wanted supplies from Romagna,
> that is peace on occasion,
> and the salt-works at Cesena.
> (p. 24)

This cynical remark about Venice's ulterior motives in securing the Church's peace with Sigismondo leaves us with the impression that Malatesta is now simply a pawn in the hands of both his enemies and his "friends": he has become "invisible," having dropped out of the poem eleven lines earlier. Compared to the humorous, "upbeat" ending of the final version (11.52.1–9), this focusing on the Venetians falls flat because it does not allow the defeated hero to bow out gracefully (and graciously). Although there is a coda to the Malatesta saga at the beginning of "Watson 13,"[12]

>   So that he had his run, on the whole
>   and got up the buildings. . . .
>   . . . .
>   He left provision, you know, /testamentum,/
>   "Lien on my goods in Ragusa, and my heirs
>   To continue the tempio . . ."
>   which they didn't,
>   (p. 27)

we nevertheless feel that Pound could have engineered a more memorable exit for one of his most powerful characters.

But by far the most interesting feature of "Watson 12" (indeed of the entire typescript) is the long passage that brings the Malatesta Cantos to a close, a revised version of the scene at Verona with Eliot and Bride Scratton already discussed in Chapter 1. The main outlines of the passage are similar to those of the corresponding scene in the five-page typescript that I consider to be Pound's first typed draft (Folder #50), but by the time of the Watson Typescript there has been some pruning of dispensable details. Nevertheless, the passage still runs to fifty-one lines, divided into a four-line address to Eliot soon after the opening of "Watson 12,"

>   Tomas, amics, we sit here,
>   For fourty-four [sic] thousand years,
>   at least I have, at this tin, rickety table,
>   Painted with ripolin,
>   (p. 21)

and, three pages further on, a forty-seven-line stretch that brings the canto to a close (see Appendix C).

What is noteworthy for our purposes about this division is that it later gives rise to two widely separated interpolations into our text of Canto 11, the first, a concise version of the four-line Watson passage,

>   And we sit here. I have sat here
>   For forty four thousand years,
>   (11.50.21–22)

the second, salvaged from the long Watson scene, the sonorous line: "In the gloom, the gold gathers the light against it" (11.51.30). Though Pound trimmed away almost the entire Verona scene from the Malatesta Cantos, he decided to retain these haunting lines, shorn of their original contexts, depersonalized—and extremely effective. Whereas the four-line passage with "Tomas, amics," the rickety table, and the ripolin, strikes us as a bathetic, or at least banal, interruption of the Malatesta saga, the final version's *ex abrupto* voice, syntactically joined to what precedes and follows, but emanating from an eerie, surrealistic dimension of its own, provides the canto with a somber, sibylline resonance. Similarly, the gnomic verse about the gloom and the gold, divorced from its original association with Galla Placidia's mausoleum at Ravenna, is now free to gravitate toward the lines immediately before it:

"When he got back here from Sparta, the people
"Lit fires, and turned out yelling: 'PANDOLFO'!"

"He is the gold, their torches rhyme with the light," Kenner comments.[13] Once again, Pound rejects the specific claims made by a striking line for its own proper contextualization (the mausoleum, Galla, Ti) in order to divest it of its "outlandish" heritage, allowing it to be assimilated within the body of the Malatesta narrative. It is only at the beginning of Canto 12 (53.1–4) that the first of these two passages is expanded. We now learn that the epochal sitting of Canto 11 is to be visualized as taking place in a three-dimensional world—that of the Roman arena at (this we are not told) Verona. This clears up the mystery somewhat, but only when we have seen the last of Malatesta.

While on this topic of the Verona scene and of its almost total excision from the final text of Cantos 8–11, we may well ask what eventually caused Pound to reject a dramatic scene whose emotional content was obviously very important to him, which contained quite a few fine lines, and on which he had lavished the care of at least four separate versions—the earliest of which counterpoised in bulk what there then was of the Malatesta material (see Chapter 1).

First of all, we must remark that the Verona material did not drop out of Pound's plans immediately after the Watson Typescript: it survived at least one revision (Pound's work on the Watson carbons, to be considered shortly) before we find that it is altogether missing from an incomplete, post-Watson typed draft, "Canto 12" there ending with the gold in the gloom (Folder #62, p. 23). It is obvious that Pound's attention became more focused on Malatesta as he worked his materials over. What began as little more than a lead-in to the Verona scene (in the first typed draft) gradually grew in scope until it required four cantos for treatment—and then it forced out the Verona scene entirely, so that Eliot's presence in the final version is limited to the adaptation of the line from *The Waste Land* that opens the sequence and the anonymous "we" in 11.50.21 and 12.53.1. At some point Pound must have decided that Malatesta had been treated in such depth that to append a short personal passage to this material would be either anticlimactic or bathetic—himself and Eliot dwarfed by the epic dimensions of the Tempio-builder. In addition, the elegiac section on the passing of empires and civilizations would have subsumed the elegiac treatment of Malatesta in Canto 11 and would thus have constituted a moral lesson or "meaning" tacked onto the recitation of Sigismondo's deeds. Or perhaps the deletion of the passage was due to Eliot's profound reticence about his personal life: Pound may have felt that Eliot's *Criterion* was not likely to be receptive to details such as the "(somewhat soiled) cuff-lace." Or was the passage scrapped out of deference to Bride Scratton, whose husband divorced her in 1923, naming Pound as co-respondent?[14]

Be that as it may, Pound nevertheless managed to incorporate into the *Cantos* a fair amount of material from the deleted passage, salvaging almost all the fine lines. Thus, the forty-four thousand years and the gold in the gloom are preserved in Canto 11; the polyglot lines on the Roman arena now open Canto 12; the gonads in organdy end up in 21/99—and that memorable lace is immortalized in both 29/145 and 78/481.

But let us now turn to Pound's revision of the Watson Typescript (Folder #57), consisting of the handwritten deletions, changes, and additions made on the Watson carbons. We notice immediately that the first page of "Watson 9" is made to acquire a more "antiquarian" look by Pound's addition to it of an early form of our 8.28.7–10, the mutilated words that identify the recipient of Malatesta's letter as Giovanni de' Medici,

>   co viro tanq̄
>   compatri
>   hanni de
>   [?] fiorentia,
>   (#57, p. 81)

complete with scholarly "Tergo" to indicate that the fragments had been culled from the reverse side of the letter, where the addressee was usually indicated. Yriarte conjectures (p. 380) that the letter was destined for Lorenzo the Magnificent—who was born in the year the letter was written. Pound's correction of Yriarte is based on his examination of the original document in the Florentine archives. In this first letter Pound also archaizes the spelling of "provisione" to "provixion," and he corrects a former blunder of his own by reinstalling Alfonso as the King of "Ragona" rather than "Ragusa."

The two major additions to the canto at this stage are (1) an early form of 8.30.11-15, which constitutes an attempt to incorporate into the sequence some of the local topography and (2) a version of 8.31.19–25, which prevents Gemisthus Plethon from remaining a mere name on the page for us by providing him with the anecdote about Plato and Dionysius of Syracuse. It also seems that Pound now decided to remove from this canto the long Latin passage on the burning in effigy, discussed above, which had closed "Watson 9": the carbon of this passage is the only page missing from Folder #57 and, since this page contained *only* the Latin quotation, it was probably inserted into some other draft at a different location in the text.

Pound's revision of "Watson 10" begins with the addition of an early form of 9.34.6–7 and 10–12 to the story of Sigismondo's being constrained to spend three days in a marsh near Mantua. The scene now takes on a greater degree of particularization and vividness by portraying Malatesta in the water "up to his neck," by bringing "whippets" into the action, and by specifying that the villain was Astorre Manfredi of Faenza. This interpolated passage continues with an early form of what is now 8.33.3 and 5–9, events culled from the very beginning of Sigismondo's martial career. Pound was later to transpose this material from the early part of his second Malatesta canto to the very end of the first, but the two lines from our present Canto 9 (34.14–15) that tell about the "street fight" in Fano, and which repeat the information provided in 8.33.6, have retained their position after the "Mantuan marsh" passage, where Pound first placed them in his revision of the Watson Typescript. The transposition of most of this material seems highly justifiable: our present text now prefaces the events from Sigismondo's youth with the lines that recall his ancestors, Paolo and Francesca, in Dante's Hell (8.32.33–8.33.2), thus creating a plausible link between the history of the Malatesta family and the very beginning of Sigismondo's active career, whereas Pound's earlier placement of the lines showed us Malatesta in the marsh, only to be followed, anachronistically, by "He was 12 when his uncle died" and the rest of it (#57, p. 87).

It is at this stage of revision that Pound deletes the poorly told "Alfonso affair," as well as the lines about Sigismondo's character and his having lost his soul by activity. An indication that Pound is losing interest in retaining Novello as his narrator is afforded by his changing "my brother" to "he" in the line that read in "Watson 10": "And my brother missed fire some how" (#56, p. 8). We also notice that Pound is trying to get rid of some of the platitudinous dead wood of the Watson Typescript, replacing it with sprightlier material, such as the lines telling of "the emparadisèd spirits" who "pewk from their jeweled terrace," and the passage that transcribes Pius's Latin comment on the "elegant oratory" he had just heard (the vile invective against Malatesta) and that ends with the narrator's nasty pun: "stone in his bladder / *testibus idoneis*" (10.45.17–22).

When we come to Pound's revision of the first page of "Watson 11" (page 14 of the Watson Typescript), we notice that he crosses out the "XI" at the beginning of the canto and renumbers the page "11." Since the intervening pages of the Watson Typescript (which deal for the most part with the Church's condemnation of Malatesta) have been either deleted or left unrevised, it is reasonable to assume that Pound decided at this point to rearrange his material, placing the trouble with Pius *after* the post-bag section. Furthermore, it is absolutely clear that Pound now wished to present the post-bag letters *before* breaking for a new canto, and thus he adds to the top of the page, beneath his cancellation of "XI," the words "& this is what they found in post bag" (#57, p. 1). When we turn to the last letter of the Watson carbons, we discover that Pound has added beneath it "That's what they found in the post bag"—the two phrases indicating that he had now changed his original strategy of having us eavesdrop on Malatesta scanning his mail to one in which we are presented with what the Sienese found in Sigismondo's deserted headquarters. In line with this shift, Pound now deletes Malatesta's three exclamations ("ugh!" "who the devil!" and "blast the silver") from the post-bag section and, after indicating that the new Canto 11 is to begin after the lines on the sarcophagi by San Vitale, he changes Trachulo's "unread epistle" to a "damn'd epistle," once again calling attention away from the original dramatic scene. The emphasis is now on the variegated personality of Sigismondo, revealed to us and the Sienese at the same time: we now read over the shoulders of the Sienese and feel some of their consternation at being confronted with the Tempio, a jealous mistress, and a little boy enjoying his "ronzino baiectino," instead of with a clutch of treasonous documents. But we notice an inconsistency here: the letters have been left untouched (as Sigismondo had originally read them), but surely the Sienese, in the heat of pursuit, would not have read the personal letters through. On the other hand, they *would* have read all of Trachulo's—as "damn'd" implies they did.

The only other changes of any interest made onto the Watson carbons are the addition of the five lines about Carlo Gonzaga's refusal to shelter Malatesta from the Sienese—one of the three commanders in the war against Pitigliano, he too had angered the Sienese by appropriating Orbetello for his own uses (10.42.30–10.43.3)—and the inclusion of Pius's comment on the betrayal of King Alfonso, to the effect that Sigismondo's action had saved the Florentine state from destruction—and this from Malatesta's fiercest enemy (9.35.19–20).

After Pound revised the Watson carbons he must have sensed that his last Malatesta canto was still in a very unsatisfactory state—a jumble of unrelated anecdotes. He thus wrote out a ten-page draft in longhand, labeling the sheets "A" to "K" ("C" and "D" appear on the same sheet), seven pages of which eventually found their way into our Canto 11.[15] What is striking about this draft is its fluency: there are hardly any cancellations or false starts in the entire sequence, and many of the passages that Pound first introduced into his work at this point were retained with very little subsequent revision. Indeed, he seems to have been composing without the benefit of his notes, for at several places in the manuscript he leaves a blank space where some specific name or number is meant to be inserted at a later time.[16] Much of the new material that now comes into the poem seems to result from Pound's perusal of Broglio's manuscript. It corresponds to our 10.47.4–11.50.6 and deals with the following topics:

1. The battle of Nidastore, in which Sigismondo defeated the papal forces;
2. The siege of Rimini by the papal forces under Federigo d'Urbino;
3. The disastrous peace terms forced on Malatesta;
4. The anecdotes about the "huntin' dogs" and the "old woman" (11.49.27–11.50.6).

In addition, there is a slightly expanded version of Malatesta's expedition to Morea and some new material dealing with the relations between Sigismondo and Paul II.

We notice that the subjects enumerated above provide Pound with a unified opening for his last Malatesta canto: they allow Sigismondo a heroic last stand, proceed to tell of his final defeat, and furnish us with a glimpse of the despoiled hero in his private persona. It is only after this that Pound returns to the material that had opened "Canto 12" in the Watson Typescript, that is, to "the writs run in Fano" and so on. By the time Pound typed up a new version of the Malatesta Cantos,[17] not only had he incorporated the above passages, but he had also added the brief story of the "castelan of Montefiore" (11.51.26–29), and, more important, he had excised all of the Verona sequence, "Canto 12" here ending with the gold in the gloom. The last of the Malatesta Cantos had now acquired its all but final form.

It is in this incomplete typescript that we first find the amusing tale of how Sigismondo stole the marble from S. Apollinare in Classe (#62, pp. 24, 26), and we also come upon a passage that has been reduced in the final version to the single word "nuns" (10.44.22):

> And that he ordered an whole sacred nunnery
> to lie with him and undergo his lust,
> thus making Christ a cuckold by as many times
> As were Christ's brides within that holy wall.
> (#62, p. 17)

Pound deleted this blasphemous passage himself (although it is merely paraphrased from Benzi's denunciation of Malatesta), whereas the "Christus cacat" distich, as we saw in Chapter 1, was "inadvertently" omitted by both the *Criterion* and the Three Mountains Press.

Onto the corrected carbons for this draft (Folder #63), Pound first added the passage about Francesco Sforza's "wiggling" and "wangling" (9.34.30–9.35.9) — a *trouvaille* translated from Broglio, whose diction and syntax chart out a linguistic equivalent for Francesco's sinuous duplicity:

el 1444, al 16 di marzo, lo Illo Sgr. Mes Alisandro Sforza dovento Sgr. d pesaro per mezentia delo Ill° S^gr mess Fedricho conte d orbino, il quale tramo dicta facenda col S^gr Galiazzo per mozentia dello Ill° mess Francisco, la quale trama fo facto ch¹ Sgr. Galiazzo vend pesaro al Sgr. miss Alexandro e la citta d fossanbrone al Sgr. miss fedricho. . . .
(*Cronaca*, p. 191)

The last three additions I have mentioned (the marble, the nunnery, and the wiggling) all testify to Pound's growing interest in the humorous presentation of at least part of his subject matter. He was apparently beginning to realize that too much of his narration was dry and lifeless—that it was doing a disservice to the hero he hoped to immortalize. Thus, if Malatesta's appropriation of the marble is presented from the point of view of his irritated employers, their own consternation can be used against them:

Foscari doge, to the prefect of Ravenna
"Why, what, which, thunder, damnation????"
(9.36.8–9)

And when we come to "grnnh! rrnnh, pthg" (line 22), we at first ascribe these grunts to the anger of Foscari, before we rightly associate them with the "oxen under night-shield" in the next line, straining to haul off the marble. Pound sets up the situation such that, instead of having recourse to moral categories, we feel the same delight at Sigismondo's successful strategem as we do when the Cid

. . . left his trunk with Raquel and Vidas,
That big box of sand, with the pawn-brokers,
To get pay for his menie.
(3/12)

This mode of treatment attempts to elicit the same outpouring of sympathy for the crafty hero that we so often experience in the *fabliau* and the picaresque tale.

Pound's increasing emphasis on the risible led him to find, at this stage of revision, a satisfactory ending to his Malatesta sequence—the curious contract between Sigismondo and Enricho de Aquabello that is now found on 11.52.1–9.[18] Here, our last view of Sigismondo as both generous master and practical joker is in line with Pound's admiration for Odysseus as "the live man among duds" (*LE*, p. 212), but it also serves to end the sequence on a positive note, stressing Malatesta's ability to retain a sense of fun, even after the shattering defeats he has suffered. However, Pound does not tell us (nor should he have) that the document is dated May 31, 1460—*before* Malatesta's excommunication, the burning in effigy, the defeat by Federigo, and the problems with Pope Paul.

The latest version of the Malatesta Cantos that we have among Pound's papers is a typescript corrected in hand (Folder #66). In my discussion of this typescript I will mention some of the chief differences between it and our present text, as well as indicate which passages came into the Malatesta sequence at this stage. To facilitate our survey of this draft I will deal with each point in the order of the text itself rather than attempt a thematic grouping of topics. (It is to be remembered that this typescript still enumerates the cantos 9 through 12.)

Toward the very beginning of this draft we notice that our lines 8.28.2–4A are still missing. Because they constitute a very late addition to the poem, they will be discussed when we come to survey the various published versions. A conspicuous feature of the letter from Malatesta to Giovanni de' Medici in this typescript is Pound's reliance on very long lines of verse, which, in the final version, are often divided into two shorter lines. For example,

> So that he may come to live the rest of his life in my lands
> (#66, p. 2)

becomes

> So that he may come to live the rest
> Of his life in my lands.
> (8.29.13–14)

Two very minor changes are here effected with regard to Sigismondo's poem (8.30.16–22): the word "Lyra" is used to introduce the poem, and the initial word "O" is changed to "Ye" in order to avoid the jarring assonance between "O" and "olde" in the first line.

It is in this draft that Pound first quotes Broglio's word *"bestialmente"* (*Cronaca*, p. 191), used with reference to Sforza's dishonesty in the Pesaro affair (8.32.7 and 9.35.7). Pound culled it from the same passage in Broglio that had given rise to the "wiggling" episode, discussed above. He also first applied two Greek words to Malatesta here: "Poliorcetes" ("besieger of cities") and the Odyssean "POLUMETIS" (#66, p. 12), the latter epithet[19] serving to remind us that Malatesta antagonized the Venetians by asking for "six months vacation" in order to besiege Pesaro while he was under contract to fight for them (9.36.28–30).

Pound's scorn for Pius II now results in a curious fusion of two previously unconnected passages:

> . . . that monstrous swollen, swelling s.o.b. cacat Christus
> Papa Pio Secundo
> (Cacat Christus ac restat sedia Petri
> Cacat Christus, pontificis officium restat)
> Aeneas Silvius Picolomini [sic]
> da Siena.
> (#66, p. 24)

The nunnery passage is still with us (placed after 10.44.29), and, to the charge that the young Sigismondo filled the holy water fonts in a church with ink, are appended the ironic lines:

> Which might be considered youthful levity
> but was really a profound indication.
> (10.45.5–6)

The lines about the alum at Tolfa and the Church's "devilment" are still missing from this draft (10.46.22–23).

We discover from this version that Pound originally intended to place the passage dealing with the bow-shot at Borso and Novello's relations with Giacomo Piccinino (10.46.30–10.47.3) after the line "But we got it next August" (11.48.29); Pound here amended his typescript so that the passage was moved to where we now find it in Canto 10—his ostensible purpose being that he did not want to dilute his epic presentation of Sigismondo, at the beginning of Canto 11, with the presence of Borso, Novello, and Piccinino.

A diacritical mark missing in our text is supplied by the draft under discussion: "grädment" indicates that an *n* is to be understood between *a* and *d*, whereas our reading of "*gradment*" in 10.47.7 and 11.48.1 causes the word to be easily confused with some such word as *gradevolmente* ("pleasingly, agreeably")—a minor point, admittedly. It is in this draft that Sigismondo's desperate journey to Tarentum first comes into the text (11.48.31–11.49.3), as well as Malatesta's offering "a decent price" for a peasant's horses (11.50.8–9). We also see Pound toying with the exact form he should give to the enigmatic phrase in 11.50.13:

> Zezena de'" be"
> Zezena d"e b
> Zezena d'"e be"e colonne;
> (#66, p. 31A)

what is meant is "Cesena delle belle colonne," Cesena of the beautiful columns, now in the possession of the Papacy, after the death of Novello.[20] Finally, this draft introduces the lines about Paul II's vain ambition of having himself crowned "Pope Formosus" (11.51.16–21).

Before considering the printed versions of the Malatesta Cantos, we should note how the first four lines of our Canto 12 ended up in their present location. It seems that when Pound first decided to remove the Verona material from his last Malatesta canto, he intended to shift at least some of it to the following canto, "Canto 13." This would have enabled him to salvage this cherished episode and, at the same time, to minimize its potential for distracting the reader from the saga of Malatesta. We thus find Pound opening an incomplete typescript of "Canto 13" with the four lines that now open Canto 12, but appending to them a shortened version (eleven lines) of the Verona scene, followed by the handwritten note "Baldy Bacon:" (#69, p. 1). But apparently realizing that the elegiac mode of the scene would contrast too jarringly with Baldy's shenanigans, Pound decided to eliminate most of the passage, striking out all but the first four lines, which now serve as a stately but enigmatic link between the activities of Sigismondo and those of a debased modern counterpart.

The MSS also contain another interesting rejected plan for our Canto 12, in which the link to the Malatesta Cantos deals exclusively with Sigismondo himself. It is worth quoting in its entirety:

> Damned,
> Lost, caschio son io in interdecto,[21]
> fallen in interdict, lost neither by good nor evil
> but by continual action.
>
>   and his bait, his god-trap,
> the carved wreaths, his tempio, but
> the treaders of aether, the high olympian gods.
> if they come. if they come they will come of themselves.
> not needing our altars?
>
> Baldy Bacon.
>   ///
>
> A speech more real than speech,
>   the form cut into the stone.
>
> Dos Santos.
>
> Honest Sailor.

(#70, p. 1)

By rejecting this version of the Malatesta link in Canto 12, Pound was avoiding the trap of evaluating his hero in terms redolent of religious piety—even if some of the words were Sigismondo's. This is another aspect of the same authorial strategy that led Pound (and D'Annunzio—see Chapter 3) to make no mention of the fact that when Malatesta saw himself surrounded by seven stalwart Cardinals, he abandoned his plan of stabbing Paul II, dropping to his knees and begging forgiveness instead. In addition, the second part of this rejected opening seems to imply that Malatesta's building of the Tempio was "wrong from the start"—that it represented an attempt to externalize what are, ultimately, psychic modes of being. But is not *all* art just that? And why present Malatesta in such depth, only to conclude on a note of skeptical hindsight? Ultimately, only the lines about the arena were retained, an arena that had witnessed the events of Diocletian's time, and from which that mysterious "we" looks upon the spectacle of Malatesta's world—and Baldy Bacon's.

The Malatesta Cantos were first published in the *Criterion* for July 1923. In a letter to Watson, Pound urges him to compare what we have been referring to as the Watson Typescript with the version in the *Criterion*, and proudly claims that "you will be able to see that the three months sweat in Italy was not wasted. And that the skeleton had been brought to life."[22] (I shall relegate to Appendix A the major differences between this text and the 1972 New Directions version.)

It will be seen that the *Criterion* text differs from ours in no essential details—except for the omission of our first five lines:

>These fragments you have shelved (shored).
>"Slut!" "Bitch!" Truth and Calliope
>Slanging each other sous les lauriers:
>*That* Alessandro was negroid. And Malatesta
>Sigismund:
>
>   (8.28.1-5)

The first line might well have been omitted in deference to Eliot, in whose *Criterion* these cantos were to appear. Lines 2-4A constitute the latest addition to Pound's text, first coming into the poem with *A Draft of XVI Cantos*. (In any event, line 4A would have made no sense in the *Criterion* text, since it refers to the passage at the end of our Canto 7, which did not immediately precede the Malatesta Cantos at this time.) Pound also left out any mention of Malatesta's name at the beginning of the poem, leaving the reader in suspense until he came to the signature appended to the first letter. As for some of the other divergences, we know that Richard Aldington was responsibe for censoring "s. o. b." from the poem (see Chapter 1), and it seems that the proper readings for the obvious New Directions misprints "Arimininum" (9.36.15) and "*scienta*" (11.52.9) are the *Criterion* "Arimnium" and "*scientia*."

In Pound's first book of Cantos, *A Draft of XVI Cantos*, published in Paris by William Bird's Three Mountains Press (1925), the Malatesta group finally receives its present numeration, VIII through XI. (See Appendix A for this edition's divergences from the New Directions text.) Besides the obvious typographical errors ("*carissimc*," "Poliocetes," "*poten*") and the readings "Arimnium" and "*scientia*" recurring here, there is very little to capture our attention in this text. Perhaps it should be pointed out that the reading "*permissa*," which occurs here, in the *Criterion* text, and indeed in all the early editions of the *Cantos* instead of our "*premissa*" (9.40.4), probably represents a temporary inadvertence on Pound's part: in his source, the reading is "premissa," to which it was subsequently corrected (see Yriarte, p. 406).

Hugh Kenner tells of how "Nancy Cunard later bought Bird's assets, and in 1930 her Hours Press issued [in Paris] *A Draft of XXX Cantos* (200 copies). Bird's and her printers' vagaries still infest the New Directions edition, for which the Hours Press book once served as copy-text."[23] The only point that need be made about this text is that here the New Directions misreading "*scienta*" (11.52.9) first creeps into the Malatesta sequence (see Appendix A). In 1933, the first American edition of the *Cantos* appeared, *A Draft of XXX Cantos*, published in New York by Farrar and Rinehart—an edition reissued in 1940 by New Directions. The differences between the 1972 New Directions text and (1) the Farrar and Rinehart edition and (2) the Faber edition of the *Cantos* (London, 1954) are listed in Appendix A.

Now that we have concluded our study of the evolution of the Malatesta Cantos, it may be useful to summarize the main points made in our discussion:

1. Pound's early drafts are often diffuse, prosaic, and crammed with details.[24] As his own familiarity with the historical background of the period increased, Pound tended to excise this explanatory matter, almost as if the reader had done his research along with him. Hence, many passages in our final text are so condensed and enigmatic that the general reader finds them baffling.

2. The early drafts abound in editorializations on Sigismondo. They talk a great deal *about* him in an attempt to persuade the reader to admire him. These generalizations and evaluative comments about Malatesta are also often used to excuse his dubious conduct.

3. In the early stages of composition Pound felt compelled to present Malatesta with all his faults, in the interests of historical objectivity. Thus, he often lists Malatesta's shameful deeds and proceeds to expatiate on them—either by justifying his hero's conduct or, when this proves impossible, by criticizing his vices. Later, when Pound came to realize that thematic coherence was paramount, he deleted many of his references to Malatesta's inexcusable actions.[25]

4. The early drafts display an excessive concern with the minor characters (that is, everyone else besides Sigismondo). Pound often states their motivations flatly, instead of allowing them to be gleaned from the characters' words and deeds.

5. Pound's frequent digressions from his main subject gradually give way to a unified highlighting of Malatesta himself: these cantos become *his* poem, rather than a jumbled account of fifteenth-century Italian petty rivalries.

6. The early versions embody a number of descriptions of the Tempio that shower the author's direct, lavish praise upon it. In our text the Tempio keeps reappearing, but not in the context of these early set pieces.

7. Pound's initial choice of Malatesta Novello as his overt narrator is ultimately rejected in favor of multiple narrators: a contemporary of Sigismondo, a modern historian/scholar, and Pound himself in the lyrical and elegiac passages.

This strategy enables us to see Malatesta from a number of different but complementary viewpoints.

    8. The tone of Pound's writing is much more strident in the early drafts, relying more heavily on obscenity and scatology for its effects.

    9. The later drafts seek to incorporate more humor into the Malatesta Cantos: there is a greater interest in sprightly diction and sardonic anecdotes.

    10. Pound struggled with the problem of ordering his material, continually shifting and reshifting the numerous tile-like pieces of his mosaic. He finally settled on a schema that presents the main events of Sigismondo's life in chronological order, but that allows the minor events to be grouped thematically rather than in order of occurrence.

    11. The lengthy scene with Eliot at Verona is reduced in the later drafts to a few impersonal lines.

In the next chapter I shall make use of what we have learned from this examination of Pound's MSS in order to shed light on the Malatesta Cantos as we now have them.

3
The Deflated Epic Style of the Malatesta Cantos

> "'MA QVESTO,'
> said the Boss, 'è divertente.'
> catching the point before the aesthetes had got
> there"
> —Canto 41

In the terza rima "Commiato" (or Envoi) to his tragedy *Francesca da Rimini* (1902), Gabriele D'Annunzio bids his poem travel through Romagna, the ancient domain of the Malatesti, in search of the family's greatest scion, Sigismondo.[1] He describes the ghosts of the long-dead individuals who will rise up to greet it: Ginevra d'Este and Polissena Sforza, both weeping, and then "divine Isotta with her proud lover, to whom Pallas was propitious." The poem continues:

> As unrestrained as a hymn of mirth and fruitfulness, there rises in view the Tempio, which inaugurates the new cult. Lovely Spring herself was the artist who sculpted the marbles, animating Leon Battista's designs with eternal joy. Like a nymph in her maternal tree, Joy pulsates ceaselessly within the marble pillars, and an internal melody, like flames amid alabaster, seems to arise ardently from every column, shimmering over the garlands and knots of ribbon. Here, Youth with its dreams . . . seems to crave an immortal love. Aphrodite, the embodiment of human voluptuousness, is housed in the tomb supported by the elephants; young Bacchus dwells in the bronze of the vine. The biform satyrs and bacchantes have filled their baskets with grape-clusters and, when they are touched, the marble seems to sing. The curving ornaments are laden with the loveliest fruits of the earth, and never was laurel so richly woven into wreaths by more skillful artisans, nor did any more joyous chorus of spirits . . . ever raise a hymn to golden Aphrodite.
> Thick-maned Sigismondo hearkens to the hymn—that tempestuous imperial soul who ruled over a few castles instead of the world. Flower of eternity, this fateful son of Desire and Death remains enclosed within the triumphal round. His locks, which had been blown about by the whirlwind of destiny, and smoothed by divine Isotta, now flow down over his powerful neck. His learnèd lips cease to roar: fixed upon beauty, his lynxlike eyes are aflame. . . . Through Art, the mighty tyrant conquers Time: he is more alive now than when he coursed through cities and provinces.
> I want to draw forth from the marble his voice of love and command, and his very deeds. O

bloodstained poem, I send you to him. I send you to Sigismondo Malatesta in the name of the two spirits buffeted about by the relentless infernal storm, so that I may see him do battle again, as on the day of Piombino, with those arms that he bears on the medallion; riding across the Apennines, escorted only by his desperate thoughts and trusty dagger; arriving tight-lipped at the gates of Rome, having carved his argument with the Pope on the blade of his knife; and dealing with Fortune after his own fashion.

This Italianate view of Sigismondo would hardly have appealed to Symonds or Burckhardt. Here, the summit of human achievement is embodied in *virtù*—the quality of being a man, with all that it once implied: absolute dedication to art, beauty, and sensual pleasures of all kinds; physical strength, courage, perhaps even a potential for cruelty; intelligence and learning, feline instincts, a passionate and turbulent disposition; pride, complete self-reliance, scorn for the forms of organized religion or civic order; trusting only in one's avenging dagger, brooking no insults, and taking Fortune by the hair and treating her like the strumpet that she is. It is a picture of man worshiping his own superiority to everything on earth, above it, or beneath it, refusing to bend the knee to anything except his own indomitable will. As much as Pound might have admired these qualities—his obsession with Mussolini is partly explicable in these terms—he nevertheless was astute enough to realize that a totally straightforward encomium of Malatesta was not the best way of proceeding to celebrate his hero's "virtues." Between the time of D'Annunzio's paean and that of Pound's Anglo-American audience there loomed the ugly shadow of World War I: proud, amoral belligerence had too recently been associated with the Enemies of Civilization for Pound to have presented Malatesta in a D'Annunzian light.

Indeed, even before the War, Pound had ventured to depict this kind of personality mainly through the distancing modes of dramatic monologue or translation, as in all but one of his evocations of Bertran de Born.[2] Moreover, his attitude toward martial or heroic poetry was always a profoundly ambivalent one: on the one hand, he reveled in the reckless assertiveness of wily characters like Odysseus the liar, Bertran the "stirrer up of strife," and the crafty Cid; on the other hand, he repudiated what he considered to be sycophantic poems glorifying military exploits, and thus had little use for poems such as the *Aeneid*—a work which, along with those of the Augustan chroniclers, he debunks in *Homage to Sextus Propertius*. Aeneas seemed to typify the stuffed-shirt as hero, too pious and conventional for Pound's palate (or palette), the representative of duty, self-effacement, reverence toward religion and country—a gigantic cog in the state's machinery. Pound had no investment in heroes like these: he felt that the modern world was already swarming with them. And although there are many fine poems dealing with war in Pound's early verse, they either focus on the personality of the warrior rather than on his deeds (the Bertran poems), or they handle the theme of war from the perspective of the sorrow it causes (the *Cathay* poems and the section in *Mauberley* dealing, in embittered elegiac tones, with World War I).

Thus, after Pound had fastened on Malatesta, there remained the crucial problem of presentation. Pound's contempt for adulatory verse (even if directed toward a long-dead individual)[3] became implicated with the issue of a war-weary audience—an audience not likely to be captivated by a godless, debauched tyrant, howsoever great his devotion to learning and art. And so, Pound gradually adopted the technique of ironic presentation: he assembled all the materials necessary for an epic, heroic treatment of Sigismondo, but he deflated the potential windiness of such an undertaking by the use of irony, humor, and bathos, thereby creating the sense of a controlled confusion out of which emerges the dauntless figure of Malatesta, scheming and contriving to build his Tempio and defend his patrimony. This parody of epic modes is joined to a comic juxtaposition of styles and levels of diction (Renaissance pomposities side by side with modern American slang, nicknames, and name-calling)—yet all in the service of lavishing as much praise on Sigismondo as Pound possibly could. The ironies that have been detected in this sequence are thus not directed against Malatesta (as several critics have claimed): they are simply an effective means of highlighting Sigismondo's heroic stature by setting it off against the slightly ludicrous and certainly nonheroic milieu into which it was his misfortune to be born.

When, for example, Thomas H. Jackson all too sweepingly concludes that Sigismondo is "a man of his times like his enemies," and describes the Tempio as a "cathedral, celebrating ten or so years of adultery, built with bootlegged marble stolen from an abbey and fenced by a cardinal,"[4] he sounds curiously like Pius II: "Aedificavit tamen nobile templum Arimini . . . , verum ita gentilibus operibus implevit, ut non tam Christianorum quam infidelium daemonis adorantium Templum esse videtur."[5] But Sigismondo's deft manipulation of the "swindling Cardinal" whose venality is discovered and denounced by Doge Foscari (9.36.5–26) belongs in the same category—that of outfoxing greedy foxes—as the Cid's preying on the credulity of the moneylenders in Canto 3, and as Bertran's advice to the barons to pawn their castles *before* they go to war: "Baros metetz en gatge!" (85/548).[6]

Too often, Poundian morality is confused with our own:

> . . . Sigismundo is depicted as a man torn between his love for the arts and his concern for war-politics and "service money." . . . If Sigismundo was responsible for the architectural splendors of the Tempio at Rimini, he was also the first man to use metal cannonballs. If he wrote beautiful love poems to Isotta degli Atti, he also engaged in the most petty materialistic power struggles with the Sforza and Medici dynasties.[7]

But if it were not for Malatesta's "service money" (8.28.24), there would be no way to assure the *"Maestro di pentore"* that

> . . . he can work as he likes,
> Or waste his time as he likes
> . . . .
>   never lacking provision.
>   (8.29.17–18,21)

Temples were expensive things to build, even in 1449. And the metal cannonballs, besides being more efficient tools for doing one's work, appear in the following context:

> And he set up the bombards in muck down by Vada
> where nobody else could have set 'em
> and he took the wood out of the bombs
> and made 'em of two scoops of metal.
> (9.37.11–14)

This supposedly dubious achievement is later explicitly associated with Mussolini's famous clearing of the swamps:

> Having drained off the muck by Vada
> From the marshes, by Circeo, where no one else wd. have drained it.
> (41/202)

And the "petty materialistic power struggles" were actually feverish attempts, on Sigismondo's part, to hold on to his domain. Pesaro might, in itself, have been an "old brick heap" (9.36.31), but its loss

> . . . cut us off from our south half [Fano]
> and finished our game, thus, in the beginning.
> (9.35.10–11)

This being the case, "What could he do but play the desperate chess, / And stir old grudges?"[8]

Furthermore, any evaluation of Sigismondo must take into account the fact that Pound makes use of multiple narrators in the Malatesta sequence in order to present his hero from three different but mutually complementary viewpoints. The most prominent narrator (originally Novello, whose voice is still heard in a few passages)[9] is presumably one of Sigismondo's soldiers, a man of action rather than thought, who speaks like an epic poet *manqué*, inspired, no doubt, by the sluttish Calliope of 8.28.2. The second voice is that of a somewhat pedantic modern historian, who, in the service of "Truth," painstakingly transcribes a number of Renaissance documents for us, sometimes citing his sources directly in the text.[10] Finally, we hear the unmistakable elegiac voice of Pound himself, in several lyric passages infused with pathos.

But while this last voice, in its authorial capacity, attempts to enlist our sympathies for Malatesta, and while "the historian's" voice casts over the sequence an aura of authenticity, it is the voice of deflated epic that must bear the main burden of narration and sustain our interest in a hero quite remote from modern sensibilities. Our attention is as much drawn to the curious "telling" as to "the lesson" itself. By means of a strategy that may be called, in both senses of the word, diversionary, Pound has managed to focus our gaze on the whimsicalities of his narration to such an extent that we are deceived into thinking that Malatesta is being ironically distanced from the speaker as well as from ourselves. Only on closer consideration does this illusion yield to the realization that, for all our "distance" from Pound's hero, we have nevertheless assimilated the main theme of these cantos: that there once was an individual who, in spite of the chaotic society in which he lived, with its bigotry, superstition, and treachery, managed to erect a monumental edifice, fill it with a pagan beauty, give employment to dozens of artists,[11] earn a precarious living from warfare, write poetry to his mistress, and never lose his sense of humor. Indeed, it is perhaps this "sense of the sleight-of-hand man" behind these cantos that has disturbed some readers—the feeling that Pound, like any good prestidigitator, has beguiled our attention to one hand so that we remain unaware of what the other is doing.

The main thrust of the Malatesta Cantos is that of an exemplum.[12] Pound's depiction of an enlightened and benevolent despot (whatever the real Sigismondo might have been like) is held up to the gaze of a "half savage" America—for Malatesta's domain smacked not a little of the frontier-town, with its "cattle thieves" (8.32.17) and its lack of a propitious "setting" (8.32.24). Yet, if one man could bring such a high degree of civilization to Rimini (and this, Malatesta *did* do), surely it should be possible for a vast and wealthy nation to achieve "what I believe in the end to be inevitable, our American Risorgimento. . . ."[13]

Presenting a controversial figure from an obviously partisan point of view and alluding to recondite matters only in barest outline—as if the modern reader were a contemporary of Malatesta—may seem to be arbitrary (and problematic) ways of skirting the issue of historicism. But it must be remembered that in the Malatesta Cantos, Pound was primarily concerned with presenting the parable of Sigismondo's struggle to preserve himself and his dream of the Tempio against the prejudice and hostility of a greedy and insensitive society.[14] If handled from a sober, "modern" viewpoint, the contours of this "parable" would be blurred by numerous moral dilemmas which, for Pound's purposes here, were largely irrelevant. If treated in forthright epic terms, the resultant twentieth-century *Malatestiad* would risk bathos at every turn. Pound's solution consisted in presenting his hero, for the most part, through the eyes of a biased contemporary of Sigismondo—an amusing, irascible narrator, unaware that he is writing "deflated epic verse" (indeed, he thinks of himself as a "tough guy," just stating the "facts"), and completely engrossed in the figure of Malatesta. Pound seems to have hoped that this narrator's obvious fascination with Sigismondo would set the proper tone for the ideal reader of the Malatesta Cantos.[15]

Before taking a closer look at the text, I wish to point out a few curious similarities between Pound's strategy in Cantos 8–11 and the ironic advice offered to poetasters in Alexander Pope's *Peri Bathous: or, of the Art of Sinking in Poetry*.[16] Among Pope's many suggestions to prospective poets are that they learn to make use of synecdoche, whereby "you may call a young woman . . . Snotty-*nose*" (p. 331),[17] metaphor, whose "first rule is to draw it from the *lowest things*" (p. 331),[18] and anticlimax, "where the second line drops quite short of the first, than which nothing creates greater surprise" (p. 336).[19] He goes on to counsel "the *Choice* of *low Words*" (p. 342)[20] and the employment of "*Technical Terms*" (p. 343).[21] In addition, Pope explains "the method of turning a vicious Man into a Hero," namely by availing oneself of "the *Golden Rule* of *Transformation*, which consists in converting Vices into their bordering Virtues" (p. 353), and he suggests in his "Receipt to make an Epic Poem" that, "for the FABLE," one should "throw all the adventures you fancy into *one Tale*" (pp. 353–54).

My point is not that Pound read Pope, but that, if *Peri Bathous* represents all that one should *not* do in attempting to write dignified or heroic verse, Pound seems to have been very assiduous indeed in his flouting of poetic decorum. What he does in these cantos, however, must not be confused with Pope's forte, the mock epic, which treats of trivial subject matter in a lofty style in order to satirize or ridicule the protagonists. On the contrary, Pound's deflated epic technique treats of potentially epic actions[22] in the low style—a peculiar admixture of Renaissance bombast and Anglo-American persiflage, to mention only two of its components. This "domestication" of the epic for a modern audience does not imply that Sigismondo and his values are being denigrated in any way. In fact, Pound "leaves little doubt that *his* sympathies are with Malatesta."[23] The irony that arises from this mode of narration is directed against a social milieu that trivializes itself by its deceitfulness and, by implication, against ourselves, who, in the dozens of clichés strewn across these cantos, hear our own voices jabbering away, while beauty dies aborning.

The obverse side of this slangy component of Pound's language is his use of Italian snippets, Latinate legalisms, and elaborate Renaissance forms of address.[24] At about the time that Pound was beginning his work on the Malatesta Cantos, he remarked that his translations from the troubadours had been cast into an archaic linguistic mold because "the Provençal feeling is archaic, we are ages away from it" (*SL*, p. 179). In Cantos 8–11, although a great deal of the language is extremely colloquial, Pound never lets us forget for long that we are dealing with the fifteenth century. He thus tries to capture many of the idiosyncratic tonalities of Renaissance Italy while, at the same time, he leads us to realize that the period we are reading about, unlike that of the troubadours, is essentially a modern one.[25] The end result is *not* that Pound distances Malatesta's era from us by his use of Latin and Italian, but that he allows *us* to become contemporaries of Malatesta. Rather than bring the Renaissance to us, Pound chooses to bring *us* back to the Renaissance.[26]

By translating foreign expressions immediately before or after or even in the midst of quoting them,

>   . . . work chucked away
>   *(buttato via),*
>   (8.28.31–32)

>   *"rem eorum saluavit"*
>   Saved the Florentine state,
>   (9.35.20–21)

>   So that he can work as he likes,
>   Or waste his time as he likes
>   *(affatigandose per suo piacere o no
>   non gli manchera la provixione mai)*
>   never lacking provision,
>   (8.29.17–21)

or by writing a sort of macaronic verse,

>   For two days' pleasure, mostly *"la pesca,"* fishing,
>   *Di cui* in the which he, Francesco, *godeva molto,*
>   (8.31.12–13)

Pound enables us to witness our language "turning into" Latin or Italian right before us on the page. Related to this technique of translucency is one that Marjorie Perloff has labeled "satiric super-literalism,"[27] best exemplified in Pound's translation of the stilted letter by Malatesta's six-year-old son (9.39.14–33). In spite of the humorous effect, this mode of rendering one language into another is highly commended by Walter Benjamin, who claims that

> . . . it is not the highest praise of a translation . . . to say that it reads as if it had originally been written in that language. . . . A real translation is transparent; it does not cover the original, does not block its light, but allows the pure language . . . to shine upon the original all the more fully. This may be achieved, above all, by a literal rendering of the syntax. . . .[28]

The illusion effected by these various procedures (previously brought to perfection in "The Seafarer" and *Cathay*) is that of being exposed to an earlier age (or a different culture) in such a way that we seem to perceive its language, sensibility, and modes of thought via the medium of what is, ostensibly, our own language. Only in this way did Pound feel that he could both present Malatesta in his own milieu and convey to us, simultaneously, his relevance for our times.

So far, we have considered Pound's deflated epic style in general terms, examining the broad contours of this strategy and defining its relationship to the tone and theme of the Malatesta Cantos. The rest of this chapter will adduce specific instances of Pound's deflation of epic modes, drawing attention not only to the linguistic and rhetorical component of these cantos but also to their parodic adaptation of epic conventions. This reading of the Malatesta sequence seeks to demonstrate that Sigismondo is a hero of potentially epic dimensions trapped in a world of little men,[29] that he whom D'Annunzio saw as "that tempestuous imperial soul who ruled over a few castles instead of the world" is portrayed by Pound as the inevitable pariah of a purblind, insensitive society.

Pound chooses to emphasize the difference in stature between Sigismondo and his adversaries not by amplifying the dimensions of his hero (that would be the mode of true epic), but by the "Lilliputianization" of men like Pius II, Federigo d'Urbino, and Francesco Sforza. This latter mode, that of deflated epic, often involves radical distortions of perspective, as when Pound devotes thirty-four stirring lines to Malatesta's defeat of "the papishes" (10.47.4–11.48.26), but only a few vague words to Federigo's thrashing of Sigismondo: "But we got it next August" (11.48.29). We must, however, keep in mind that what most interested Pound about Malatesta was not that he was a greater man than his enemies (though Pound certainly seems to think so), but that he chose to take an unorthodox path to greatness—one that led, paradoxically, to a failure "worth all the successes of his age."

We have already traced the growth of the Malatesta sequence to its final four-canto structure; it remains for us to observe that this tetradic organization calls to mind the short epic (the epic "deflated" in size), sometimes consisting of four books, as do the *Argonautica* of Apollonius of Rhodes, Milton's *Paradise Regained,* and, perhaps most appropriately, *The Dunciad.* At the opposite pole, that of the individual line of verse, we notice that Pound's lines are often lengthy and prosaic, suggesting a parodic relationship to the swelling hexameters of classical epic (Arnold's "grand style simple" with a vengeance). Pound has said of this aspect of the Malatesta sequence:

> I don't think, either, that I ought to give preface, or defence of the form. For a work of this length (i.e. the ten thousand or more cantos as a whole), I think I have a right to rhythm units, longer than the single octo or octo-decasyllabic verse.
>
> Besides the Ship canto (VIII) [the present Canto 2] is supposed to have given the lecteur, for the nonce, his melodic apricot.[30]

Certainly no one has accused the Malatesta Cantos of constituting a "melodic apricot"—not with lines like "But dey got de mos' bloody rottenes' peace on us" (11.49.14) and the bovine "grnnh! rrnnh, pthg" (9.36.22). But Pound's "mighty line" reaches a point of *reductio* (or *amplificatio*) *ad absurdum* in the post-bag letters, where, for the first time in the *Cantos*, the sweep of the individual lines is fortuitously determined merely by the width of the page:

> "Sence to-day I am recommanded that I have to tel you my
> "father's opinium that he has shode to Mr. Genare about the
> "valts of the cherch...etc...
> (9.37.35–9.38.2)

Undisguised prose here enters the *Cantos*, often of a kind that prompted Pound to instruct Watson: "I DO want the mis-spellings in the documents, letters, etc. kept VERY carefully. Also the abbreviations."[31]

The Malatesta Cantos begin with a feigned slip of the pen that purports to mimic a plausible slip of the tongue:

> These fragments you have shelved (shored).

His revision of *The Waste Land* still fresh in his head, Pound here indulges in a bit of gratuitous "emendation" of his friend's line, "These fragments I have shored against my ruins," perhaps in order to suggest that

> . . . Eliot's poetic method in *The Waste Land*, far from making the useful part of the past more available, rather "shelves" it again. Pound, on the other hand, will "unshelve" the useful part of the past, as he does in the Malatesta Cantos.[32]

Pound has fumbled his way into the sequence, only to follow this *lapsus linguae* with a parodic epic invocation in which the patronesses of History and Epic, Truth and Calliope, reveal their testy natures and utter incompatibility: where there is epic in the conventional sense, there is no truth; where there is historical truth, epic sublimity is impossible. Truth thus accuses Epic of being the "Slut" of almost any legendary or historical character: all that is needed is a poet willing to distort, exaggerate, or embellish the facts. Calliope, on the other hand, considers History a "Bitch," for she exposes the vileness and sordidness that often lurk beneath the surface of "heroic deeds."

While Pound, on the level of structure, seems to ally himself unequivocally with History,[33] which presents, in Aristotle's formulation of the distinction between Epic and History, "not a single action, but a single period, and all that happened within that period to one person or to many, little connected together as the events may be,"[34] he nevertheless chooses, on the level of individual details, an overtly fictive mode. This is not to say that historians are "objective" or that Pound falsifies the historical record on Malatesta: my point is merely that Sigismondo's misdeeds have been deemphasized by Pound, whereas those of his enemies have been foregrounded.

Pound does his best to cast a veneer of authenticity over the Malatesta Cantos by incorporating a large number of original or translated documents into his poem. Especially at the beginning of the sequence, he is careful to rely heavily on "the facts": the letter from Sigismondo to Giovanni de' Medici, the contract between Malatesta and Florence, Sigismondo's love lyric, the snippet from his letter in 8.30.24–32, and so on. There is even the demystifying gesture toward the murdered Alessandro de' Medici, treated elegiacally in Canto 7, where he is associated with Dante's Manfred, "E biondo, with glass-grey iris, with an even side-fall of hair" (7/27),[35] only to be introduced into Canto 8 as "*That* Alessandro was negroid."[36] Pound here deflates his own earlier elegiac mode in order to prepare the reader for the very different tone of the Malatesta Cantos, but the debunking implications of the line have more to do with rhetoric than with "Truth": Pound's deflated epic style purports to shear the past of its legendary accretions, yet it nevertheless manages to avoid subjecting Sigismondo to the cold scrutiny of objective investigation. This shuttling back and forth between Truth and Calliope, History and Epic (deflated or otherwise), pusillanimous foes and embattled hero, is built into the linguistic component of the line describing Truth and Calliope as "Slanging each other sous les lauriers." Calling to mind the antitheses featured in the "gonads in organdy" line,[37] this verse epitomizes the *concordia discors* achieved in these cantos: the slangy English phrase joined to the "poetic" French one—a slangy English phrase, moreover, whose chief element is the word "slang" itself, and a poetic French phrase whose referent is the laurel tree, sacred to Apollo and all his tribe.

Pound next states his epic subject or theme: "And Malatesta / Sigismund." The epic hero is usually a central figure of national importance; here, he is an Italian princeling whose deeds are, by and large, buried in musty tomes, which it is Pound's self-appointed task to "unshelve." His casual alluding to events long forgotten inverts the epic's typical retelling of familiar tales, and his adducing of an introductory document dated 1449 plunges us *in medias res*—here, into the exact midpoint of Sigismondo's active career, which spanned the years 1430–68.[38] But we are also plunged into the middle of words themselves:

> ...hanni de
> ..dicis
> ...entia.

With regard to the Tempio, Pound had written that "the word [was] made stone,"[39] but these particular words of Malatesta have crumbled beneath the weight of centuries, and it is only the poet's dedication which "shores" these fragments for us and translates them into English:

> Equivalent to:
> > Giohanni of the Medici,
> > Florence.[40]

Pound's transcription of the mutilated words confers an air of scholarly authenticity over the sequence, as does the untranslated salutation of Sigismondo's letter: "*Frater tamquam / Et compater carissime.*"[41]

The letter itself is sprinkled with legalistic and business English ("with all due dispatch," "memoranda," "party to," "adherent," "to make due provision"), as well as with a few slangy expressions ("chucked away," "cash," "Unless you put him off it"), but it nevertheless serves to introduce Malatesta to us in an extremely favorable light: "arranging peace" between Florence and "the King of Ragona" would give him "the greatest possible pleasure"; the "service money" that he requests from the Medici will presumably go, at least in part, to the "*Maestro di pentore*," who, like his future patron, also "needs cash"; and the leisure that Pound claimed is the only thing with which a patron can provide an artist[42] will seemingly be guaranteed by the terms of Malatesta's offer to the painter. The conscientious "historian" who is presumably translating this letter for us also transcribes some snippets from the original Italian document—as if he were translating a philosophical treatise, which often demands that all the technical terms be provided in both languages.[43] But in one of these instances, there is an obviously humorous deflation of this gesture when the text provides the Italian "technical term" for "chucked away":

> And it wd. be merely work chucked away
> (*buttato via*).

Lest there be any doubt that we have left behind the world of saga and entered the domain of lawyers and clerks, Pound next provides a translation of part of an agreement between Sigismondo and the city of Florence, in which he retains a goodly amount of the original's legalistic jargon:[44]

> Therefore between the aforesaid Illustrious Sigismund
> And the respectable man Agnolo della Stufa,
>   ambassador, sindic and procurator
> Appointed by the ten of the baily, etc., the half
> Of these 50,000 florins, free of attainder,
>   (8.29.31–8.30.1)

and so on. These letters and legal documents (by means of which much of the communication between the various characters in the Malatesta sequence takes place) stand in ironic contrast to the extended formal speeches of epic verse: there, the heroes praise or vilify each other face to face; here, they often do so via the mediation of a text, whether it be a letter, an agreement, an invective, or a historical work such as Pius's *Commentaries*. The preponderance of the written over the spoken word is part of the overall deflationary strategy of the Malatesta Cantos, in which the characters (with the significant exception, for the most part, of Sigismondo) are not so much dramatized as "memorialized" on the page by means of their own written traces. This "absence" of theirs throws into high relief the omnipresence of Sigismondo, who is thereby rendered, in the words Pound once used of Odysseus, "the live man among duds" (*LE*, p. 212).

Immediately after the two introductory documents, Pound provides the reader with a bit of "epic geography" that falls far short of the national, international, or even cosmic scope of many epic works: "Romagna, teeming with cattle thieves" (8.32.17) is here represented by "the mud-stretch full of cobbles" (8.30.15), and instead of the twin peaks of Parnassus, we read of "the forked rocks of Penna and Billi, on Carpegna" (8.30.11). A little further on, Pound states explicitly that "here they wanted [that is, "lacked"], a setting, / By Marecchia [hardly a Scamander], where the water comes down over the cobbles" (8.32.24–25). The Pesaro that helps to ruin Malatesa, and that Galeaz sold "'to get pay for his cattle'" (which the "cattle thieves" had presumably carried off), is no more than an "old brick heap" (9.36.31),[45] and Malatesta almost loses his life in the squabble over Sorano, "a ten acre lot, / Two lumps of tufa / ...with six hundred pigs in the basements" (9.37.19–20, 24). Even when Sigismondo is despoiled, the "epic" catalogue that enumerates his losses can speak only of places with names like

>   Sogliano,
> Torrano and La Serra, Sbrigara, San Martino,
> Ciola, Pondo, Spinello, Cigna and Buchio,
> Prataline, Monte Cogruzzo,
>   and the villa at Rufiano,
>   (11.49.16–20)

constituting in part the "few castles" that Malatesta ruled over, "instead of the world."

Between the bleak setting of "the mud-stretch full of cobbles" and the "interruption" of Sigismondo's military engagements ("it rains here by the gallon"), there appears Pound's exquisitely wrought lyric—a greatly "deflated" pastiche of Malatesta's interminable poem—by which a mythological or epic motif is introduced into the sequence in the person of Helen of Troy, who, along with "Yseut" and "Batsabe," is not considered the peer of Isotta degli Atti (8.30.16–22). Here, however, the theme of destructive feminine beauty ("Κύθηρα δεινά" [76/456]) plays no part, as it does in Cantos 2 and 7, with their Aeschylean puns on Helen's name,[46]

> ". . . ἐλέναυς and ἐ λέπτολις!" (2/6)
> Ἔλανδρος, (7/24)

and with the Trojan elders' plaint that "doom goes with her in walking" (2/6). It is not the worship of beauty that destroys Malatesta, but the absence of that predilection among his foes, who, in the words of Canto 14, may be likened to "the perverts, who have set money-lust / Before the pleasures of the senses" (14/61). The hypocrisy of one of them, Pope Paul II, is revealed by Pound's recording of the fact that he wished to assume the rather un-Christian name of "Formosus" upon his elevation (11.51.18-21), but that he afterwards proceeded to jail and torture Platina and the rest of the neo-pagan Roman Academy "For singing to Zeus in the catacombs" (11.50.33).[47] Indeed, most of the mythological allusions in the Malatesta Cantos are introduced ironically:[48] Pius II is scornfully referred to as "'this Aeneas'" (10.46.13),[49] Malatesta is seen to be "a bit too POLUMETIS" (9.36.29), and the name of "POSEIDON" is followed immediately by the philosophical term "*concret Allgemeine*" (8.31.20), suggesting that we are viewing Gemisthus Plethon's Poseidon via the mediation of some scholarly German tome.[50]

But classical mythology plays a relatively small role in these cantos. Much more in evidence is a "demythologizing" of some of the most prominent of Sigismondo's contemporaries. Thus, Francesco Sforza, the foremost *condottiere* of the day, is introduced to us, by means of a legal document, as the "most illustrious / Duke of Milan" (8.29.25–26), but he is soon revealed to have been a "peasant's son" (8.31.9) with a penchant for fishing. Nothing is said of his numerous military victories, yet we read of "an excellent hiding" he once received (8.31.15). Even his seizure of a powerful duchy is downplayed: "And old Wattle-wattle slipped into Milan" (9.35.32). Whereas Malatesta's betrayal of King Alfonso is euphemistically referred to as a "change-over" that even Pius II had to admit "Saved the Florentine state" (9.35.19–21), Sforza's shiftiness is disproportionately foregrounded, syntactically as well as thematically:

> With wattle Sforza against him
> Sforza Francesco, wattle-nose,
> Who married him (Sigismundo) his (Francesco's)
> Daughter in September,
> Who stole Pèsaro in October (as Broglio says "*bestialmente*"),
> Who stood with the Venetians in November,
> With the Milanese in December,
> Sold Milan in November, stole Milan in December
> Or something of that sort,
> Commanded the Milanese in the spring,
> the Venetians at midsummer,
> The Milanese in the autumn,
> And was Naples' ally in October.[51]
>
> (8.32.3–15)

Against this "general indefinite wobble" (35/173), we are presented, in the very next line, with Malatesta's "rock-like" steadfastness of purpose, "He, Sigismundo, *templum aedificavit*"—the Latin phrase constituting, once more, a grudging concession to Malatesta on the part of Pius.[52] Pound works another of these "syntactic see-saws" into Canto 9, where we read:

> And old Sforza bitched[53] us at Pesaro;
>   (*sic*) March the 16th:
> "that Messire Alessandro Sforza
>   is become lord of Pesaro
> through the wangle of the Illus. Sgr. Mr. Fedricho d'Orbino
> Who worked the wangle with Galeaz
>   through the wiggling of Messer Francesco,
> Who waggled it so that Galeaz should sell Pesaro
>   to Alex and Fossembrone to Feddy.
>   (9.34.29–9.35.5)

Pound implies that the duplicity and capriciousness of these characters is so pronounced that even the pronouns used in speaking of their actions must be immediately rescued from any possible ambiguity (9.35.7-9):

> And this he did *bestialmente*; that is Sforza did *bestialmente*

[for it could also have been Galeaz, Alex, or Feddy],

> as he had promised him, Sigismundo, *per capitoli*

[for he could also have promised to Galeaz, Alex, or Feddy],

> to see that he, Malatesta, should have Pesaro

[but he made sure it ended up with Alex].

    The three other chief antagonists of Sigismondo are treated in much the same way. A great general and illustrious patron of the arts is reduced to "that nick-nosed s.o.b. Feddy Urbino" (11.49.5);[54] an outstanding humanist becomes "old bladder" (9.35.20), "that monstrous swollen, swelling s. o. b." (10.44.14), who often "lost his pustulous temper" (10.46.21); and Pius's successor is trivialized as "fatty Barbo, 'Formosus,'" and "Little fat squab 'Formosus'" (11.51.2,18). But Pound does not, in a merely facile way, invest Malatesta with a sublime grandeur at the expense of his foes: quite a few specimens of *sermo humilis* are put into his mouth, or those of his friends and supporters. Indeed, Malatesta's first spoken words in the sequence (unconsciously ominous in light of his final despoliation) are no more dignified than

"Now you have me,
    Caught like a hen in a coop."
            (8.31.31–32)

After Federigo succeeds in tricking him over the Pesaro affair, Malatesta confides to Broglio that "'I'm the goat'" (9.37.4). And Valturio is made to give his cynical advice on the betrayal of Alfonso by means of a homely proverbial expression: "'as well for a sheep as a lamb'" (9.35.18).

Although Sigismondo and his party are not immune from the lower registers of diction, it is nevertheless true that the lyrical or elegiac moments in these cantos are reserved for Malatesta alone, or—as in the brief descent to Dante's Hell near the end of Canto 8—for members of the Malatesta clan. This scene (8.32.26–8.33.2), with its evocation of two cases of incest leading to murder,[55] serves as an introduction to the last segment of the canto (8.33.3–9), which draws on the earliest events of Sigismondo's public life. His *first* attempts to defend his patrimony are thus proleptically viewed as *ultimately* futile, in light of the *past* retribution meted out to the Malatesti for their passionate dispositions. The sweep of Canto 8 is from the exact midpoint of Sigismondo's career to the very beginning of it—or from *in medias res* to earliest flashback—and from the middle of words (". . . *hanni de* . . .") to the middle of a sentence, "And that year he crossed by night over Foglia, and . . ." —the ellipsis here suggesting that it is useless to continue listing these precocious attempts at self-preservation ("he was twelve at the time"), since, given the tragic history of the family, defeat is a foregone conclusion: "For this tribe paid always."[56]

The ninth canto opens with an evocation of the hostility of the elements,[57]

> One year floods rose,
> One year they fought in the snows,
> One year hail fell, breaking the trees and walls,

soon succeeded by the hostility of man, in the person of Astorre Manfredi, who sets his hounds on Malatesta, "down here under Mantua"—the narrator now locating himself in Sigismondo's milieu.[58] The end of this canto, however, focuses on the realms of love and art—Isotta and the Tempio—counterbalancing the destructiveness of man and the elements: destructive nature / the construction of a work of art; man's hate / woman's love. Between these two pairs of polarities, Pound elaborates on the more pernicious of the two evils (man's hostility: the "street fight," the sale of Pesaro, Federigo's deception of Malatesta, Sigismondo's dismissal by the Venetians, Sforza's not paying him promptly, the Sienese fiasco) and on the more perdurable of the two "loves" (the Tempio, as it surfaces in almost all of the post-bag letters).

Since a true epic "includes history" (*SL*, p. 247), a deflated epic might very well occasionally imitate the most debased form of historical writing—the chronicle, "which enumerates events one after the other with frequent and somewhat abrupt shifts from one scene to another."[59] Thus, in a passage of twenty-four lines soon after the opening of Canto 9 (9.34.6–29), we notice that eighteen of them begin with "and," while the subject at hand changes no fewer than eleven times.[60] In addition, the chronology is that of the chronicle gone awry. For example, Sigismondo's court poet, Basinio, is seen going out to "Where the lists were, and the palisades / had been set for the tourneys" (9.34.19-20) to engage in a purely verbal rather than martial duel with Porcelio Pandone, "the anti-Hellene," who had espoused the thesis that one may be an elegant Latin poet without having studied the Greek authors assiduously. The outcome of this "single combat," which took place in 1456, is that Basinio "talked down" Pandone. But in the next two lines we jump back to 1437, with the birth of "an heir male to the seignor," and to the death of Ginevra d'Este in 1440. A few lines farther down the page we are told that Malatesta "built the great Rocca to his plan" (his fortress and palace)—yet this edifice was completed in 1446, eight lines after and ten years before Basinio walks out into its courtyard to commence his forensic duel. The perpetrator of this anachronistic chronicle is soon seen to be our "epic" narrator, one of Sigismondo's companions, who proudly associates himself with his master:

> And this cut us off from our south half
>   and finished our game, thus, in the beginning,
> And he, Sigismundo, spoke his mind to Francesco
>   and we drove them out of the Marches.
>   (9.35.10–13)

After Sigismondo "Poliorcetes"[61] (9.36.28) is shown besieging, not Troy, but Sorano, with its "six hundred pigs in the basements" (9.37.24), we jump to what the indignant Sienese found in the confiscated post-bag. Searching for treason, they uncover an assortment of oddments: trivial domestic matters, sundry mundanities and fripperies, plans for the Tempio—and a bit of dirty laundry concerning "Sr. Galeazzo's daughter" (9.38.14–15). It is nevertheless in these sometimes illiterate letters that we obtain our first extended view of Sigismondo, by means of the ways in which his servants and family communicate with him. The "Rex Proditorum" of the next canto is here presented as a man whom his household feels free to address on a variety of topics in a cordial, intimate tone:

> "The man who said young pullets make thin
> soup, knew what he was talking about."
>   (9.38.15–16)

> "Everyone wants to be remembered to you."
>   (9.38.25–26)

> ". . . noboddy hear can do anything without you."
>   (9.39.5–6)

">... in consideration of yr. paternal affection...."
(9.39.23–24)

These humble "epic speeches" are contrasted with the excerpts from the papal diatribe against Malatesta presented in Canto 10. The remarks of Pius, who had religious, political, and economic motives for detesting Sigismondo, are thus carefully prepared for by the favorable picture of Malatesta drawn by his domestic circle.[62]

The ninth canto draws to a close with a description of Sigismondo's two loves: Isotta and the Tempio. Once again, Pound uses Pius's words to praise Malatesta—here, in the Italian lines,[63]

> "*et amava perdutamente Ixotta degli Atti*"
> e "*ne fu degna,*"
> (9.41.4–5)

but he also translates the Pontiff's condemnation of the Tempio as being "full of pagan works." This, of course, is one of the very reasons why Malatesta was so important for Pound: his temple was one of the first edifices in Europe to ensure that pre-Christian canons of sculpture and architecture should survive "'Past ruin'd Latium'"—that is, beyond the decline of paganism in the West.[64] The canto ends with a brief *ekphrasis* of the Tempio in Pound's own voice:

> The filigree hiding the gothic,
> > with a touch of rhetoric in the whole
> And the old sarcophagi,
> > such as lie, smothered in grass, by San Vitale.

The "filigree" and "touch of rhetoric" succeed in transforming the Gothic shell of the edifice into something new—an amalgam of classical and medieval motifs that inaugurates the "new style" of Renaissance architecture.[65] Pound admits that the eclecticism of the Tempio is not entirely successful when he later portrays Sigismondo inspecting the interior and "noting what was done wrong" (11.49.33). Yet, more than a decade after the completion of the Malatesta Cantos, Pound was to write:

> The Tempio in Rimini would have been a far less daring synthesis had all its details been fully digested and reduced to a unity of style, à la Palladio. As a human record, as a record of courage, nothing can touch it.[66]

The last two lines of Canto 9, with their evocation of the Tempio's sarcophagi, inject a note of doom into the sequence: the next two cantos will trace the trajectory of Sigismondo's decline and fall. By comparing the stone tombs with those that "lie, smothered in grass, by San Vitale," Pound is once again emphasizing the cultural overlaying that went into the Tempio by suggesting that Malatesta might have gotten the idea for his Renaissance tombs from having seen the ancient Roman sarcophagi that are to be found near the Byzantine (medieval) church of San Vitale. The grass that smothers the Roman tombs takes us back full circle to the inclemency of the elements at the beginning of the canto, reminding us that even carved stone is subject to the inexorable law of dissolution.[67] But we must also remember that the mortal remains of Plethon are buried in one of the Tempio's sarcophagi—thus establishing Malatesta in the role of a worthy Dionysius to Gemisto's Plato.[68]

In Canto 10 we return to the account of the siege of Sorano, which had been interrupted by the transcription of the post-bag letters. The unauthorized peace that Sigismondo made with Count Pitigliano is dismissed by a hardly disinterested narrator with the words "And what of it *any*how?" (10.42.10), though farther down on the same page we revert to the supposedly impartial narration of the historian—one who would introduce into his text the citation:

> *Florence, Archivio Storico, 4th Series t. iii, e*
> *"La Guerra dei Senesi col conte di Pitigliano."*

In any event, from whatever point of view we examine the situation, one thing is evident: Sigismondo's fortunes are on the wane. The Sienese seek to entrap him, he and Federigo exchange "epic boasts" (" '*Te cavero la budella del corpo!*' " and " '*Io te cavero la corata a te!*' "), and Pius orders him to be burned in effigy. The description of this auto-da-fé by inanimate proxy is provided in Pius's own words, transcribed by Pound in Roman capitals in order to suggest ancient Latin inscriptions—such as those recording memorable feats on triumphal arches. But Pius's gloating over his enemy's "funeral pyre" ("INGENS PYRA EXTRUITUR") is a hollow sham, for the corpse of no Patroclus or Hector feeds the flames, but a dummy "costing 8 florins 48 bol / (i.e. for the pair, as the first one wasn't a good enough likeness)" (10.45. 29–30). Once again, Pound cites his sources in scholarly fashion, "*Com. Pio II, Liv. VII, p.* 85. / *Yriarte, p.* 288," but immediately thereafter proceeds to take a very partisan view of things:

> So that in the end that pot-scraping little runt Andreas
>   Benzi, da Siena
> Got up to spout out the bunkum
> That that monstrous swollen, swelling s. o. b.
>   Papa Pio Secundo
>   Aeneas Silvius Piccolomini
>   da Siena
> Had told him to spout, in their best bear's-greased latinity.
>   (10.44.11–18)

This tirade on the part of the narrator prepares us for an "epic catalogue" of Sigismondo's sins—a string of syntactically free-floating Latin epithets suggesting the ravings of an obsessed personality and demonstrating the true nature of the man with the elegant name of Aeneas Silvius:[69]

> *Stupro, caede, adulter,*
> *homocidia, parricidia ac periurus,*
> *presbitericidia, audax, libidinosus,*
> wives, jew-girls, nuns, necrophiliast, *fornicarium ac sicarium,*
> *proditor, raptor, incestuosus, incendiarius, ac*
> *concubinarius.*[70]
>   (10.44.19–24)

This is certainly *not* the Sigismondo we have been allowed to see so far in the Malatesta Cantos. We notice, however, that Pound chooses to present the serious charges by means of single words (the *Discipula veritatis* contains such lists, but it also elaborates on many of the accusations), whereas he lovingly translates two passages from the invective in somewhat greater detail—instances of thoroughly bathetic argumentation. The first of these deals with a prank that involved substituting ink for holy water in the fonts of a church. Pound heightens the ludicrous potentiality of such a charge by the tautological construction "fill up the same full with ink" (10.44.32), by the stilted rhetoric of "Making mock of the inky faithful" (10.45.3), and by the concessionary gesture that renders the entire passage ridiculous: "Which might be considered youthful levity / but was really a profound indication" (10.45.5–6).

The second passage that Pound chooses to present in its entirety concerns the *hypothetical* nausea of the souls of the blessed:

> "Whence that his, Sigismundo's, foetor filled the earth
> And stank up through the air and stars to heaven
> Where—save they were immune from sufferings—
> It had made the emparadisèd spirits pewk"
>   from their jeweled terrace.
>   (10.45.7–11)

The stately syntax and eloquent locutions of this vignette ("Whence that . . .," "save they were . . .," "It had made . . .") are everywhere ironically undermined. Thus, the elevated diction of "foetor" is undercut by its semantic component, "stench"—as "stank" in the next line reminds us. And the Thomistic parenthetical remark on the imperturbable bliss of the saints becomes absurd in light of the activity in which these "emparadisèd spirits" would engage, if only they were capable of it—that is, "pewk" (complete with onomatopoetic spelling). What the narrator accomplishes in this brief "epic" flight to the heavens is merely to have a host of preternatural beings vomit down on the world in order to vent their disgust—if only they were ontologically constituted to do so.

After this heady metaphysical interlude, Pius's "pustulous temper" doggedly reasserts itself in an Italian translation (Soranzo's) of thirteen more charges against Malatesta, bringing to a close this rabid trilingual assault on the Tempio-builder. The narrator's colloquial tones are heard once more as he attempts to continue with his story, but he gets entangled in his own grammatical constructions,

> and the whole lump lot
> given over to...
>
> I mean after Pio had said, or at least Pio says that he
> Said that this was elegant oratory . . . ,

and so on, for another four lines of interpolation, before he finds his thread again: "The lump lot given over / To that kid-slapping fanatic il cardinale di San Pietro in Vincoli. . . ."[71] Sigismondo's trial *in absentia* has by now taken such a pharisaical turn that the narrator is prompted to identify his hero with the crucified Christ:

> I. N. R. I. Sigismund Imperator, Rex Proditorum.
> (10.46.2)

In spite of Malatesta's excellent advice at the Crusade Council of Mantua (10.46.20),[72] Pius has set out to destroy him. But the Pope is not Sigismondo's only enemy. Francesco Sforza is interested in receiving some of the territories soon to be wrested from Malatesta (10.46.24–26); the Venetians, Sigismondo's "allies," threaten his court artist, Matteo da Pasti, with torture (10.46.28–29; see also 26/121); and Malatesta's friend, Borso d'Este, is attacked in Venice:

> And they had a bow-shot at Borso
> As he was going down the Grand Canal in his gondola
>   (the nice kind with 26 barbs on it).[73]
>   (10.46.30–32)

And although Malatesta "had three chances of / Making it up with Alfonso, and an offer of / Marriage alliance" (10.46.17–19), we have already seen what happened to Piccinino "For trusting Ferdinando of Naples" (10.43.26), Alfonso's son—this betrayal too having occurred via a "marriage alliance."

Now that we have been thoroughly exposed to "the nature of the enemy," Sigismondo is allowed to emerge, in the last verse paragraph of the canto, as a heroic warrior in the ancient Roman mold. Battle with the papal troops is imminent, and an eagle, Jove's bird, has "lit on his tent pole." Malatesta's pagan cast of mind enables him to correctly interpret this augury of divine favor, to associate it with the world of *"li antichi cavaler romanj"* (from Broglio, p. 273r), and to use it to exhort his men to victory, along with the laconic paradox:

> They've got a bigger army,
>   but there are more men in this camp.

This serious epic moment brings to a close a canto that had begun with Sigismondo's ignominious flight from the Sienese. He now has a chance to vindicate himself—as the historical Malatesta actually did at the battle of Nidastore on July 2, 1461.

The last of the Malatesta Cantos opens with a "formulaic repeat" of the Italian lines from Broglio, and seems to plunge into a straightforwardly epic description of Sigismondo's victory. On closer inspection, however, we realize that the deflationary mode is still with us, though somewhat attenuated by Pound's desire to celebrate his hero's finest hour. Thus, although the narrator emphasizes by repetition the numerical disparity between Malatesta's army and the Pope's, the way in which this is done includes some elements of the risible:

> And the papishes were three thousand on horses,
> dilly cavalli tre milia,
> And a thousand on foot,
> And the Lord Sigismundo had but mille tre cento cavalli
> And hardly 500 fanti (and one spingard).
>   (11.48.13–17)

The macaronic technique in the last two lines culminates in the use of the obsolete English word "spingard" (from Italian "spingarda," a kind of swivel-gun), added as a parenthetical, but obviously important, afterthought—yet one that remains for the reader semantically vague and phonologically outlandish. This absence of referentiality extends to the pseudo-Homeric catalogue of Malaesta's "chiefs,"[74] none of whom constitutes for us more than a name on the page:

> Bernardo Reggio, Nic Benzo, Giovan Nestorno,
> Paulo Viterbo, Buardino of Brescia,
>   Cetho Brandolino,
> And Simone Malespina, Petracco Saint Archangelo,
> Rioberto da Canossa,
> And for the tenth Agniolo da Roma
>   And that gay bird[75] Piero della Bella,
> And to the eleventh Roberto. . . .
>   (11.48.5–12)

In addition, the polysyndeton of the last two passages quoted above pervades the entire description of the battle—twenty-six lines all connected by "and," forming an enormous sentence whose semi-flippant syntactic structure functions as a safeguard against the possibility of slipping into the mode of sentimentalized bombast.

Close on the heels of Malatesta's victory, however, there follows his disastrous defeat by the papal army under the command of Federigo d'Urbino (August 1462):

> But we got it next August;
> And Roberto got beaten at Fano,
> And he went by ship to Tarentum,
> I mean Sidg went to Tarentum. . . .
> (11.48.29–11.49.1)

In apparent dismay, the narrator stumbles over his own feet and has to rewrite the ambiguous line in which "he" seems to refer to Roberto. The gloating pun of the victorious general, "that nick-nosed s.o.b. Feddy Urbino," is dutifully recorded, "*'Par che è fuor di questo...Sigis... mundo'*" (11.49.6),[76] before the narrator enunciates what is perhaps the most "deflated" line in the sequence: "But dey got de mos' bloody rottenes' peace on us" (11.49.14). This hybrid specimen of cockney and Joel Chandler Harris jars with the rest of this narrator's utterances, especially because it is followed immediately by "*Quali lochi sono questi*" and the "epic" catalogue of very obscure Italian towns lost by Malatesta (11.49.15–21).

While his enemies divide his state, Sigismondo sits in the Tempio, "On a bit of cornice . . . / Too narrow to fit his big beam" (11.49.31–32), and expresses his concern for the lowly by providing for Zuliano's "kids" and for a peasant who had suffered the loss of some horses (11.50.4–9). His fortunes, however, continue to ebb: he is sent to places with epic associations, Sparta and Lakedaemon, "to do in the Mo'ammeds," but comes back defeated, "with no pep in him"; he is foiled in his desperate attempt on the life of Paul II: "Damn pity he didn't / (i.e. get the knife into him)"; and he must finally accept service with the despised pontiff: "64 lances in his company, and his pay 8,000 a *year*."

But besides building the Tempio, Malatesta has managed to earn the respect of the humanist, Platina:

> And they want to know what we talked about?
>   "*de litteris et de armis, praestantibusque ingeniis,*
> Both of ancient times and our own; books, arms,
> And of men of unusual genius,
> Both of ancient times and our own, in short the usual subjects
> Of conversation between intelligent men."
> (11.51.3–8)

And he has also captured the imagination of the common people:

> And the castelan of Montefiore wrote down,
> "You'd better keep him out of the district.
> "When he got back here from Sparta, the people
> "Lit fires, and turned out yelling: 'PANDOLFO'!"
>   (11.51.26–29)

In short, he has functioned (at least in this poem) as the only good thing in a bad time:

> In the gloom, the gold gathers the light against it.[77]

But the elegiac tone of this majestic line is not allowed to cast its somber shadow over our last glance at Sigismondo, for the sequence ends with a description of the facetious bargain drawn up between Malatesta and his steward, Enrico Acquabello:[78]

> And one day he said: Henry, you can have it,
> On condition, you can have it: for four months
> You'll stand any reasonable joke that I play on you,
> And you can joke back
>   provided you don't get too ornry.
> And they put it all down in writing:[79]
> For a green cloak with silver brocade
> *Actum in Castro Sigismundo, presente Roberto de Valturibus*
> . . *sponte et ex certa scienta* . . . *to Enricho de Aquabello.*
>   (11.52.1–9)

Malatesta, whom we first see (via a letter) at the siege of Cremona, returns home to his palace, where (via a legal document) we see him . . . no, not exterminating suitors, but playing practical jokes on one of his courtiers. (Then again, Odysseus is "the live man among duds" [*LE*, p. 212], and Sigismondo is "an entire man" [*GK*, p. 194].) In fact, Malatesta's first quoted word in the sequence is "*Frater*" and his last is "ornry"—and the distance between these two terms serves to indicate the scope of a man who spans the entire gamut of mood and expression, as well as the scope of a poem, the *Cantos*, which will, from now on, do much the same thing.[80]

Of the individual components of *A Draft of XVI Cantos,* Hugh Kenner has said that only the Malatesta sequence "offers a wholly novel rhetoric" (*Pound Era*, p. 416). In this chapter I have attempted to trace the contours of this rhetoric, which, in the words of Ficino on Plato, allowed Pound "to joke seriously and to play most studiously."[81] After the Malatesta group, the pervasive *gravitas* of the first seven cantos gives way to a style that often weaves together the comic and the tragic so inextricably that the two demand to be seen as inseparable strands in the fabric of human existence—as in the *Pisan Cantos*, when the anguish, degradation, and loneliness of the imprisoned poet find expression in the words:

> nox animae magna from the tent under Taishan
> amid what was termed the a.h. of the army
> the guards holding opinion. As it were to dream of
> morticians' daughters raddled but amorous. . . .
> (74/437)

4

The Malatesta Mystique in the Works of Ezra Pound

> "I have seen the married,
> I have seen the respectably married
> Sitting at their hearths:
> It is very disgusting."[1]

> "All our work was the work of
> outlaws . . . ."[2]

The Figure of the "Outsider" in Pound's Early Work

Ezra Pound's lifelong preoccupation with Italian civilization may be traced to the very title of his first book, *A Lume Spento*, printed in Venice in June 1908. More important for our purposes, however, is the uncanny resemblance between Dante's Manfred, who utters the Italian phrase in the course of telling his story in *Purgatorio* III, 103-45, and Pound's Malatesta, who in 1908 was not yet even a gleam in his creator's eye. Like Malatesta, Manfred was brought low by papal enmity arising from his epicurean ways and his scorn for the Church. Dante has him admit that "my sins were horrible" (III.121), but does not elaborate on them. Manfred's enemies were more specific, charging him with the murders of his father (Frederick II), his brother, and two of his nephews. Twice excommunicated, Manfred was killed in the battle of Benevento (1266), his corpse being thereafter exhumed and transported, "with tapers quenched," beyond the borders of the kingdom of Naples and Sicily, to which he had laid claim. The excommunicate Malatesta, who had been burned in effigy by papal decree, was similarly despoiled by an envious Pope, and was, like Manfred, recovered from the obloquy of pious historians by what many have considered the sheer vagaries of the poetic imagination.[3] I am not, of course, suggesting that Pound's use of three words from the *Purgatorio* constitutes a manifesto of any sort, or that it represents his first conscious reference to an archetypal character that he was to exploit for many years to come: I am merely making use of the allusive potential embodied in the title of his first book in order to introduce a certain type of personage often encountered in his verse.

An examination of the poems in *A Lume Spento* reveals that, from the very beginning of his career, Pound was firmly committed to "wineing the ghosts of yester-year."[4] The medievalism, in both style and content, of predecessors like Rossetti, Swinburne, and the early Yeats, is united to a Browningesque fascination with the violence and unorthodoxy of the Italian Renaissance (especially as evinced in many of Browning's dramatic monologues), and results in a poetry of masks—a series of disguises through which the ambitions and frustrations of the young poet are distanced in the very process of being enunciated. This double focus of the mask, or persona, allowed Pound to disclaim any personal endorsement of the ideas and attitudes expressed by his masks ("you might as well say that Shakespeare is dissolute in his plays because Falstaff is"),[5] while enabling him to identify himself, imaginatively, with the dead masters of his soul, whose passions and ideals he saw as akin to his own: "Thus am I Dante for a space and am / One François Villon, ballad-lord and thief."[6] The aspect of this situation directly relevant to the evolution of the Malatesta-figure concerns itself with the large proportion of masks falling into the category that may be labeled, at its most inclusive, that of the "outsider"—the man who finds himself alienated from, or hostile to, the established norms of the society in which he lives. Often he is a lusty or, at least, life-affirming individual, painted against the background of a stagnating, repressed, and repressive society—in his broadest aspect, a life-force set against the powers of darkness and death. Ultimately descended from Browning's portraits of heroic failures, he is usually an extraordinary man despised and misunderstood by the masses of mediocrities numerically powerful enough to set themselves up as his judges. A failure (or worse) in the eyes of the world, he must content himself with his own appraisal of his ultimate worth or with that of posterity.

The masks of the outsider in *A Lume Spento* range from that of Miraut de Garzelas and his wise folly in "La Fraisne,"

> And now men call me mad because I have thrown
> All folly from me, putting it aside
> To leave the old barren ways of men,[7]

to the towering (and futile) ambition of Bertold Lomax in "Scriptor Ignotus," who seeks, in the eighteenth century, to write another *Divine Comedy*.[8] Between the poles of madness and obsessive artistic dedication there is the middle ground of a vagabond love-poet (Cino, whose ladies are more interested in wealthy noblemen than in "lackland" singers), a criminal-poet ("Villonaud for This Yule" and "A Villonaud: Ballad of the Gibbet"), and a warrior-poet hated by his lady (Bertran de Born in "Na Audiart"). That most of Pound's masks at this stage of his career are those of poets should not be too surprising: often the masks are semi-transparent projections of the young Pound's self-image as a *poète maudit*. More important is the fact that, of all these outsider-poets, the one who was to be preeminent in Pound's early work, Bertran de Born (introduced innocently enough in "Na Audiart"), should be the one who was most a man of action—indeed, a man whose poetic achievement seems only incidental to his primary self, that of warrior and "stirrer up of strife." Thus, from the very beginning of his career, the focus of Pound's attention was to be less on "the lonely singer" for his own sake, than on the long-range revitalizing influences of such outsiders on the very society they scorn and attack. The distinction was to be between those figures who, like the Pre-Raphaelites and the Aesthetes, cut themselves off from society in order to create a private dream-world, and those audacious enough to strive for the realization of their dream in the midst of a society not yet ready to accept it.[9]

Although Pound began his career under the guiding lights of Browning, Pre-Raphaelitism,[10] and the 1890s, he nevertheless found himself, at a much later date, writing verse as publicly oriented as

> But in Russia they bungled and did not apparently
> grasp the idea of work-certificate
> and started the N.E.P. with disaster
> and the immolation of men to machinery
>   and the canal work and gt/ mortality
>   (which is as may be)
> and went in for dumping in order to trouble the waters
>   in the usurers' hell-a-dice
> all of which leads to the death-cells.
>   (74/441)

The process that led the young Pre-Raphaelite to the death-cells spans several decades. But already in 1909, the year in which he met T. E. Hulme, Pound was dissatisfied with the feckless role that many of his contemporaries were content to assume:

> I would shake off the lethargy of this our time,
>   and give
> For shadows—shapes of power
> For dreams—men.
>
> "It is better to dream than do"?
>   Aye! and, No!
>
> Aye! if we dream great deeds, strong men,
> Hearts hot, thoughts mighty.
>
> No! if we dream pale flowers,

Slow-moving pageantry of hours that languidly
Drop as o'er-ripened fruit from sallow trees.[11]

In "Redondillas, or Something of That Sort," a poem withdrawn from *Canzoni* (1911), Pound dons a Whitmanesque mask in order to outline the type of poetry he hopes to write:

> I believe in a love of deeds,
>   in a healthy desire for action. . . .
> . . . .
> Whenever we dare, the angels crowd about us.
> There is no end to the follies
>   sprung from the full fount of weakness;
> There is great virtue in strength
>   even in passive resistance.
> . . . .
> I sing of the special case,
>   The truth is the individual.
> . . . .
> The chief god in hell is convention,
>   'got by that sturdy sire Stupidity
> Upon pale Fear, in some most proper way.
> . . . .
>   Mistrust the good of an age
> That swallows a whole code of ethics.
>   (*CEP*, pp. 217-21)

By the time he wrote these lines, Pound had already conjured up, in *A Lume Spento,* the shade of Villon, "thief, murderer, pander, bully to a whore" (*SR,* p. 171). In prose, he had extolled the figure of the Cid:

> . . . it is the unquenchable spirit of that very glorious bandit, Ruy Diaz, which gives life to the verse. . . . Upon learning from historical sources that the actual Ruy Diaz of Bivar was not a drivelling sentimentalist, but a practical fighting man, some people speak of disillusion. . . . If the Campeador had set out with some beautiful ideals, . . . it is unlikely that he would have taken Valencia.[12]

One of Pound's most impressive translations, "The Seafarer" (1912), focuses on the total isolation of a character separated both physically and spiritually from his fellow men. But all these "outsiders" in Pound's early work pale beside Bertran de Born: nobleman, warrior, lover, poet of love and war, and deemed worthy of a place in the *Inferno*, Bertran seemed to unite in one character all the energy, passion, and scorn for the norms of society that a penniless young American poet in London could wish to appropriate as his own.[13]

Pound wrote five poems dealing with Bertran,[14] two of which rank with his finest shorter pieces: "Sestina: Altaforte" and "Near Perigord." In the latter (and later) poem, Bertran becomes the subject of a meditation on the sphinxlike inscrutability of the past: its literary texts, historical data, biographical facts, and even those poetic re-creations of it (the *Inferno* on Bertran, for example) that have, like the past itself, grown dark with the passage of time. But in its self-consciously perplexed treatment of the central figure (a strategy derived mainly from Browning's *Sordello*), the poem uses Bertran merely as a convenient pretext for the narrator's extended rumination on the problem of interpreting the past. Pound suggests the potential equivocation with which all literary and historical documents speak to us by focusing on Bertran's "Dompna Pois de me No'us Cal"— ostensibly a love poem, which, if read "allegorically," lends itself to a "war-strategy" interpretation:

> Is it a love poem? Did he sing of war?
> Is it an intrigue to run subtly out,
> Born of a jongleur's tongue, freely to pass
> Up and about and in and out the land,
> Mark him a craftsman and a strategist?
> ("Near Perigord," *PERSONAE*, p. 153)

The emphasis here is less on the figure of Bertran as an outsider than on the modern poet's struggle to come to terms with his protean literary and historical source materials.

The sestina, however, presents Bertran as a blood-thirsty warrior, a man who can discover strife even in a sunrise:

> And I love to see the sun rise blood-crimson.
> And I watch his spears through the dark clash
> And it fills all my heart with rejoicing
> And pries wide my mouth with fast music
> When I see him so scorn and defy peace,
> His lone might 'gainst all darkness opposing.
> (*PERSONAE*, p. 29)

If Christ is the Prince of Peace, Bertran is Anti-Christ, or at least a Prince of Strife, invoking the powers of Hell three times during the course of his monologue, and even presuming to make the oxymoronic request of "May God damn for ever all who cry 'Peace!'" Pound's careful choice of end words seems, at first glance, to establish a tension between peace ("peace," "music," "rejoicing") and war ("clash," "opposing," "crimson"), but on closer inspection we realize that Bertran's "peace" is attained only through the "crimson" of bloodshed, his "music" is the "clash" of swords, and his "rejoicing" is derived from his "opposing" of men in battle. In this poem, and in various prose pronouncements on Bertran, we see most clearly an early form of the "Malatesta-figure" in Pound's work. Bertran emerges as a "type" of Malatesta—a man who revels in the overturning of traditional hierarchies of good and evil, substituting military *virtù* for Christian virtue.

Propertius and Mauberley: Major Visions of the Poet as Outsider

In "Near Perigord" Pound had mused on the difficulties of interpreting, and thereby recovering, the past. By the time he came to write *Homage to Sextus Propertius,* he was convinced that a more pressing problem, rendered inescapable by the continuing horror of the War, was that of the poet's relation to his own age. Pound had certainly addressed this issue before 1917, but always in a minor mode. The poems in *Lustra*—a volume which, with *Cathay,* marks Pound's poetic coming of age—had indulged in social criticism and raised the issue of the artist's relation to his public, often by means of Whitmanesque apostrophes to the reader or in short, satiric poems modeled on Roman epigram. Yet, although *Lustra* contains many of Pound's wittiest and most popular poems, the volume as a whole is much more impressive than its individual components. We sense that Pound has finally shed a great deal of his archaizing and "literariness," that there is a new limpidity of language and movement, a new bareness of style and modernity of tone. But many of the poems embodying these praiseworthy features merely strike us as being slight graftings onto the slender tree of Imagism. Before leaving the domain of "non-*Cantos* verse," however,[15] Pound attempted to define his stance vis-à-vis his era by means of two long poems that may be regarded respectively as a positive and a negative statement of essentially the same theme, that of the poet as outsider in a materialistic society.

Many of the epigrams in *Lustra* had ridiculed certain modern "types" beneath the guise of Roman or Romanized Greek names: Mumpodorus, Leucis, Arides, Florialis, Bastidides, Agathas, Phyllidula, Erinna, Lalage, Aurelia, Phidippus, and Candidia. It is clear that Pound saw some connection between the mores of Roman society and those of the modern age, and he makes this yoking explicit in his oft-cited comment on *Propertius:*

> . . . it presents certain emotions as vital to me in 1917, faced with the infinite and ineffable imbecility of the British Empire, as they were to Propertius some centuries earlier, when faced with the infinite and ineffable imbecility of the Roman Empire. These emotions are defined largely, but not entirely, in Propertius' own terms. If the reader does not find relation to life defined in the poem, he may conclude that I have been unsuccessful in my endeavour.
> (*SL*, p. 231)

The "relation to life" consists in the representation of Propertius as an outsider-poet, a man involved in a struggle, albeit a nonphysical one, against "the current of power," a love-poet who chooses to realize his own potentialities, at the expense of popularity and patronage, in the attempt to create a living work of art. He sets himself apart from the subsidized patriotic poetry of his contemporaries[16] by concentrating on mastery of technique and by a return to the theme of love:

> Out-weariers of Apollo will, as we know, continue
>   their Martian generalities,
> We have kept our erasers in order.
> ....
> Annalists will continue to record Roman reputa-
>   tions,
> Celebrities from the Trans-Caucasus will belaud
>   Roman celebrities
> And expound the distentions of Empire,
> But for something to read in normal circumstances?
> For a few pages brought down from the forked hill
>   unsullied?
>   (*PERSONAE*, p. 207)

> The primitive ages sang Venus,
>   the last sings of a tumult.
>   (p. 216)

"Propertius" believes that the "official" poets of his day have abdicated their primary responsibility to their own craft in the attempt to resurrect a dead past as propagandistic underpinning for a turbulent present:

> Alba, your kings, and the realm your folk
>   have constructed with such industry
> Shall be yawned out on my lyre—with such industry.
>   (p. 210)

The main defect of Virgilian and Horatian verse is seen to be its remoteness from emotional verities: "my ventricles do not palpitate to Caesarial *ore rotundos*" (p. 218). Propertius thus chooses to focus his work on the aspect of existence that he feels temperamentally equipped to deal with—the theme of love:

> And if she plays with me with her shirt off,
>   We shall construct many Iliads.
>   (p. 217)

Although his relationship with the mercurial Cynthia is often distanced by a Laforguean irony, Pound's Propertius remains satisfied with his poetic task because it enables him to present the subject of his passion truthfully and in a way that is as meaningful for other lovers as it is for himself:

> And in the mean time my songs will travel,
> And the devirginated young ladies will enjoy them. . . .
>
> (p. 208)

In *Propertius* we see the outsider-figure removing himself from the social and political arena of his day in order to create a personalized poetry of potentially universal interest and appeal, as opposed to the rhetoric and bombast of official poetry, written according to accepted party lines for the glorification of the new imperial system. In this light, the isolation sought and achieved by "Propertius" is a laudable one: rather than hoodwink himself and others by means of pseudo-historical fictions, he adopts the guise of a cultivated man speaking frankly to other cultivated individuals and bypassing the militaristic preoccupations of his age. Indeed, even Pound's structuring of his poem into twelve parts (complete with descent to Hades in Part VI) reinforces Propertius's claim of serving an artistic function at least as important as that of Virgil and the other epic poets of his day.

The salutary consequence of Propertius's withdrawal from public events and controversies consists in his tending the hearth of primordial impulse: "the primitive ages sang Venus." Once again, as in much of Pound's early verse, we are confronted by an outsider-figure who keeps the flame of instinct artistically alive during a historical period characterized by propaganda, materialism, and repression. Scattered individuals like Propertius become, in Pound's view, the guardians of certain cherished traditions that otherwise would be permanently mislaid.[17] There can be no doubt that Malatesta belongs to this same class of preservers, especially in his defiant role of neo-pagan builder in a hypocritically "Christian" age. (The essential difference between them, however, is important for understanding Pound's later development of the outsider in the *Cantos*: as a ruler, Malatesta was in the position of marshaling men and money into the service of his artistic vision, whereas Propertius had to rely entirely on the efficacy of his art itself: "We have kept our erasers in order.") But what happens when a poet, possessing neither wealth nor political power, withdraws so far from the bourns of a repressive society that he renders himself sterile and ineffectual even in the realm of his own art? This question is taken up in *Hugh Selwyn Mauberley,* a work roughly contemporaneous with *Propertius* and dealing with the gloomy obverse side of many issues raised half-humorously in the latter poem.

Although Pound suggested that *Propertius* could be read in light of the British Empire and the War, the distancing achieved by the poem's ancient setting allowed him to treat what had once been the realities of bloodshed in a farcical manner:

> "The Euphrates denies its protection to the Par-
> thian and apologizes for Crassus,"
> And "It is, I think, India which now gives necks to
> your triumph,"
> And so forth, Augustus. "Virgin Arabia shakes in

> her inmost dwelling."
> If any land shrink into a distant seacoast,
> it is a mere postponement of your domination.
>
> (*PERSONAE*, p. 216)

In *Hugh Selwyn Mauberley*, with its modern setting and unmediated treatment of World War I, armed conflict ceases to be amusing:

> Daring as never before, wastage as never before.
> Young blood and high blood,
> fair cheeks, and fine bodies;
> ....
> hysterias, trench confessions,
> laughter out of dead bellies.
>
> (*PERSONAE*, p. 190)

The immediacy of this war, in which Pound had lost his friends, Henri Gaudier-Brzeska and T.E. Hulme, precluded any ironic detachment. In addition, by 1918 Pound had met Major C. H. Douglas, whose attempts to integrate the cultural heritage within the economic framework of society were to have a profound influence on the *Cantos*, as well as on many of Pound's journalistic pieces. By the end of the year (1920) in which both *Mauberley* and Douglas's *Economic Democracy* were published, Pound's "regard for the individual genius, 'the favoured of the gods,' was as high as ever, but Douglas had introduced a new factor which began to place him at the mercy of contemporary events. If things were happening he had a desire always to participate . . ." (Stock, *Life*, p. 307).[18] According to Kenner, Douglas's views

> gave meaning to the present and the past alike, and relieved art from the impasse of aestheticism by absolving it of the need to demonstrate its immediate utility. The artist had only to refrain from curling up with his dreams, and set about patterning the air with forms. 'Hugh Selwyn Mauberley' (1919-20) was the first fruit of this insight, and Pound's first work to contain the word 'usury.'
>
> (*Pound Era*, pp. 316-17)

The main critical debate over *Mauberley* has centered on the difficulty of determining the exact relationship among Mauberley, "E.P.", and Pound himself. Though this difficulty is a real one—resembling in some ways the problems of reading *A Portrait of the Artist*—it is at least clear that it stems from the double-edged irony pervading the work. Pound is attempting to point out the artistic limitations of Mauberley (and of young Pound the aesthete, E.P.) at the same time that he is lambasting a society that tends to produce Mauberleys in such profusion. The strong autobiographical undercurrent in *Mauberley* seems to result in a kind of schizophrenic analysis of the artist confronted by a materialistic society: the first part of the poem explains—and goes a long way toward extenuating—Mauberley's ultimate decision to dissociate himself from a repulsive social scene, whereas *Mauberley 1920* directs a ruthless gaze on Mauberley's sterile solipsism, making use of rhythms, syntax, and imagery suggestive of his own inner chaos:

> Drifted . . . drifted precipitate,
> Asking time to be rid of . . .
> Of his bewilderment; to designate
> His new found orchid. . . .
>
> To be certain . . . certain . . .
> (Amid aerial flowers) . . . time for arrangements—
> Drifted on
> To the final estrangement.
> *(PERSONAE,* p. 199)

Where does Mauberley go wrong? Surely he starts off with the right impulses. Even in the highly ambiguous first poem of the sequence (in which I think it is possible to fuse the characters of Mauberley and E.P.), Mauberley is delineated in terms of the outsider-figure, "out of key with his time" and striving "to resuscitate the dead art / Of poetry." So far, he differs very little from Propertius. In the second stanza we even discover a premonition of Malatesta himself, who ruled "in Romagna, teeming with cattle thieves," but who dreamt of the pagan glories of Rome, erecting his Tempio in proud defiance of his enemies, though often falling prey to their strategems:

> . . . seeing he had been born
> In a half savage country, out of date;
> Bent resolutely on wringing lilies from the acorn;
> Capaneus; trout for factitious bait.
> *(PERSONAE,* p. 187)

The rest of this first poem goes on to introduce an Odyssean motif (Sirens, Penelope, Circe), which was to play, along with that of the Dantesque journey, such a crucial role in the overall conception of the *Cantos.* Indeed, the first part of *Mauberley* contains, like *Propertius,* twelve subdivisions,[19] calling our attention not only to the "epic" underpinning of the work but also to its potential affinities with Pound's earlier long poem. And surely the twelve parts of *Mauberley I* may be read as a modern analogue of Odysseus's voyage of discovery, constituting Pound's denunciation-by-survey of a society deadened by tawdry commercialism, economic wars, and the triumph of mediocrity.

But a voyage implies a destination; pointless movement is mere wandering. It is only in *Mauberley 1920* that we discover the true nature of Mauberley's Ithaca, as well as of his Penelope. The first part of the poem had exposed a society desperately in need of some remedy for its ills. The second part reveals Mauberley's response to the problem: an escape inward to an island paradise of the mind, to an aesthete's interiorized "Palace of Art" in which

> . . . his desire for survival,
> Faint in the most strenuous moods,
> Became an Olympian *apathein*
> In the presence of selected perceptions.
> *(PERSONAE,* p. 202)

"By constant elimination," Mauberley seeks to furnish himself with "an armour / Against utter consternation," but he only succeeds in paralyzing his artistic instincts by depriving them of the often unpleasant substratum of human actions and emotions. Unlike Malatesta, who struggles purposefully against a hostile world (by stealing marble, if he must, by fighting to get money for his Tempio, and by braving the Church) in order to register permanently a certain set of aesthetic values, Mauberley is content to keep his insights to himself, seeing no reason to divulge, or even to render concrete, his private intuitions:

> A pale gold, in the aforesaid pattern,
> The unexpected palms
> Destroying, certainly, the artist's urge,
> Left him delighted with the imaginary
> Audition of the phantasmal sea-surge.
> (ibid.)

According to Pound (*SL*, pp. 274-75), the last line is his version of the Homeric phrase *para thina poluphloisboio thalasses* ("by the loudroaring sea," *Iliad*, I.34). If so, the adjective "imaginary" certainly undermines whatever pretensions Mauberley may have had toward setting himself up as a modern Odysseus: not only is his sea an ersatz one, but so, as we shall see, is the Aphrodite/Penelope that rises out of it.

In order to illuminate the precise nature of Mauberley's failure, I wish at this point to consider briefly two poems, "The Seafarer" and "Exile's Letter," which, along with *Propertius*, Pound once referred to as examples of his "major personae" *(Umbra*, p. 128). Although these poems, which Pound seemed to single out for special attention, all deal with outsider-figures, each differs from the others in the nature of the separation involved. "The Seafarer" presents a man physically and spiritually separated from the mass of men,

> Burgher knows not—
> He the prosperous man—what some perform
> Where wandering them widest draweth,

but nevertheless compelled to sing of the loveliness left behind, "Bosque taketh blossom, cometh beauty of berries," as well as of the rigors of his solitary life at sea. Each "mindscape" adds poignancy and depth to the other: the pleasures of life on land are accentuated by contrast with the grim seafaring life; the harshness of wandering is rendered more intense by the speaker's nostalgic reminiscences:

> Sea-fowls' loudness was for me laughter,
> The mews' singing all my mead-drink.

The sacrifices involved in the way of life presented in "The Seafarer" are justified by the exquisite song they make possible, indeed, wrench out of him. Though the speaker claims that he sings it "for my own self," it nevertheless enters our landlubber consciousness and comments insightfully upon it, in a way that "a view from the inside" could not.

In "Exile's Letter," on the other hand, the separation is purely physical: the two friends presumably remain as intellectually and emotionally compatible as they have been in the past. But once more the isolation of the speaker, "far away over the waters," results in a compensatory heightening of sensibility—the speaker's, certainly, but potentially that of his readers too. Those events which, through repetition, might have become cloying, assume instead the character of "spots of time," precisely because they may never occur again—as in the speaker's evocation of the last time he feasted with his friend:

> And what a reception:
> Red jade cups, food well set on a blue jewelled table,
> And I was drunk, and had no thought of returning.

This outsider's predicament has not resulted in sterility of any kind; on the contrary, it has enabled him to send a letter "a thousand miles, thinking." In the case of Pound's Propertius, as indicated above, his emotional and aesthetic dissociation from patriotic verse has freed him to pursue a theme closer to the core of human existence.

Mauberley's separation, however, has led to

> Nothing, in brief, but maudlin confession,
> Irresponse to human aggression,
> Amid the precipitation, down-float
> Of insubstantial manna,
> Lifting the faint susurrus
> Of his subjective hosannah.
> *(PERSONAE*, p. 202)

The emphasis here is on Mauberley's lack of sustenance: the "insubstantial manna" of his reveries does not provide him with the strength to think coherently, fight off his adversaries, or sing above a whisper—and that to a god of his own delirious devising. He has chosen to "starve" himself, rather than derive power, direction, and determination from feeding on the harsh realities of modern existence:

> Mouths biting empty air,
> The still stone dogs,
> Caught in metamorphosis, were
> Left him as epilogues.
>
> (p. 200)

Mauberley's failure as an artist results, in large part, from his failures as a human being, exemplified in his sexual sterility. The woman who serves as his Muse might well have become his lover, but

> He had passed, inconscient, full gaze,
> The wide-banded irides
> And botticellian sprays implied
> In their diastasis.
>
> (ibid.)

What then, we may ask, has this outsider—unable to read the passion in a woman's eyes—reinjected into a stagnant society? What would allow him to say, with Pound,

> I bring you the spoils, my nation,
> I, who went out in exile,
> Am returned to thee with gifts.[20]
>
> (*CEP*, p. 209)

Mauberley's "gift" consists of his poem "Medallion," a charming exercise in the aesthetics of the glimpse. It is a little gem that Arthur Symons, for example, would have aspired to. Its success as a poem underscores Mauberley's essential failure as an artist: it presents a "portrait of a lady" that treats a woman (she of the "wide-banded irides," no doubt) as if she were a work of art, rather than as the subject around which a work of art may be created. Looking at the woman, Mauberley sees nothing but colors, shapes, volume, line, the play of light, and so on, "inconscient" of whatever else these may "imply." Thus, the interplay of these optical stimuli serves to remind him only of certain works of art—*reproductions* of works of art at that, remembered from Reinach's *Apollo*. The extremely mediated nature of his perceptions and associations has led Mauberley to attempt in verse what a painter could have done better:[21] the woman's face is twice referred to as the "face-oval," it is seen "beneath the glaze" and has a "bounding-line," her hair resembles artifacts in the Minoan style, and her eyes, in a certain lighting, turn the color of topazes. This, then, is the Penelope toward whom Mauberley has been wandering, an Anadyomene as seen "in the opening pages of Reinach." She is portrayed superficially, in the literal sense of the word: woman as a complex of thoughts, emotions, and desires (as in Propertius's Cynthia) has been trivialized to the level of woman as *nature morte*. In addition, the last line of "Medallion," "the eyes turn topaz," echoes Ariel's song: "Those are pearls that were his eyes." The irony here consists in Mauberley's apparent claim to have brought about a "sea change" in the woman, to have transformed her, by means of literary artistry, into "something rich and strange," while overlooking the fact that Ariel's song presupposes, on a literal level, the physical death of the artistic subject. Instead of bringing something dead to life, Mauberley has "killed" something living in order to endow it with an eerie luster, such as might adorn a bride for Huysmans's Des Esseintes. In brief, Mauberley's aesthetics compels him to view life in terms of art, rather than the other way around. It reminds one of Wilde's remark when he was asked to look at a lovely sunset: "Oh, it's probably just a bad Turner." And this was the topsy-turvy kind of aestheticism that Pound was exorcising in *Mauberley*.

By pushing the isolation of Propertius to an unacceptable degree in Mauberley, Pound was refining and restricting his conception of the outsider-figure: the removal of oneself from the center of society was henceforth to be conceived as a socially responsible act. It had to be accompanied by compensatory powers of insight, productivity, and inspiration. Anything else was mere narcissism:

> "I was
> And I no more exist;
> Here drifted
> An hedonist."
>
> (*PERSONAE*, p. 203)

In *Mauberley* the poet has painted himself into a corner of preciosity and fastidious inconsequence. His lack of engagement, of "resistance to current exacerbations," renders him useless to himself, to poetry, and to the society he scorns as useless. He has cultivated his "outsideness" as if it were a quality valuable in itself, and it is this that earns him his absolute insignificance. Far from being part of the solution, he has become, if anything, part of the problem: he furnishes society with yet one more instance of the spineless childishness of the modern artist, one more reason for denying its support to those who represent, in its pompous terms, "no adjunct to the Muses' diadem."

While Pound's repudiation of Mauberley's aestheticism stems partly from embarrassment at his own early tendencies toward the school of limp wrists, lisps, and sunflowers, it also owes a great deal to his growing conviction that the arts can best thrive in an atmosphere of social, political, and economic sanity.[22] In Pound's view, a poet like Mauberley has evaded his responsibility to use art as a weapon in the struggle for a better society, for one which—unlike the London of *Mauberley I* —will welcome the serious artist. But Pound also realized that the influence of the artist constituted, at best, a long-range solution for the ills of society. More immediate in its effects was the type of action open to those with political and economic power. Thus the *Cantos* feature a number of warriors, rulers, and statesmen who are depicted as active bringers of civilization. These "factive personalities" concern themselves with discarding the dead wood of their particular social system and with bringing about immediate, decisive changes in the structure of political, economic, or cultural life. Their motto, in short, is "make it new"—but the "newness" may result from the reviving of lapsed traditions as well as from radical or innovative changes. Pound's vision of the just society was therefore one in which much depended on the wisdom and the noble intentions of its ruler, the man who could accomplish the greatest amount of good in the shortest space of time.

By placing so much emphasis on the leader who could effect change most expeditiously, Pound was gradually required to diminish the importance of the outsider-figure. As the *Cantos* progress, we notice a movement away from the wandering singers, exiles, and independent warriors of the early cantos toward the presidents, emperors, and dictators of the middle section of the poem—that is, a movement away from the isolated heroes who stand (albeit temporarily) at the peripheries of social structures (Odysseus in Hades, the Cid proscribed, Malatesta excommunicated and baited by his enemies) toward the dedicated leaders who sit at the center of power. It is ironic that, while the subject matter of Pound's verse was moving closer to the political core of various societies (including that of America), he himself was drifting farther away from the ideologies of his fatherland and embracing those of Fascist Italy, with the result that, in the *Pisan Cantos*, the theme of the outsider powerfully reasserts itself, receiving its most movingly elegiac treatment in all of Pound's verse—with the caged poet himself in the role of defeated hero.

The Cantos: From Outsider to Factive Personality . . . and Back Again

Mauberley is the last major outsider in Pound's verse who is purely aesthetic in orientation. After him, there is an attempt to depict characters who have a significant *public* aspect to them: "If *Mauberley* presents Pound's conception of the poet as decadent, the *Cantos* presents Pound's conception of the poet as hero, whose ideal role is actively to exert a determining influence on the social environment. Odysseus is the archetype for all those later 'heroes' of active, creative will who crop up in the *Cantos*. . ." [23] Odysseus, who stands in the same relation to the Lotophagoi (20/93-94) as Propertius does to Mauberley, is indeed the first Poundian hero encountered in the *Cantos,* but it must be remembered that, in addition to his role as Ithacan king, he is also the narrator of the "Nekuia"—in fact, of four books of the *Odyssey* (9-12). And Malatesta, though portrayed primarily as an embattled outsider, is also a patron of the arts and the builder of the Tempio. But in the 1930s, Pound's interest in the solitary outsider was displaced onto another kind of "solitary" figure—not the man alone on the *outside*, but the man alone at the *top*—and thus the so-called "middle Cantos" (31-71) concern themselves with figures like Jefferson, John Adams, Mussolini, and the Chinese emperors, who, while often interested in the arts, are principally engaged in the practical, constructive tasks of leadership. Just how far behind Pound had left the outsider (and to what an extent he had replaced him by the "factive" personality) may be gauged from a remark made in 1935: "Let us deny that *real* intelligence exists until it comes into action" (*J/M*, p. 18). These leaders celebrated by Pound—builders not merely of edifices, but of nations—came to be seen as purveyors of the social, political, and economic stability that facilitates the flourishing of the arts: "When the vortices of power and the vortices of culture coincide, you have an era of brilliance" (*GK*, p. 266).

In Canto 1, however, Odysseus stands remote from "the vortices of power." In this translation from a translation of part of Book 11 of the *Odyssey* (the "Nekuia" or "Book of the Dead"), Odysseus and his men, "Heavy with weeping," sail "to the bounds of deepest water, / To the Kimmerian lands," where "Swartest night stretched over wretched men" (1/3). This tenebrous journey to the ends of the earth must be undertaken in order to commune with the shade of Tiresias, who alone can tell Odysseus how to return home to Ithaca in spite of Poseidon's wrath. Pound associates this "man of ill star" (1/4) with that other outsider, the "Seafarer" poet, not only by means of the Anglo-Saxon rhythms that pervade the canto, but also by the grim note of solitude that haunts the two poems:

> "Odysseus
> "Shalt return through spiteful Neptune, over dark seas,
> "Lose all companions;"
>
> (1/4-5)

and the "Seafarer" poet, who must traverse "the salt-wavy tumult" alone,

> knows gone companions,
> Lordly men, are to earth o'ergiven. . . .
>
> (*PERSONAE*, p. 66)

But the wider significance for Pound's poem of the journey to the Underworld in quest of Tiresias is made explicit in Canto 47, where Circe informs Odysseus:

> First must thou go the road
> to hell
> ....

> Through overhanging dark, to see Tiresias,
> ....
> So full of knowing that the beefy men know less than he,
> Ere thou come to thy road's end.
>   Knowledge the shade of a shade,
> Yet must thou sail after knowledge
> Knowing less than drugged beasts.
>   (47/236)

By this point in the *Cantos*, we have already been apprised of the cowardly compromise made by those of Odysseus's men who were content to remain "drugged beasts":

> Eurilochus, Macer, better there with good acorns
> Than with a crab for an eye, and 30 fathom of fishes
> Green swish in the socket;[24]
>   (39/194)

in Canto 47, which remembers Dante's Ulysses,

> "fatti non foste a viver come bruti,
> ma per seguir virtute e canoscenza,"[25]

we are enabled to perceive Odysseus's journey in Canto 1 as a paradigm for Pound's creative act itself—a voyage through the farthest reaches of historical time and geographical space, in quest of the knowledge needed to return "home." The price paid for the knowledge gained by these two outsiders is recorded in the first and the last of the cantos: Odysseus shall "lose all companions" (1/5), and Pound prays

> Let those I love try to forgive
> what I have made.
>   (120/803)

    Pound's self-identification with the outsiders of the early cantos is also evident in Canto 3, which opens with the penury of the young self-exiled poet (Venice, 1908),

> I sat on the Dogana's steps
> For the gondolas cost too much, that year,

before proceeding to tell of the Cid's proscription by the resentful King Alfonso:

> That no man speak to, feed, help Ruy Diaz,
> On pain to have his heart out, set on a pike spike
> And both his eyes torn out, and all his goods sequestered.
>   (3/11)

But we next see the Cid engaging in a bit of Odyssean trickery in order to repair his fortunes:

> And left his trunk with Raquel and Vidas,
> That big box of sand, with the pawn-brokers,
> To get pay for his menie;
> Breaking his way to Valencia.
>   (3/12)

Pound was later to claim that "The Anglo-Saxon is particularly inept at understanding the Latin clarity of 'Qui veut la fin veut les moyens.' Who wills the end wills the means" (*J/M*, p. 34); in Canto 3 we are invited to meditate on what would have happened to the Cid if he had been content to live "morally" and merely wait for the King's pardon—for a crime he had never committed.[26] By using his wits, however, the Cid is eventually enabled to capture Valencia from the Moors and regain the favor of Alfonso. Indeed, it is his own sense of being wronged that spurs him to victory after victory for the Christian cause—an instance of the compensatory gain that Pound expected the heroic outsider to pluck from the most adverse of circumstances.

In the Maltesta Cantos, this compensatory gain is obviously the Tempio and the Riminese *paideuma*:

> The Tempio Malatestiano is both an apex and in verbal sense a monumental failure. It is perhaps the apex of what one man has embodied in the last 1000 years of the occident. A cultural "high" is marked.
> In a Europe not YET rotted by usury, but outside the then system, and pretty much against the power that was, and in any case without great material resources, Sigismundo cut his notch. He registered a state of mind, of sensibility, of all-roundness and awareness.
> He had a little of the best there in Rimini. He had perhaps Zuan Bellin's best bit of painting. He had all he cd. get of Pier della Francesca. . . . Intaglio existed. Painting existed. The medal has never been higher. All that a single man could, Malatesta managed *against* the current of power.
> You can contrast it with St. Hilaire. You can contrast it with ANY great summit done WITH the current of power.
> If ever Browning had ready an emphasis for his "reach and grasp" line it was waiting for him in Rimini.
>   (*GK*, pp. 159-60)

Pound here stresses the remarkable depth of Sigismondo's achievement in spite of his having been "one man . . . outside the then system": "All that a single man could, Malatesta managed *against* the current of power." This emphasis on the solitary individual standing in an adversative relation to his contemporaries derives from the Malatesta Cantos themselves, in which we see Sigismondo "With the church against him, / With the Medici bank for itself, / With wattle Sforza against him . . ." (8.32.1-3), and with the Sienese against him, and Astorre Manfredi, and Federigo d'Urbino, and King Alfonso, etc. But in two other passages from

Guide to Kulchur, Pound focuses his attention only on Malatesta's "constructivity" and his public persona:

> No one has claimed that the Malatesta cantos are obscure. They are openly volitionist, establishing, I think clearly, the effect of the factive personality, Sigismundo, an entire man.
> (p. 194)

> S. Malatesta gave away a lot of castles on, or shortly after, his accession. Such acts have a meaning and a social significance.
> (p. 261)

Writing in 1938, Pound is casting a backward glance at his hero that seeks, at the same time, to view him as the embattled outsider of the early cantos (as in the first long quotation from *GK*) and as one of the "factive personalities" that people his middle cantos (as in the two short quotations from *GK*, in the second of which Malatesta is presented at the center of power in Rimini, rather than at its peripheries in Italy as a whole). It is in these middle cantos that we find the heads of state who can institute the changes toward which the outsider can often only point.

Thus, our first glimpse of Thomas Jefferson in the poem, in Canto 21, seems to afford us nothing more than an interesting "subject rhyme" with Malatesta: we see the American rebel leader ("June 1778 Montecello") writing in wartime to a friend of his in Burgundy (from the residence that he himself designed), requesting the services of a gardener who could double as a musician. Pound stresses the similarity of this gesture to Sigismondo's writing to the Medici in quest of a painter (8.28.6–8.29.24) by introducing into the text of Jefferson's letter the phrase *"affatigandose per suo piacer o non"* from Malatesta's missive—immediately after Jefferson's assertion, "A certainty of employment for / Half a dozen years" (21/97), which calls to mind "So that he may come to live the rest / Of his life in my lands" (8.29.13-14). But in the first of *Eleven New Cantos: XXXI-XLI* (1934), Jefferson is not presented merely as a dilettante with an interest in "garden variety" musicians:

> Jefferson was *polumetis*, many-minded, and as literature wasn't his main job, this multiplicity is now recorded item by item in his letters, one interest at a time, and the unreflective reader gets simply the sense of leisure without perceiving the essential dynamism of the man who did *get things* DONE.
> *(J/M,* p. 89)

The "factiveness" of this man—who, though overtly compared with both Odysseus ("*polumetis*") and Malatesta ("Tempus loquendi, / Tempus tacendi"),[27] represents a different type of Poundian hero—is reflected in Canto 31's documentary presentation of his multifarious activities and pursuits: modernity in the arts ("'modern dress for your statue'"), the construction of canals (the Erie and the Ohio), the restriction of slavery to the southern states, botany, mechanics, economics, diplomacy, law, and architecture ("for our model [for the Virginia Capitol], the Maison Quarrée of Nismes"). The outsider of the early poems and cantos has ceded to the man at the center of power, a man who has many more possibilities for putting his ideas into action—and *that* within a political system partly of his own devising. Although the middle cantos are replete with "factive personalities," leaders such as John Adams, John Quincy Adams, Martin Van Buren, Ferdinand II of Tuscany (founder of the Sienese bank, the Monte dei Paschi), and various Chinese emperors, I wish to focus on only one of them, Benito Mussolini, in whose nation Pound was residing during the entire time that he was waxing enthusiastic over American patriots, Tuscan Grand Dukes, and Chinese Confucians.

Mussolini is introduced innocuously enough into Pound's poem—in Canto 38, where we are informed that "Italian marshes / been waiting since Tiberius' time" (38/188-89).[28] This much-touted draining of the Pontine marshes prepares the way, in Canto 41, for a more extended look at il Duce, composed after Pound's only meeting with Mussolini in January of 1933. The canto opens with a polite remark made by "the Boss" after he had perused *A Draft of XXX Cantos*:

> "MA QVESTO,"
>   said the Boss, "è divertente."[29]

Although Mussolini was probably using the word "divertente" in its broadest sense ("entertaining"), Pound seems to have interpreted it in light of its more restricted meaning ("amusing" or "humorous"), and thus a vapid compliment is seized upon as a manifestation of the dictator's literary perspicacity:

> catching the point before the aesthetes had got
>   there.[30]

In all, there are three links between Mussolini and Malatesta in Canto 41, one of them probably unconscious on Pound's part:

> "Noi ci facciam sgannar per Mussolini"
>   said the commandante della piazza.
>   (41/202)

The man who claimed that "We'd be willing to have our throats cut for Mussolini" was a hotelkeeper and Fascist functionary in Rimini who enabled Pound to examine Broglio's *Cronaca* even though the library was officially closed.[31] The two other links with Sigismondo are more explicit:

> Having drained off the muck by Vada
> From the marshes, by Circeo, where no one else wd. have
>   drained it.
>   (41/202)

And he set up the bombards in muck down by Vada
where nobody else could have set 'em.
(9.37.11-12)

Over Udine . . .
wd. have called that eagle a portent.
(41/204)

. . . the eagle lit on his tent pole.
And he said: The Romans would have called that an augury.
(10.47.5-6)

Thus, although Mussolini is praised for having provided the Italians with more food, water, and housing, and for having exiled some predatory businessmen (41/202), we sense that Pound's fascination with il Duce stems at least in part from the fanciful kinship he envisioned between the strutting dictator and the Quattrocento *condottiere*:

> Don't knock Mussolini, at least not until you have weighed up the obstacles and necessities of the time. He will end with Sigismondo and the men of order, not with the pus-sacks and destroyers.[32]
>
> Mussolini is the first head of a state in our time to perceive and to proclaim *quality* as a dimension in national production. He is the first man in power to publish any such recognition *since*, since whom?—since Sigismond Malatesta. . . .
> (*SP*, p. 230)[33]

Indeed, by 1933, Pound seems to have perceived Mussolini as a Sigismondo on a cosmic scale, fashioning the entire country of Italy into one enormous "Tempio":

> I don't believe any estimate of Mussolini will be valid unless it *starts* from his passion for construction. Treat him as *artifex* and all the details fall into place. Take him as anything save the artist and you will get muddled with contradictions.
> (*J/M*, pp. 33-34)

"Men of order," "*quality* . . . in national production," "passion for construction"— it is obvious that Pound is associating Mussolini with the "factive" Malatesta, rather than with Malatesta the outsider (and, in the process, shifting the emphases of his own earlier presentation of Sigismondo). But after the fall of Mussolini in 1943—after the man with the "passion for construction" had become the outsider at Salò—Pound's bitter disappointment with what be considered to be the cowardly fickleness of the other Fascist leaders led him to compose two cantos in Italian (still missing from all the editions of his poem), which he sent to the ex-Duce, hoping they could be of some practical use.[34]

Cantos 72 and 73 are written in an Italian free verse that occasionally makes use of rhyme in order to suggest the *canzone* and *ballata* forms of Guido Cavalcanti (the main character of 73). The two poems are structured along the lines of the Dantesque journey to the world of the dead—except that here the shades seem to seek out Pound, rather than he them. In all, Pound sees the shades of four Italians, two of them long dead and the other two his contemporaries. The first speaker is the Futurist poet and propagandist, Marinetti, who asks Pound for the use of his body in order to continue fighting for the Fascist cause. After Pound's polite refusal and his suggestion that he make a hero of some brainless young man by inhabiting his frame, there appears the shade of Manlio Torquato Dazzi,[35] who had been a librarian at Cesena's Malatestiana and who had translated from Latin into Italian the *Eccerinis*, a tragedy by Albertino Mussato (1261-1329). But before Dazzi has a chance to do more than recite two lines from his translation, the hero himself of Mussato's play rends the air with his melodramatic entrance—Ezzelino da Romano, the thirteenth-century tyrant of Padua whom Dante places, for his violence, in the river of boiling blood.[36]

In his anguish over Mussolini's fall from power, Pound has resuscitated the shade of an outsider who clearly out-Malatestas Malatesta:

> This Azzolino was the most cruel and feared tyrant who ever existed in Christendom . . . he did away with large numbers of the citizens of Padua, and he put out the eyes of even the best and most noble in great numbers, depriving them of their possessions and sending them begging through the world. He caused many others to die by various tortures and torments and at one time had eleven thousand Paduans burned . . . and under the pretext of a rough and wicked justice, he did much evil. . . .[37]

Pope Alexander IV proclaimed a crusade against Ezzelino, who, after a war lasting three years, was captured and left to die in prison in 1259. Pound makes use of this diabolic character—in Mussato's play, he is literally the son of Satan—in order to excoriate the new premier (Badoglio) and the Church for having betrayed the Fascist cause. Ezzelino's unbounded capacity for violence presents itself to Pound as the only possible cure for a fainthearted nation that had allowed itself to be overrun by the Allies. In the course of his indignant speech, the as yet unidentified Ezzelino inveighs against those who have enabled the invading forces to destroy the Tempio,[38] with its tombs of Gemisthus and "the divine Ixotta." This concern of his prompts the narrator to ask him: " 'Sei tu Sigismundo?' "

By way of reply Ezzelino states his name and proceeds to exonerate himself from what he considers to be the slanders of Mussato,[39] claiming, in any event, that a single traitor does more harm than all of his own violence ever did. Toward the very end of the canto, Pound (who is speaking in his own person) sees and feels Ezzelino's disembodied hand clench him by the wrist, and he hears the dead tyrant's voice predict the revival of Fascism. One of the interesting features of this macabre poem is its inability to exorcise the ghost of Malatesta, in the very process of dredging the sloughs of Italian history for an even more infamous reprobate. Canto 73, of which all but the first five lines are narrated by Cavalcanti, displays a similar inability to dissociate the outsider-figure from Malatesta.

The canto opens with the narrator's vision of a shade on horseback—Cavalcanti— who proceeds to make use of the diction and tone of the *pastourelle* in order to relate a grim tale of Samsonian vengeance.[40] Guido, whom even his close friend, Dante, saw fit to exile for his political violence, begins his speech by lambasting the Allied leaders and decrying the shameful fickleness of the Italian people. He then tells of how, passing by Rimini, he had seen the joyful shade of a pretty peasant girl, who, after having been raped by Allied soldiers, had led a troop of twenty Canadians to their deaths by conducting them onto a minefield. As in the previous canto, the specter of Sigismondo manifests itself indirectly when we learn that the minefield was located where "the lovely Ixotta's Tempio" had stood.[41] Canto 73 ends with Cavalcanti's marching-song celebration of the young martyr's heroism and with yet another prediction of the rebirth of Fascism. Yet, after the strident broadcasts over Rome Radio, after the execution of Mussolini, after the Allied victory, there remained of Pound's hopes nothing but a searing reminder of their essential futility: the steel cage in the American army's detention camp near Pisa.

The total collapse of Pound's dream for Italy, "To build the city of Dioce whose terraces are the colour of stars" (74/425), and his own incarceration as a political prisoner inevitably led to the most sustained treatment of the outsider-figure in the Poundian canon. In the *Pisan Cantos* we witness the return of all the major outsiders of Pound's earlier work, as well as the introduction of a host of new ones, including the caged poet himself—a man whose lifelong fascination with a certain type of personage eventually resulted in the self-embodiment of his dominant literary motif.[42] It was perhaps this realization that, sometimes, "life imitates art" that induced Pound to resurrect even Mauberley in the *Pisan Cantos*, the aesthete who had seemingly been exorcised so many years before.[43] And though Pound remains firmly committed to "commitment," he nevertheless suffuses the Pisan sequence with a plangent lyricism long absent from the *Cantos* and with a sense of the ultimate futility of human endeavor:

> I believe in the resurrection of Italy   quia impossibile est
> ....
> now in the mind indestructible.
> (74/442)

This internalization of the "paradiso terrestre," this retreat to a Miltonic paradise within, for "the drama is wholly subjective" (74/430), may remind us of Mauberley's escape to a tropical paradise of the mind. But the significant difference consists in Mauberley's shirking of the struggle, the *agon*, and Pound's affirmation of it—even if it prove materially unsuccessful:

> But to have done instead of not doing
>   this is not vanity
> ....
>   To have gathered from the air a live tradition
> or from a fine old eye the unconquered flame
> This is not vanity.
>   Here error is all in the not done,
> all in the diffidence that faltered . . .
>   (81/521-22)

The opening movement of the *Pisan Cantos* concerns Mussolini, erstwhile factive personality, now a corpse exposed to the jeers of the crowd:

> The enormous tragedy of the dream in the peasant's bent
>   shoulders
> Manes! Manes was tanned and stuffed,
> Thus Ben and la Clara *a Milano*
>   by the heels at Milano
> That maggots shd/ eat the dead bullock
>   (74/425)

Like the ill-fated original Manichean, Mussolini has paid the price of being a "bullock" among "maggots"— human counterparts of that "Conqueror Worm" which ineluctably devours great as well as small. On this same initial page of the Pisan sequence, Pound collocates two other major outsiders, Malatesta and Odysseus, the first as a transmitter of the "precise definition," the latter on his way to destruction for having ventured beyond the pillars of Herakles, flouting their terse inscription of "ne plus ultra."

But Odysseus is also presented as a prisoner in the cave of the Cyclops,

> ΟΎ ΤΙΣ, ΟΎ ΤΙΣ? Odysseus
>   the name of my family,

this giving rise to a double parallelism with Pound's situation at Pisa that runs through Canto 74—his captivity at the hands of a hostile giant and his consequent enforced anonymity:

>   ΟΎ ΤΙΣ
>   ΟΎ ΤΙΣ
> "I am noman, my name is noman"
>   (74/426)
>   ΟΎ ΤΙΣ
> a man on whom the sun has gone down
>   (74/430)

And, unlike the Odysseus of Canto 39 who enters Circe's bed, Odysseus/ Pound at Pisa finds himself in her pigsty ("harum" for "haram"):

> ac ego in harum
> so lay men in Circe's swine-sty;
> ivi in harum *ego* ac vidi cadaveres animae[44]
> (74/436)

Pound even provides a schema for the *Cantos* in terms of Odysseus's adventures,

> between NEKUIA where are Alcmene and Tyro
> and the Charybdis of action
> to the solitude of Mt. Taishan,
> (74/431)

by means of which the first thirty cantos (introduced by the "Nekuia" of Canto 1), and their preoccupation with mythology, beautiful women, and the more remote past, are designated in the first line; the middle cantos, with their "whirlpool" of factive personalities, are alluded to in the second; and the Pisan cantos, with their stream of meditative reminiscences, are evoked by the third.[45] When we last see Odysseus in the Pisan group, he is in danger of drowning, having been hurled from his skiff by a tempest sent by Poseidon (*Odyssey* 5):

> when the raft broke and the waters went over me.[46]
> (80/513)

The Dantean Odysseus whom we have already encountered on the first page of the Pisan group, audaciously sailing beyond the bourns of the known world, is soon joined by a cohort of his fellow sinners from the *Inferno*—rebels and outsiders of various sorts—beginning with Dante's Lucifer, who, according to Pound's rewriting of the myth, "fell in N. Carolina."[47] Farther along in the *Pisan Cantos*, Pound alludes to the murdered lovers, Paolo and Francesca (83/533; *Inf.* 5), the blasphemer Capaneus, struck down by Jove's lightning, but still defiant in Hell (79/487; *Inf.* 14), the false counselor, Guido da Montefeltro (74/435; *Inf.* 27), Count Ugolino, the traitor starved to death by the Pisans in a tower visible from the cage (74/436, 438; 79/486; *Inf.* 33), and, most significantly, Farinata the heretic, who rises from his fiery tomb in *Inferno* 10 "as if he held all Hell in great disdain," and who was the only man among the Ghibellines to speak out against the planned destruction of Florence:

> who resisted at Arbia when the fools wd/ have burnt down
> Florence "in gran dispitto" "men used to obeying orders"[48]
> (77/473)

Clark Emery has observed that "the rebel-hero has been a main character . . . all through the poem."[49] But nowhere in the *Cantos* has Pound donned so many masks of the outsider as in the Pisan sequence, as even a partial listing would demonstrate.[50]

One of the most prominent of these masks is, of course, Malatesta,[51] whose motto Pound now reverses by way of asserting his right to speak out, "Tempus tacendi, tempus loquendi" (74/429), and whose topics of conversation he appropriates as his own: "books, arms, men, as with Sigismundo" (80/512). His memories of Olga Rudge's house at Venice, with its marble bas-relief of Isotta,[52] move him to identify himself with the despoiled Malatesta:

>   . . . the great Ovid
> bound in thick boards, the bas relief of Ixotta
>   and the care in contriving
> Olim de Malatestis
>   the long hall over the arches at Fano
> olim de Malatestis.[53]
>   (76/462)

Pound even imagines Malatesta journeying on the Via Aurelia, near which the prison camp was located:

> Sigismundo by the Aurelia to Genova
>   by la vecchia sotto S. Pantaleone.[54]
>   (76/452)

There are certain passages in the *Pisan Cantos,* however, that indicate how the outsider-figure has been modified by the poet's personal confrontation with society's rejection and punishment. Thus, although we come upon quite a few virulent denunciations of "the enemy,"

> and merrda for the monopolists
>   the bastardly lot of 'em
>   (78/479)

> Geneva the usurers' dunghill
>   Frogs, brits, with a few dutch pimps
>   as top dressing to preface extortions
>   and the usual filthiness,
>   (78/481)

there is nevertheless on Pound's part a recognition that his plight at Pisa has not been merely foisted upon him by hostile external forces, but that it is the consequence of a failure of his own:

> Mr. K. said nothing foolish, the whole month nothing foolish:
> "if we weren't dumb, we wouldn't be here"
> (74/428)

> first must destroy himself ere others destroy him.
> (74/430)

> "Master thyself, then others shall thee beare"
> (81/521)

In much the same way that Sigismondo, after his final defeat, begins to take an interest in the hardships of others (11.50.4-9), Pound admits that

> J'ai eu pitié des autres
> probablement pas assez, and at moments that suited my own con-
> venience,
> (76/460)

and begins to reflect on the pathos of his fellow prisoners, one of whom had surreptitiously constructed a makeshift table for him:

> and Mr Edwards superb green and brown
> in ward No 4 a jacent benignity,
> of the Baluba mask: "doan you tell no one
> I made you that table"
> . . . .
> and the greatest is charity
> to be found among those who have not observed
> regulations.
> (74/434)

The very names of some of the prisoners suggest to Pound an originary American dream that has turned to nightmare:

> of the slaver as seen between decks
> and all the presidents
> Washington Adams Monroe Polk Tyler
> plus Carrol (of Carrolton) Crawford.[55]
> (74/436-37)

Pound's sense of his own degradation ultimately gives rise to a new note of humility in the *Cantos*, often expressed by means of animal imagery:

> As a lone ant from a broken ant-hill
> from the wreckage of Europe, ego scriptor.
> (76/458)

> Pull down thy vanity
> Thou art a beaten dog beneath the hail,
> A swollen magpie in a fitful sun,
> Half black half white
> Nor knowst'ou wing from tail
> Pull down thy vanity
> How mean thy hates
> Fostered in falsity,
> Pull down thy vanity,
> Rathe to destroy, niggard in charity,
> Pull down thy vanity,
> I say pull down.
>
> (81/521)

After the catharsis of the Pisan section, the "Malatesta-figure" drops out of the *Cantos* almost entirely. In addition to a few late appearances by Odysseus (see note 46 above), there is a final linkage established between Mussolini and Malatesta in *Thrones*,

> And Muss saved, rem salvavit,
> in Spain
> il salvabile,
> (105/746)

and a final allusion to the Malatesta Cantos in Pound's rewriting of his parody of Eliot's line:

> From time's wreckage shored,
> these fragments shored against ruin.
> (110/781)

It is thus quite true that "the sense of human heroism is not so well communicated in the post-Pisan historical Cantos."[56] Having weathered the cage and the asylum, Pound had earned the right to place less premium on merely human heroism.

In a recent book, Sigismondo Malatesta has been described as "perhaps Pound's most complex persona, and the model of the subsequent historical-poetical ventures of the *Cantos*."[57] We have seen how it cost Pound a year of intensive work to rescue the historical Malatesta from the depths of infamy into which Pius II's hardly disinterested philippics had hurled him. In the process of disentangling Sigismondo from this web of irresponsible accusations, Pound gradually developed a manner of presentation that allowed him to celebrate his hero's achievements without falsifying the historical record or assuming a tone of lugubrious indignation. The resultant mode of deflated epic obviated the necessity of criticizing Sigismondo's misdeeds, such as they were, or of overtly lauding his accomplishments, for the focus of attention had been shifted to the spectacle of a heroic figure ultimately defeated by adversaries in whom epic gestures survive only in the form of parody. But it is not Malatesta's "atavism" that Pound ridicules in these cantos: it is the perversity of an era that no longer knows how to accommodate the exceptional individual. Indeed, Pound's grafting of a distorted epic frame onto these events of the early Renaissance suggests that the programmatic relationship between Renaissance values and those of the ancient world is, for the most part, a meretricious one. Much of the humor in the Malatesta Cantos thus arises from the incongruity and futility of erecting a neo-pagan temple in a milieu still effectively dominated by the bugbears of the medieval imagination:

> Where—save they were immune from sufferings—
> It had made the emparadisèd spirits pewk
> from their jeweled terrace.

Yet, beneath the humor of these cantos and the stylistic innovations that it summoned forth, there lies the serious substratum of the sequence: an exemplum (this, too, a medieval form) of the heroic individual striking a memorable blow for civilization "*against* the current of power." Although Pound had conjured up many such outsiders before Sigismondo, it was only in Cantos 8-11 that he fastened on a historical character who seemed to exhibit a Bertran's fierce energy as well as the finely honed sensibility of a Propertius. Malatesta was to retain his exemplary status for Pound long after he first entered the *Cantos* in 1923: versions of the phrase "*templum aedificavit*" assume a mantra-like quality in installments of Pound's poem published as late as 1955 and 1959.

It will be recalled that, in a canceled passage, Sigismondo's Tempio had been compared to the *Cantos* (see pp. 15–16 above). It is entirely fitting that the greatest verse epic of the present century has emerged from the undeserved neglect often directed not so much against the unevenness of the poem as against the ideological vagaries of its creator—that the "great bulk, huge mass, thesaurus" which is the *Cantos* is being assessed without resort to the type of blanket condemnation that had all but smothered with ignominy the positive accomplishments of Sigismondo Malatesta five centuries earlier.

Appendix A

Major Textual Variants in the Published Versions of the Malatesta Cantos

Divergences in lineation, spacing, positioning, punctuation, capitalization, and minor orthographic matters have not been included. In each case, the variant readings are compared with the 1972 New Directions text of the *Cantos,* from which the page and line references are also drawn.

New Directions	Criterion[1]
Canto 8	Canto IX
28.1–5	(missing)
29.19: *no*	*non*
31.13: *Di cui* in the which he	*Di cui* the which he
33.9: Foglia	the Foglia
Canto 9	Canto X
34.18: Basinio	Bassinio
34.23: Ginevra	Genevra
35.16: anyway	anyhow
35.19: (*haec traditio*)	(*hoc traditio*)
36.15: Arimininum	Arimnium
36.27: that German-Burgundian female	the German-Burgundian female
37.5: *(m'l' ha calata)*	*(m'l' a calata)*
37.15: getting	kept getting
37.27: *die xxii Decembris*	*die Decembris*
38.6: Sagramoro	Sagramoro has
40.4: *premissa*	*permissa*
Canto 10	Canto XI
42.19: then	now
42.28: *Florence, Archivio Storico, 4th Series t. iii,e*	*Archivio Storico, 4th series t,III. Florence e*
43.2: *Caro mio*	*Cara mio*
43.3: *is*	is

116   Appendix A

43.4: Lolli.	Lolli!
44.6: SCRIPTURAM	SCRIPTURUM
44.14: swelling s. o. b.	swelling
45.32: *novità*	*novita*
46.27: jailed	jaild
47.7: *gradment*	*grädment*
Canto 11	*Canto XII*
48.1: *gradment*	*grädment*
48.8: Saint	St
49.11: God	god
50.12: *palatium*	*Palatiam*
50.16: to do in the	to do the
51.21: Paolo Secondo	Paulo Secundo
52.5: ornry	ornrey
52.9: *scienta*	*scientia*
New Directions	*Three Mountains Press*[2]
Canto 8	*Canto 8*
30.14: Marecchia	Morecchia
30.24: *carissime*	*carissimc*
32.27: Paolo	Paulo
Canto 9	*Canto 9*
34.23: Ginevra	Genevra
36.15: Arimininum	Arimnium
36.28: Poliorcetes	Poliocetes
37.5: (*m'l'ha calata*)	(*m'l'a calata*)
37.27: *die xxii Decembris*	*die xx Decembris*
39.12: *potens*	*poten*
40.4: *premissa*	*permissa*
41.13: filigree	filagree
Canto 10	*Canto 10*
44.6: SCRIPTURAM	SCRIPTURUM
47.3: Piccinino	Piccinini
47.7: *gradment*	*grādment*
Canto 11	*Canto 11*
48.1: *gradment*	*grādment*
52.9: *scienta*	*scientia*
New Directions	*Hours Press*[3]
Canto 9	*Canto 9*
34.23: Ginevra	Genevra
36.15: Arimininum	Arimnium
37.5: (*m'l'ha calata*)	(*m'l'a calata*)

37.27: *die xxii Decembris*   *xx Decembris*
39.12: *potens*   *poten*
40.4: *premissa*   *permissa*
41.13: filigree   filagree
Canto 10   *Canto 10*
44.6: SCRIPTURAM   SCRIPTURUM
New Directions   Farrar and Rinehart[4]
Canto 9   *Canto 9*
37.27: *xxii Decembris*   *xx Decembris*
39.12: *potens*   *poten*
40.4: *premissa*   *permissa*
41.13: filigree   filagree
Canto 10   *Canto 10*
44.6: SCRIPTURAM   SCRIPTURUM
New Directions   Faber[5]
Canto 8   *Canto 8*
31.19: Delphos   Delphi
Canto 9   *Canto 9*
34.23: Ginevra   Genevra
36.15: Arimininum   Arimnium
37.5: *(m'l'ha calata)*   *(m'l'a calata)* has sunk it
37.27: *xxii Decembris*   *xx Decembris*
39.12: *potens*   *poten*
40.4: *premissa*   *permissa*
41.13: filigree   filagree
Canto 10   *Canto 10*
43.15: *Te cavero*   *Ti cavero*
43.17: *te cavero*   *ti cavero*
44.6: SCRIPTURAM   SCRIPTURUM
46.12: Alfonso   Alfonso, Alfonse le roi, etc.

Appendix B

Some Sources for the Malatesta Cantos

At the time that an earlier version of this book was submitted to Yale University as a doctoral dissertation (March 1981), I believed that none of the following sources had been discovered. Since then, Ben D. Kimpel and T. C. Duncan Eaves, in "Pound's Research for the Malatesta Cantos," *Paideuma*, 11, 3 (Winter 1982), 406–19, have tracked down all of them (though I disagree with them on Pound's source for the contract between Sigismondo and Enrico de Aquabello). In any event, I include this appendix because it provides the sources in their original context and language, and also translates the Italian and Latin passages.

9.35.14: "Alphonse le roy d'Aragon"
10.46.12: *"tiers Calixte"*
These two phrases are taken from the first stanza of Villon's "Ballade des Seigneurs du Temps Jadis" (lines 357–64 of *Le Grand Testament*):

> Qui plus, ou est le tiers Calixte,
> Dernier decedé de ce non,
> Qui quatre ans tint le papaliste?
> Alphonce le roy d'Aragon,
> Le gracieux duc de Bourbon,
> Et Artus le duc de Bretaigne,
> Et Charles septiesme le bon?
> Mais ou est le preux Charlemaigne?[1]

10.46.27-28: "And they nearly jailed a chap for saying / The job was *mal hecho*"
The ultimate source of these lines is a letter written from Rome by a Mantuan priest (April 27–28, 1462); Pound's immediate source was Giovanni Soranzo, *Pio II e la politica italiana nella lotta contro i Malatesti (1457–1463)* (Padua, 1911), pp. 288–89:

> Racconta l'oratore mantovano un curioso aneddoto: un fiorentino, spirito arguto, stava tra la folla spettatrice in Campo dei Fiori: tutto ad un tratto si mise a gridare ad alta voce: "Per Dio, è mal fatto!" Le guardie subito lo presero e vollevano menarlo in prigione. "Perchè fate questo?" disse il fiorentino, "io non dico che Nostro Signore faccia male, dico solo che Sigismondo è mal riprodotto perchè non gli somiglia." E in mezzo alle risa degli astanti fu lasciato libero.

120   Appendix B

> (The Mantuan orator tells an amusing anecdote. A certain Florentine, a witty soul, was among the crowd of spectators in Campo dei Fiori. All of a sudden he started shouting out: "By God, that's pretty bad!" The guards immediately seized him, intending to lead him off to jail. "What are you doing?" said the Florentine. "I'm not saying that our Lord [the Pope] has done anything bad. What I mean is that it's a bad dummy of Sigismondo: it doesn't look like him at all." And so they released him, amid the laughter of the spectators.)

11.49.5-6: "And that nick-nosed s.o.b. Feddy Urbino / Said: '*Par che è fuor di questo . . . Sigis . . . mundo'*"
Ultimate source: a letter of Federigo d'Urbino to Francesco Sforza (?), Oct. 21, 1463; Pound's source: Soranzo, *Pio II*, Appendix, Doc. 46, p. 510:

> . . . et el Signore Sigismondo, per quanto intendo, pare che sia fora de questo mondo et va là e qua como balordo senza saper pigliare alcuno partito a cosa che luy habia ad fare. . . .
>
> (. . . and Lord Sigismondo, from what I understand, seems to be out of this world [*mondo*], and he runs here and there like a dimwit, without being able to make up his mind about what to do. . . .)

11.49.27–29: "And he wrote to young Piero: / Send me a couple of huntin' dogs, / They may take my mind off it."
Ultimate source: a letter from Sigismondo to Pier Francesco de' Medici, Dec. 5, 1463; Pound's source: Soranzo, *Pio II*, p. 457:

> " . . . retrovo la conditione mia essere diversa, l'opposito de quello che volgarmente se sole dire che chi ha poca roba ha pochi pensieri; a mi è remasta poca roba e assai pensieri e per dare loco alle bizzarie e melanconie ho deliberato per mio esercito cacciare et uccellare"; gli chiede perciò in dono una coppia di buoni levrieri . . .
>
> (" . . . I find my situation to be very different from—indeed, the total opposite of—the proverb that says, 'No wealth, no worries,' for I have little wealth left and many worries indeed. And so, to distract myself from anger and melancholy, I have decided to get some exercise by going hunting and hawking"; he thus asks him for the gift of a couple of good greyhounds. . . .)

11.50.4–9   "And he thought:
Old Zuliano is finished,
If he's left anything we must see the kids get it,
Write that to Robert.
And Vanni must give that peasant a decent price for his horses,
Say that I will refund."
Source: Carlo Grigioni, "Documenti inediti intorno a Sigismondo Malatesta," *La Romagna*, 7, 8–9 (Aug.-Sept. 1910), p. 382:

> Magnifice filii noster poy che quello poverecto de giuliano agulante e morto voglio che se dal lato de la se trova niente del suo chel sia de glie figliolecti soy . . . Ex Ariminio XVIII iunii 1463 Sigismundus pandulfus de Malatestis. (Doc. XII)

(Magnificent Son of Mine [Roberto]: Since poor old Giuliano Agulante is dead, I want anything that he may have left behind over there [Fano] to go to his little children . . . Rimini, June 18, 1463.)

Magnifice filii noster . . . quelli doy ronzini che ha uno contadino . . . che dicto Giohanne riccio li habbia per omne modo in vendita e del pregio che convenerrano . . . remanero Io lo pagadore arimini die XXIV martii 1463 Sigismundus pandulfus de Malatestis. (Doc. XI)

(Magnificent Son of Mine [Roberto]: . . . those two horses that the peasant has . . . by all means let Giovanni Riccio buy them for whatever price they're worth . . . I'll bear the expense. Rimini, March 24, 1463.)

11.52.1–9: (The contract between Sigismondo and Enrico de Aquabello.) Source of contract: Archivio Notarile di Rimini, Atti di Bartolomeo di Ser Sante, Vol. 1460, fol. 75r; Pound's source: Carlo Grigioni, "Un Capriccio di Sigismondo Malatesta," *Arte e Storia* (Florence), 3rd Series, 5–6 (Mar. 1908), 40–41.[2]

È una scomessa buffonesca corsa tra il Sigismondo e il suo scalco Enrico Acquabello di Argenta, con la quale quest' ultimo s'impegna di non adirarsi per qualunque scherzo *sopportabile* voglia fargli il suo Signore e di accorrere ad ogni chiamata di questo, pena in caso di non osservanza, la perdita di una giornea donatagli dal munificente padrone.

Il documento è del 1460 (31 Maggio), uno degli anni meno burrascosi e più calmi ne la vita di Sigismondo.

"Magnificus et eximius dominus Sigismundus pandulfus de Malatestis arimini Sponte et ex certa scientia et sua mera Magnifficentia et liberalitate dedit tradidit et donavit Nobili viro Enricho quondam Alberti de Aquabello de argenta presenti et acceptanti unam giorneam drappi viridis brochatum de argento Ad habendum tenendum possidendum et utendum ad eius Enrici beneplacitum cum pactis et condicionibus infrascriptis videlicet.

Quod ipse Enricus debeat et teneatur per quatuor menses prossime futuros acedere cum prefato Magnifico domino ad Aucumpaiandum (?) ad Requisitionem ipsius Magnifici domini et equo animo supportare omnes nugas et omnia scripza fienda per ipsum Magnificum dominum in rebus et persona ipsius Enrici que sint tamen suportabilia nec ex ipsis altercari nec molestus esse nec Indignationem aliquam suscipere ex ipsis nugis et scripzis Dans ipse Magnificus dominus dicto Enricho etiam plenam licentiam nugandi et scrizandi cum ipso Magnifico domino ac promicens non molestam facere (?) aliquam nugam sive scrizum fiendos contra ipsum Enricum contra donationem suam Que sint tamen suportabilia et Recipienda.

Quod si ipse Enricus molestus ferret et non supportabit pacienter et equo animo tollerabit nugas sive scrizos fiendos per ipsum Magnificum dominum et non accederet continuo ad omnem ipsius Magnifici domini Requisitionem cum donatione sua ut supra toto dicto tempore quatuor mensium ex nunc prout ex tunc et ex tunc prout ex nunc liceat dicto Magnifico domino subtraere et acipere dictam giorneam ut supra donatam sibi per dictum Magnificum dominum omni exceptioni et condictioni remota Et Refficere et Restituere ipsi Magnifico domino omnia eius dampna expensas et Interesse que et quas fecerit vel substinuerit quocumque.

Actum in castro Sigismundo. . . . presente Roberto de valturibus. . . ."

(This is a comical wager struck between Sigismondo and his steward, Enrico Acquabello of Argenta, by means of which the latter agrees not to get angry over any *tolerable* joke that his Lord might wish to play on him, and to be at his every beck and call—the penalty for nonobservance being the loss of a cloak that his generous master had presented him with.

The document dates from 1460 (May 31), one of the calmest and least tempestuous years in the life of Sigismondo.

"The magnificent and distinguished Lord, Sigismondo Pandolfo Malatesta of Rimini, out of sheer magnificence and liberality, freely and knowingly gave, handed over to, and bestowed upon the noble gentleman, Enrico (son of the late Alberto Acquabello of Argenta), who was present to accept it, a cloak of green cloth with silver brocade, which the said Enrico may hold, keep, possess, and use, provided that he consent to the following terms and conditions, to wit:

That said Enrico pledge himself for the next four months to be at the beck and call of the aforesaid magnificent lord in order to comply with (?) the requests of that magnificent lord, and to bear with equanimity any and all tricks and practical jokes played by that magnificent lord on the person and effects of the said Enrico—provided, however, they be tolerable—and not to grow quarrelsome and peevish, nor to evince the slightest indignation over said tricks and practical jokes, the magnificent lord also according the said Enrico free license to play tricks and practical jokes on the said magnificent lord himself—provided, however, they be tolerable and bearable—and furthermore pledging to do no harm, to either Enrico himself or to his cloak, in retaliation for any trick or practical joke that Enrico might play on him.

That if the said Enrico grow angry and not bear patiently and tolerate with equanimity the tricks or practical jokes to be played by said magnificent lord, and not always be ready to attend (wearing his cloak) to the every need of said magnificent lord for the entire term of four months, as stipulated above, both prospectively and retrospectively, retrospectively and prospectively, it shall be lawful for the said magnificent lord to repossess and receive the aforesaid cloak (presented to Enrico, as stated above, by said magnificent lord), free of all exceptions and conditions—and Enrico must furthermore make restoration and restitution to said magnificent lord for all damages and expenses (with interest) that his lord shall have undergone or suffered, in any way whatsoever.

Drawn up in the castle of Sigismondo. . . . Witness: Roberto Valturio. . . .")

Appendix C

Pound and Eliot at Verona:
A Passage from the "Watson Typescript"

[From "Watson 12," Folder #56, pp. 21, 24–26.]

      Tomas, amics, we sit here,
For fourty-four [sic] thousand years,
  at this tin, rickety table,
Painted with ripolin.[1]
. . . .
And
  We sit here under the wall
Inside it: the footlights, the clowns, dancers,
Performing dogs, arena romana (Diocletian's)
  and the lady in tights has got to the fourth table,
that's on the third, that's on the table with two legs
  that's on the first table.
"quarante trois rangées de gradins en calcaire"
    And /As/ we sat over Girart Borneil's old bake-oven
Level with the town spire
    But I have been here
Forty four thousand years,
    "poi gli affina" for you, possibly,
Me swinging the burning head
  peering, uselessly into crevices,
That bitter Bonomelli is a worse red than Egypt's
The stuff painted into the stones,
  And our roman takes form from stones, here,
And Ti, Galla?
      Byzantine? disintegrates,
Puts on Venetian clogs, plucks at your (somewhat soiled)
      cuff-lace
At which time I was lifting sedan-chairs,
  Paying the bill for my banquet (Veronese's)
And never learning, no never learning,

And she's buried in Ravenna,
    yellow, sun-yellow,

Lit by the alabaster panes,
                yellow, ~~yellow~~ sun-yellow
In the gloom, the gold,
                gathers the light against it.
Byzance gone,
                the empire?
The empires slide to nothing here in the marsh-drift,
                there in the marsh-drift, gone
Caesarea, between the town and Classe, gone,
                roof-deep in the marsh.

Behind the great phalloi of the temple. . . .
            winding path,
Mosaic wall, and the souls,
        gonads in organdy
Rose-flakes in arid darkness,
          the wing shows for a moment,
                and fades,
An emerald lizzard [sic]
                        peers through the border grass.
Fatal August.

Appendix D

Allusions to the Malatesta Cantos in the *Cantos* of Ezra Pound

A Draft of XXX Cantos (1930)

4/16: (Reference to the Roman arena.)

12/53: (Reference to the Roman arena.)

16/69: (References to Sigismondo and Malatesta Novello.)

16/70: (Reference to the Silk War.)

17/78: (Reference to the gold in the gloom.)

17/79: (References to Borso, Carmagnola, and Sigismondo.)

20/90: (References to Agostino di Duccio.)

20/90–91: (References to the execution of Parisina Malatesta by her husband, Niccolò d'Este, to his son, Borso, and to the "arras" that figures in the murder of Paolo and Francesca in 8.32.28.)

20/94: (References to Sallustio Malatesta and Isotta.)

20/95: (Reference to Borso.)

21/96: (Reference to Borso.)

21/96-97: (References to Cosimo de' Medici.)

21/97: (Reference to Piccinino.)

21/97: (*affatigandose per suo piacer o non*)

21/98: (References to the gold in the gloom, Placidia's mausoleum, and the Roman arena.)

126   Appendix D

23/107: (References to Gemisto and Malatesta Novello.)

23/108: (Indirect reference to Parisina Malatesta by means of the "arras" of 20/91 and 8.32.28.)

24/110–13: (References to Parisina Malatesta and Niccolò d'Este.)

24/111: (Reference to the marriage of Roberto Malatesta—not Sigismondo's son, but his elder brother, Galeotto Roberto.)

24/114: (References to Niccolò and Borso d'Este.)

26/121–22: (References to Matteo da Pasti's imprisonment in Venice [see 10.46.28–29], to Roberto Valturio, to Venice's efforts to arrange a peace between Pius II and Sigismondo and Malatesta Novello, to Borso d'Este, and to the secret aid provided to Malatesta Novello by the Venetians.)

26/123-24: (References to Niccolò d'Este, the Greek Emperor, Cosimo de' Medici, Sigismondo, and Gemisto—and to their association with the Council of Ferrara-Florence.)

26/124: (References to the military services provided to the Venetians by Sigismondo's uncle, Carlo, and his father, Pandolfo; and to Cosimo de' Medici.)

26/125: (Reference to Sigismondo.)

26/125–26: (References to Francesco Sforza and Pisanello.)

29/145: (Reference to the Roman arena. The "Arnaut" who appears before this passage is Eliot on a trip to Provence with Pound; he is also the one with the "lace at the wrist," this time in Verona.)

30/148-49: (Reference to Fano, where the printer Soncino is preparing an edition of Petrarch's *Rime* for Cesare Borgia in 1503, using as text a codex that once belonged to the Malatesti.)

Eleven New Cantos (1934)

31/153: (This book of Cantos begins with Sigismondo's personal motto.)

34/171: Constans proposito. . . .

37/185: Placuit oculis . . .

41/202:   Having drained off the muck by Vada
From the marshes, by Circeo, where no one else wd. have
         drained it.

41/204: wd. have called that eagle a portent

The Fifth Decad of Cantos (1937)

42/214: ex certe scientia . . .

45/229–30:   (References to Agostino di Duccio and Piero della Francesca.)

Cantos LII-LXXI (1940)

54/283:   (Reference to Valturio.)

56/302:   Hail breaking the trees and walls

57/312:   (Reference to Valturio.)

62/345:   no word, orationem, probably not elegantissimam

Cantos LXXII-LXXIII (1945)

72:   (References to the Allied bombing of Rimini during World War II, to the sepulchers of Gemisto and Isotta in the damaged Tempio, to Sigismondo, and to Placidia and the gold of her mausoleum.)

73:   (References to Rimini, the Tempio, and Isotta.)

The Pisan Cantos (1948)

74/425:   (References to Sigismondo and Agostino di Duccio.)

74/429:   (Reversal of Sigismondo's motto.)

74/430:   (Reference to Isotta.)

74/437:   (References to Matteo da Pasti and Pisanello.)

74/446:   (Reference to the Biblioteca Malatestiana at Cesena.)

74/448:   (References to Sallustio Malatesta and Isotta.)

76/452:   (References to Sigismondo and Isotta.)

76/453:   (References to Agostino di Duccio's bas-relief of Diana in the Tempio, here referred to as "la scalza," "la luna," and "the huntress.")

76/455:   (Reference to Galla Placidia and her mausoleum.)

76/459:   (References to Sigismondo, Isotta, and the Tempio.)

76/462:   (References to Isotta and the Malatesti.)

78/481:   (Reference to the Roman arena. "Thiy" is Bride Scratton, and "il decaduto" is Eliot, whose *Criterion* failed to follow the "literary program" mentioned here.)

128 Appendix D

80/497:   (Reference to the damaged Tempio.)

80/501:   (Reference to the Malatesti.)

80/502:   (Reference to Rimini.)

80/503:   ne povans desraciner

80/511:   (Reference to Agostino di Duccio's bas-relief of Diana "in the moon barge.")

80/512:   (Reference to Sigismondo.)

80/518:   (Reference to the shouting-match between Sigismondo and Federigo d'Urbino.)

82/524:   (Reference to Basinio.)

83/528:   (References to Gemisto and the Tempio.)

83/529:   (Reference to the Malatesti.)

Rock-Drill (1955)

89/596:   POPULUM AEDIFICAVIT

90/605:   Templum aedificans . . .

91/614:   (Reference to the Roman arena.)

92/620–21:   (References to Sigismondo's uncle, Carlo, and to the Tempio's bas-reliefs.)

93/624:   (Reference to the discovery of alum at Tolfa.)

93/626:   . . . both of antient times and our own

Thrones (1959)

96/653:   (Reference to Rimini ["Arimnium"].)

96/654:   (Reference to Galla Placidia.)

98/685:   (Reference to Gemisto.)

98/688:   (Reference to Gemisto.)

98/690:   (Reference to Gemisto.)

103/736:   nec Templum aedificavit

104/740:   (References to Basinio and Carlo Malatesta.)

105/746:   And Muss saved, rem salvavit,
                                  in Spain
                                              il salvabile.
            (Reference to Cesena and its beautiful columns.)

106/755:   Aedificavit

107/758:   Templum aedificavit

108/765:   (Reference to Carlo Malatesta.)

Drafts and Fragments of Cantos CX-CXVII (1969)

110/780:   (Reference to Galla Placidia's mausoleum.)

110/781:   From time's wreckage shored,
                 these fragments shored against ruin

Notes

Introduction

1. Ezra Pound, "James Joyce et Pécuchet," *Pound/Joyce*, ed. Forrest Read (New York: New Directions, 1967), p. 204. (Hereafter cited as *P/J*.)

2. *Guide to Kulchur* (New Directions, 1970; 1938), frontispiece. (Hereafter cited as *GK*.)

3. John Addington Symonds, *A Short History of the Renaissance in Italy* (New York: Henry Holt, 1925; 1893), pp. 48–49.

4. Jacob Burckhardt, *The Civilization of the Renaissance in Italy*, trans. S. G. C. Middlemore, 2 vols. (New York: Harper and Row, 1958; 1860), I, 50; II, 442.

5. All quotations from the *Cantos* are from the 1972 New Directions edition. In citing from the Malatesta Cantos, I supply canto number, page of the New Directions text, and line number. Thus, 10.45.23–27 means: Canto 10, page 45, lines 23 to 27. For passages quoted from cantos other than the Malatesta group, I supply only canto number and page, separating them by a slash: 26/123 (Canto 26, page 123).

6. P. J. Jones, *The Malatesta of Rimini and the Papal State: A Political History* (London: Cambridge Univ. Press, 1974), pp. 176–77.

7. Gabriele D'Annunzio, *Tragedie sogni e misteri*, 2 vols. (Milan: Mondadori, 1939), I, 708–12. Since the view of Malatesta evinced in the "commiato" anticipates Pound's, I translate parts of the poem in Chapter 3 in order to register at least one other modern poet's veneration of this morally dubious *condottiere*.

8. Dante sees two of them in Hell: Paolo and Francesca (V. 73–142). The other three were still alive in 1300, but their eventual damnation is strongly implied: Gianciotto (V.107), Malatesta da Verrucchio (XXVII.46–48), and Malatestino (XXVII.46–48 and XXVIII.76–90).

9. Luigi Tonini, *Rimini nella signoria de' Malatesti*, vol. II (Rimini, 1880) and *Storia civile e sacra di Rimini*, vol. V (1882); Giovanni Soranzo, *Pio II e la politica italiana nella lotta contro i Malatesti* (Padua, 1911); Charles Yriarte, *Un condottiere au XVe siècle* (Paris, 1882).

10. Hugh Kenner, *The Pound Era* (Berkeley: Univ. of California Press, 1971), pp. 77–78.

11. P. J. Jones, *The Malatesta of Rimini*, p. 186, n. 3.

Notes for Introduction

12. At Piombino, in September 1448, when Sigismondo drove Alfonso's son Ferdinando "out of the / Terrene of the Florentines" (10.46.13–15). Pound quotes Pius's Latin, *"rem eorum saluavit,"* in 9.35.20.

13. Pound claims that "the *Isoteus* probably contains more fine poetry than is to be found in the work of any of the men mentioned in my foregoing essay ["Poeti Latini"] . . ." in *The Spirit of Romance* (New York: New Directions, 1968; 1910), p. 240 (one of the additions made to the text in 1929). (This book will hereafter be cited as *SR*.) He refers to Basinio as "the most intelligent of the Quattrocento Latinists" in *ABC of Reading* (New Directions, 1960; 1934), p. 48. (Hereafter cited as *ABC*.)

14. "The Tempio was stopped by a fluke? or Sigismundo had the flair when to stop it?" (*GK*, p. 159).

15. Pius II, *Commentarii* . . . (Rome, 1592), bk. II, p. 92. (My translation.)

16. For Pound's comments on the Tempio, see: *GK*, frontispiece, and pp. 159-60, 301; *Jefferson and/or Mussolini*, p. 31. On the Tempio, see Adrian Stokes, *The Stones of Rimini*, and Corrado Ricci's monumental *Il tempio malatestiano*. Kenner's *The Pound Era* contains some excellent photographs of the Tempio and its artistic treasures (pp. 73, 253–54, 332, 341, 429, 480; see also pp. 343–44 for photos of other places figuring in the Malatesta Cantos). John Pope-Hennessy's *Italian Renaissance Sculpture* is also useful: pp. 68–73, 309–14; Plates 100–03. This scholar claims that "the Tempio Malatestiano is the most richly sculptured Renaissance building in Italy" (p. 312).

17. D. D. Paige, ed. *The Selected Letters of Ezra Pound, 1907–1941* (New York: New Directions, 1971; 1950), p. 212. (Hereafter cited as *SL*.)

18. *SL*, p. 53; Mar. 8, 1915. On Quinn as patron of modern art and literature, see B. L. Reid, *The Man from New York: John Quinn and His Friends* (New York: Oxford Univ. Press, 1968).

19. *SL*, pp. 172–73, n. 1; enclosed in a letter to W. C. Williams, March 18, 1922.

20. See Noel Stock, *The Life of Ezra Pound* (New York: Avon, 1970), pp. 320–22. (Hereafter cited as Stock, *Life*.)

21. "And Piccinino was out of a job" (10.43.6).

22. P. J. Jones, *The Malatesta of Rimini*, p. 228.

23. Giovanni Soranzo, the foremost authority on Pius's relations with Sigismondo (and Pound's major source for these relations), claims that not one of the grave charges against Malatesta was proven conclusively, in "Un'invettiva della Curia Romana contro Sigismondo Malatesta," *La Romagna*, 7 (Nov.-Dec. 1910), 462–89; p. 485.

24. See 26/121–22.

25. Sixtus IV later annulled this provision.

26. This line seems to be freely translated from Broglio's phrase "una cattiva pace, una sententia molto aspra et indebita" (quoted by Soranzo, *Pio II*, p. 131, n. 1), but Broglio was referring to the terms formulated at Mantua in 1459, not to the treaty of 1463.

27. Jones, *The Malatesta of Rimini*, pp. 238–39.

28. One of the members of the Roman Academy who had been imprisoned and tortured by command of Pope Paul.

29. Part of a passage cancelled from a very early typescript of "Canto IX," at a stage when only one Malatesta Canto was envisioned (Beinecke Library at Yale, Pound Archive, *Cantos* Folder #50, p. 16; p. 3 of typescript).

30. *GK*, frontispiece.

31. Donald Davie, *Ezra Pound: Poet as Sculptor* (London: Routledge and Kegan Paul, 1965), pp. 130–31.

32. George Dekker, *Sailing After Knowledge: The Cantos of Ezra Pound* (London: Routledge and Kegan Paul, 1963), p. 138. See also Noel Stock, *Reading the Cantos*, p. 28.

33. Niccolò Machiavelli, *The History of Florence*, in Myron P. Gilmore, ed., *Machiavelli: The History of Florence and Other Selections*, trans. Judith A. Rawson (New York: Washington Square Press, 1970), p. 219.

34. Karl Shapiro, "The Meaning of the Discarded Poem," in C. D. Abbott, ed. *Poets at Work* (New York: Harcourt Brace, 1948), p. 121.

35. Folders #69–70 are labelled "Canto 12," but they deal, at least in part, with various codas to the Malatesta Cantos that Pound had envisioned for the beginning of what is now the "Baldy Bacon Canto" (12).

36. Conversation, Sept. 30, 1980. See also her *Ezra Pound, Father and Teacher: Discretions* (New York: New Directions, 1971), p. 159.

Chapter 1

1. Paige Collection in the Pound Archive at Yale's Beinecke Library, #601, p. 6; hereafter, *Paige* and letter number.

2. *SL*, p. 176.

3. Letter quoted in Daniel D. Pearlman, *The Barb of Time: On the Unity of Ezra Pound's "Cantos"* (New York: Oxford Univ. Press, 1969), p. 302.

4. Ibid., pp. 302–3.

5. See 8.28.27–8.29.22.

6. In 1934, Pound was to write of D'Annunzio: "The only living author who has ever taken a city or held up the diplomatic crapule at the point of machine-guns, he is in a position to speak with more authority than a batch of neurasthenic incompetents or of writers who never having swerved from their jobs, might be, or are, supposed by the scientists and the populace to be incapable of action" (*Literary Essays of Ezra Pound*, ed. T. S. Eliot, New Directions Paper, 1968, p. 192; hereafter cited as *LE*).

7. Pound Archive, Beinecke Library, Yale University, *Cantos* Folder #46, first two pages.

8. Letter to Dr. James Sibley Watson, Jr., Jan. 4–5, 1923, p. 1. (Dr. Watson has kindly provided me with a copy of this and of four other letters to him from Pound.)

9. Charles Yriarte, *Un condottiere au XVe siècle* (Paris, 1882). Pound's primary debt in these cantos is to this book, from which he culled the following material: Sigismondo's letter to Giovanni de' Medici, and the contract between Malatesta and the Florentines (8.28.14–8.30.10); the poem on 8.30.17–22, based on two poems by Malatesta; the translated bits of a letter from Sigismondo on 8.30.26–32; the phrase "*templum aedificavit*" (8.32.16); the epithets "Atreides" (8.32.32) and

"Poliorcetes" (9.36.28); *all* of the post-bag letters, with the exception of a few excerpts (9.37.27–9.40.35; 10.42.4–8); the phrases on 9.41.6–10; Carmagnola's execution "between the two columns" (10.42.22); Strozzi's remarks (10.42.25–27), in spite of the citing of an Italian scholarly article; the Latin describing the burning in effigy (10.43.29–10.44.8); the "8 florins 48 bol" (10.45.29); Platina's remarks (11.51.4–8); and many other facts and incidents.

10. Cesare Clementini, *Raccolto istorico della fondazione di Rimino* . . . (Rimini, 1617), II, 296–476; Francesco Gaetano Battaglini, "Della vita e de' fatti di Sigismondo Pandolfo Malatesta," *Basini Parmensis poetae opera praestantiora* (Rimini, 1794), II, 259–698, for both of which books there are undated call-slips from an unspecified French library among Pound's MSS; Giovanni Soranzo, "Un'invettiva della Curia Romana contro Sigismondo Malatesta," *La Romagna*, 7 (Nov.–Dec. 1910), 462–89; 8 (Mar.-Apr. 1911), 150–75; 8 (May-June 1911), 241–84; Pius II, *Commentarii* . . . (Frankfort, 1614). Soranzo's painstakingly researched defense of Malatesta against the irresponsible accusations of the Papacy demonstrates that Pound, far from choosing a monster as his hero, simply followed the leads emanating from the most respectable scholarship of his day in attempting to rehabilitate Sigismondo's reputation.

11. Giovanni Soranzo, *Pio II e la politica italiana nella lotta contro i Malatesti, 1457–1463* (Padua: Drucker, 1911). Among Pound's MSS is a bill from Hoepli, dated Dec. 31, 1922, for this book as well as for a two-volume study of Francesco Sforza by Rubieri, a life of Alberti by Mancini, and other books relating to this period of Italian history (Folder #40, p. 5).

12. Carlos Baker, *Ernest Hemingway: A Life Story* (New York: Scribner, 1969), p. 107; Stock *Life*, p. 328. Baker claims that, after visiting Orbetello, the Pounds returned to Rapallo, but this seems improbable in light of the fact that, by February 17, Pound was in Rome. Stock claims that "about the middle of February 1923 the Pounds went to Sicily with Yeats and his wife." This is even more improbable: according to one of Pound's letters (*Paige*, #711), the Yeatses were due to arrive in Sicily, where the Pounds had already been for a while, on January 9, *1925*. Stock refers to this excursion on page 337, but with no mention of Yeats.

13. Letter to Quinn, reproduced in Pearlman, *The Barb of Time*, p. 303. Among the MSS are six call-slips, dated February 23, 24, and 26, 1923 (Folder #44, pp. 45–47). In this same folder are transcriptions, not in Pound's hand, of five papal documents relating to Sigismondo, all culled from the Vatican Archives.

14. Quoted in Stock, *Life*, p. 330.

15. Ben D. Kimpel and T. C. Duncan Eaves, "Pound's Research for the Malatesta Cantos," *Paideuma*, 11 (Winter 1982), 406–19; p. 411.

16. In Folder #45 there is a letter to Pound dated March 26, 1923, and addressed to him at the Hotel Palace, Rimini, from where he had presumably wired on March 22.
    I have been able to examine a copy of Broglio's *Cronaca universale*, for, thanks to the efforts of Mary de Rachewiltz, there is now at Yale's Beinecke Library a copy of the portion of the MS dealing with Sigismondo (pp. 148–303r).
    Pound was later to write of this visit to Rimini: "The local librarian had shut up the library, and the Comandante had damn well decided that if I had taken the trouble to come to Romagna to look at a manuscript, the library would cut the red tape" (*J/M*, p. 27).
    He says of one of his visits to the Tempio: "Idea that there could be clean and beneficent Christianity restarted in Tempio Malatestiano. Country priest not the least disturbed that I shd. be making my farewells *solo ai elefanti*. Namely that I had come for friendly word with the stone elephants and not for altar furniture" (*GK*, p. 301).

17. Letter to James Sibley Watson, Mar. 26, 1923. (Copy furnished by Dr. Watson.) Although the dateline of this letter is Pound's Paris address, there is no doubt that he is writing from Italy: in his letter to Watson of January 4, he had instructed him to send all correspondence to his Paris address, from where it would be forwarded to him in Italy.

18. He adds that he "found Divus *Iliad* this p.m.," clearing up the doubt he had expressed as to the existence of that work in his "Early Translators of Homer" (*LE*, p. 265n).

19. In a letter to John Quinn (May 29, 1923), Pound writes: "Have been snowed under, or at least working on my Malatesta Cantos steadily and without let up from middle of Feb. until about five weeks ago. . . ." (Letter reproduced in Pearlman, *The Barb of Time*, p. 303).

20. Nicholas Joost, *Scofield Thayer and "The Dial"* (Carbondale, Ill.: Southern Illinois Univ. Press, 1964), pp. 169–70.

21. Joost, pp. 170, 173; letter from Pound to Watson, June 27, 1923. (Copy furnished by Dr. Watson.)

22. Letter to me from Dr. Watson, July 10, 1980.

23. Quoted by Joost, p. 111.

24. Letter from Pound to Watson, June 27, 1923, p. 2. "To inspect said Cantos" is Pound's version of Burke's words.

25. Letter dated May 29, 1923. (Copy furnished by Dr. Watson.)

26. Joost, p. 170. The *Dial* went on, however, to publish part of Canto 27 in Jan. 1928 and Canto 22 the following month—and even to confer on Pound the Dial Award for 1927 (Joost, p. 172).

27. Letter from Pound to Watson, Jan. 4–5, 1923, p. 1. See also *SL*, p. 187: "*The Criterion* wants me to send in stuff. . . ."

28. Letter to Watson, Aug. 4, 1923. (Copy provided by Dr. Watson.)

29. Charles Norman, *Ezra Pound* (New York: Funk and Wagnalls, 1969), p. 259.

30. For an extended discussion of Pound's revision of the early cantos, see Ronald Bush, *The Genesis of Ezra Pound's Cantos* (Princeton Univ. Press, 1976). Myles Slatin, in "A History of Pound's Cantos I-XVI, 1915–1925" (*American Literature*, 35 [May 1963], 183–95), emphasizes the importance of the Malatesta sequence in the overall structure of the early *Cantos*: ". . . the fission of Canto IX [into "9" to "12"] was to delay his progress drastically and crucially; only after he had gone through the struggle to shape these next Cantos was Pound able to reshape all he had so far done and really begin his work on the poem" (p. 190), and ". . . only after he had finished the Malatesta group was Pound able to rethink the poem sufficiently to change drastically those parts of it left untouched since the appearance of the *Lustra* volumes" (p. 192).

31. Folder #48, p. 11, among other instances. Soranzo mentions that contemporary invectives against Pius II were fairly common (*Pio II*, p. 267n).

32. Pound drew this from Clementini, *Raccolto istorico*, II, 325–26.

33. Plutarch, "Life of Alexander," *The Lives of the Noble Grecians and Romans*, Dryden/Clough trans. (New York: Modern Library, n.d.), p. 801.

34. Folder #43, p. 37; cf. 11.50.4–9. See Appendix B for a transcription of the two letters from which these lines are derived.

35. Folder #42, pp. 130, 132, 156–57; #43, pp. 3–5, 10, second page 2. See Soranzo, *Pio II*, pp. 227, 290.

36. For example, see 8.28.8–10; 9.36.14; 9.37.33–34; 9.39.14–17; 11.49.22; 11.50.5,13.

37. From Clementini, *Raccolto istorico*, II, 325.

38. The most significant of these are the following: I: #41, pp. 22–24 ff.; II: #41, pp. 1–7; III: #41, p. 13; IV: #42, pp. 53–56; V: #43, pp. 17–20; VI: #65, pp. 8–9; VII: #65, pp. 1–10; VIII: #65, pp. 10–12, 14–15 f.

39. Folder #46, 18th and 19th sheets. (I have silently corrected obvious typographical errors, here and elsewhere.)

40. The epithet had been applied to the sympathetic Cino (*Personae: The Collected Shorter Poems of Ezra Pound*, rev. ed. [New York: New Directions, 1971], p. 7). (Hereafter cited as *PERSONAE*.)

41. Michael André Bernstein, *The Tale of the Tribe: Ezra Pound and the Modern Verse Epic* (Princeton: Princeton Univ. Press, 1980), p. 74.

42. Folder #46, sheet 30; typescript. (I have placed Pound's handwritten additions within slash-marks.)

43. Though this very abruptness suggests the narrator's skepticism about the charge.

44. "Don't be descriptive; remember that the painter can describe a landscape much better than you can, and that he has to know a deal more about it" (*LE*, p. 6).

45. In his translation of the letter in Folder #48, Pound substitutes "Caesar" for Trachulo's "Haniballe" (letter in Yriarte, *Un condottiere*, p. 444). He later reverts to the original reading, thus providing Malatesta with another reason for not finishing the letter, for Sigismondo claimed descent from Scipio Africanus. (See transcription from Broglio, p. 273r, quoted above.)

46. But see R. P. Blackmur's 1933 essay, "Masks of Ezra Pound," in *Form and Value in Modern Poetry* (Garden City, N. Y.: Doubleday, 1957), 79–112, especially pp. 97–100.

47. Folder #49, nine sheets.

48. See, for example, 9.34.16 and 10.45.28.

49. Edward Hutton, *Sigismondo Pandolfo Malatesta, Lord of Rimini: A Study of a XV Century Italian Despot* (London: Dent, 1906).

50. Pound took these words from the epigraph to Soranzo's "Un'invettiva," Part One. Their ultimate source is Broglio, *Cronaca*, p. 238.

51. Folder #50, pp. 112, 114, 16, 18, 6 (numbered by Pound, 1–5); typescript with handwritten corrections.

52. In the other drafts, as well as in the published version, "shelved" is followed by Eliot's word, "shored" (*Waste Land*, line 430).

53. See the last two lines of Canto 4, added to the poem shortly before the publication of *A Draft of XVI Cantos* in 1925; also, 29/145; and 78/481, where Scratton is referred to as "Thiy" ("Ti" in the draft under discussion) and Eliot as "il decaduto." For a personal reason for Pound's associating Scratton with Malatesta and his Tempio, see Stock, *Life*, p. 320: "Ever since their first meeting . . . they [Pound and Scratton] had shared the idea of building a temple to the true religion. . . ." See also Wendy Stallard Flory, *Ezra Pound and "The Cantos": A Record of*

Struggle (New Haven: Yale Univ. Press, 1980), p. 115. Flory discusses Pound's aversion to self-revelation on pp. 4–5.

54. Cf. 29/145, where the same two meetings are recalled and in which Eliot is referred to as "Arnaut." Eliot is here quoted as having said: "'I am afraid of the life after death.'"

55. The meeting with Eliot at Excideuil had taken place "over Borneil's bake-oven" (#50, p. 3). This collocation of Arnaut, Bertran, and Bornelh recalls what Pound had written in *The Spirit of Romance* of "the other two who form with Daniel the great triad mentioned in *De Vulgari Eloquentia* (II, 2): Giraut of Bornelh and Bertrans de Born" (p. 44).

56. At least for the time being. It re-enters subsequent drafts.

57. Incidentally, Pound here identifies the "*Maestro di pentore*" as Piero della Francesca. (So is he identified by Yriarte, *Un condottiere*, pp. 380–81.)

58. Cf. 8.31.26–34.

59. Cf. some later lines from this draft:
>   And Gemisthus . . .
> who had talked the gods, gone back to Morea,
>   but the word burning and hot. . . .
>   (#53, p. 43)

60. This presumably refers to the scene with Eliot.

Chapter 2

1. Karl Shapiro, "The Meaning of the Discarded Poem," *Poets at Work*, ed. C. D. Abbott (New York: Harcourt Brace, 1948), p. 119.

2. Letter from Pound to Watson, Jan. 4–5, 1923, p. 3. (Copy furnished by Dr. Watson.)

3. Folder #56 in the Pound Archive at Yale's Beinecke Library; sheets numbered by Pound, 1–27. All page references in this section, unless otherwise stated, are from this folder.

4. Cf. Pound's disillusioned remark to Santayana: "Gemisthus Plethon's polytheism evaporated when one got near it" (letter dated Dec. 8, 1939; *SL*, p. 331).

5. He never does.

6. Cf. Pound's lucid narration of these events in 9.34.29–9.35.13, translated from Broglio, p. 191*r*.

7. In "Watson 10," the deaths of Ginevra and Polissena—nine years apart—are separated by only eight lines; in the final version, by a more respectable thirty-three lines.

8. Cf. the present Canto 10, in which the Latin quotation is followed immediately by the events that led up to the Church's condemnation of Malatesta. Thus, our interest is captured by the strange Latin document and rewarded soon afterward with the sordid spectacle of a frenzied papacy using all the powers at its disposal in order to seize Malatesta's domain.

9. It seems that the New Directions printer was provided with no such assistance: see 10.44.12,17.

10. Pound seemed to sense this deficiency. When submitting the typescript to Watson, he let him know that "I may want to make a few alterations in XII . . ." (letter to Watson, Jan. 4–5, 1923, p. 3).

11. "Watson 12" has "beauty" for "glory" (p. 21).

12. "Watson 13" consists of a ten-line passage, from which four of the lines have been deleted. With regard to this fragmentary canto, Pound had written to Watson: "Print it if you think it helps to clarify the story" (letter to Watson, Jan. 4–5, 1923, p. 2).
13. Hugh Kenner, *The Pound Era*, p. 342.
14. Stock, *Life*, p. 319.
15. This manuscript draft comprises pages 1–10 of Folder #65.
16. Kung says in Canto 13: "And even I can remember / A day when the historians left blanks in their writings, / I mean for things they didn't know . . ." (p. 60).
17. Incomplete typescript, 25 leaves, Cantos 10–12, Folder #62.
18. Folder #65, p. 30, typed sheet with only these nine lines on it. This sheet, Folder #66 (p. 33), and Pound's source for this passage (see Appendix B), all give the reading "scientia" rather than "scienta" in the last line.
19. "Resourceful," "wily," "of many counsels"; but I think that Pound wished to shade the meaning to something like "with his mind on many different things." Indeed, one of the meanings of *mētis* is "a project."
20. The *Annotated Index* guesses that it means "double columns" (p. 49).
21. Paraphrased from a religious sonnet by Malatesta, reproduced by Yriarte, p. 393. The original line reads "Jo me veggio caschar ne glinterdecti."
22. Letter to Watson, June 27, 1923, p. 3. (Copy furnished by Dr. Watson.)
23. Kenner, *The Pound Era*, p. 384.
24. Rudolf Arnheim, in "Psychological Notes on the Poetical Process," observes that "the ways of 'practical' language seem to influence early versions of poems. The poet's primary experience may well contain a precise feeling of the perceptual qualities which carry the crucial expression. Yet as he searches for an equivalent in the medium of words he will often be inclined at first to use the most abstract practical name, which may call to mind things but not actually convey their characteristics charged with expression" (*Poets at Work*, ed. C. D. Abbott [New York: Harcourt Brace, 1948], p. 141).
25. Noel Stock raises the objection that "in the Malatesta cantos, there is no proper coverage of the less savoury aspects of Sigismundo's life" (*Reading the Cantos* [London: Routledge, 1967], p. 28). But Pound was not writing a scholarly monograph on Malatesta: he simply presented Sigismondo's virtues (as worthy of being recorded and emulated) and consigned his vices to oblivion.

Chapter 3

1. Gabriele D'Annunzio, *Tragedie sogni e misteri* (Milan: A. Mondadori, 1939), I, 708–12. (The excerpt I have translated is from pp. 710–12 of this edition.)
2. The exception is "Near Perigord"—but this poem is very different, in tone and theme, from the "Sestina" or the translations. See also Pound's 1929 note to his translation of Bertran's war-poem, "Be.m platz lo gais temps de pascor," that had appeared in *The Spirit of Romance*: "This kind of thing was much more impressive before 1914 than it has been since 1920" (*SR*, p. 48, n. 10, New Directions Paperbook, 1968).

3. "De Born writes songs to provoke real war, and they were effective. This is very different from Romantic or Macaulay-Tennyson praise of past battles" (letter dated July 8, 1922, when Pound was already working on the Malatesta sequence; *SL*, p. 179).

4. Thomas H. Jackson, "The Adventures of Messire Wrong-Head," *ELH*, 32 (1965), 238–55; p. 255.

5. Pius II, *Commentarii* . . . (Rome: 1592), Bk. II, p. 92.

6. Pound lifts the phrase from Bertran's "Be.m platz lo gais temps de pascor."

7. Marjorie G. Perloff, "Pound and Rimbaud: The Retreat from Symbolism," *Iowa Review* (Winter 1975), 91–117; p. 106. (In Perloff's last sentence, "Montefeltro" would be more appropriate than "Medici.")

8. Said of Bertran in "Near Perigord" (*PERSONAE*, p. 152). Cf. Geoffrey Hartman's apposite reminder: "Tradition provides us . . . with a definite term for the man who is so much greater than we are, not morally perhaps but in modes of being . . . that our familiar, democratic judgment is suspended, if not disabled. He is the *hero*" ("The Heroics of Realism," *Beyond Formalism: Literary Essays 1958–1970* [New Haven: Yale Univ. Press, 1970], p. 68).

9. For example, "And the Emperor came down and knighted us" (9.34.16)—where Sigismondo and Novello are meant.

10. See, for example, 10.42.28–29 and 10.44.9–10.

11. See Kung's remark in 13/59 "'When the prince has gathered about him / All the savants and artists, his riches will be fully employed.'" (Pound uses Pauthier's French version of this dictum as one of the two epigraphs to *Gaudier-Brzeska*.)

12. "It's all rubbish to pretend that art isn't didactic. A revelation is always didactic" (letter to Felix E. Schelling, July 9, 1922; *SL*, p. 180). See also *GK*: "All that a single man could, Malatesta managed *against* the current of power" (p. 159).

13. *SL*, p. 10 (Aug. 18, 1912).

14. In 1913 Pound claimed that "thoughtful men have in every age found almost the same set of things . . . to protest against; if it be not a corrupt press or some monopoly, it is always some sort of equivalent, some conspiracy of ignorance and interest" (*LE*, p. 104). Kenner says of Pound's source for the Chinese Cantos that it "uses history . . . to afford paradigms" (*The Pound Era*, p. 457). In much the same way are we to understand Pound's use of history in the Malatesta sequence. Peter Makin claims, in *Provence and Pound* (Berkeley: Univ. of California Press, 1978), that the poet's "view of history came to be . . . a succession of identifiable Montforts and Hamiltons betraying a parallel series of culture-heroes and secret cultists" (p. 35). Leon Surette, in *A Light from Eleusis: A Study of Ezra Pound's "Cantos"* (Oxford: Clarendon Press, 1979), deals at some length with this issue:

    . . . Clearly Pound wanted in Malatesta a figure who would conform to some preconceived pattern. He was anxious to achieve historical accuracy if possible, but had poetic or fictional requirements which took precedence over history. . . .
    The point to be taken here is not that the history contained in the *Cantos* is inaccurate, but that it conforms to a fictional pattern established by the poem. The fabric of history is composed of recurrences or repeats of a permanent pattern. Malatesta is another Odysseus, *Poliorcetes,* and "a bit too *polumetis,*" struggling alone in a hostile and imperciPient world toward some perception of beauty (p. 108).

As early as 1910, Pound had claimed that "All ages are contemporaneous" (*SR*, p. 6).

140 Notes for Chapter 3

15. Daniel Bornstein points out that the tone of Broglio's *Cronaca* exerted a significant influence on this narrative voice in "The Poet as Historian: Researching the Malatesta Cantos," *Paideuma*, 10 (Fall 1981), 283–91; pp. 285–86. (Bornstein is currently preparing an edition of the *Cronaca*.)

16. William K. Wimsatt, ed., *Alexander Pope: Selected Poetry and Prose* (New York: Holt, Rinehart and Winston, 1951), pp. 306–60.

17. Cf. Pound's "Sforza Francesco, wattle-nose" (8.32.4) and "that nick-nosed s.o.b. Feddy Urbino" (11.49.5). While Pound may have been remembering portraits of these princes (there is a portrait of a very hook-nosed Federigo in Yriarte, p. 276; see also *SL*, p. 191), there might also be an unconscious recollection of *Purgatorio* VII, in which three of the negligent princes pointed out by Sordello are referred to as "quel nasetto" ("little-nose"), "colui dal maschio naso" ("manly-nose"), and "nasuto" ("big-nose") (VII, 103, 113, 124). See also Pound's "Marvoil," in which the speaker refers to the King of Aragon as "poke-nose" (*PERSONAE*, p. 22).

18. From Canto 8: "Now you have me, / Caught like a hen in a coop"; Canto 9: And he fought like ten devils at Monteluro; And the King o' Ragona . . . / was the next nail in our coffin; "as well for a sheep as a lamb"; old bladder [Pius II]; Corn-salve; "Broglio, I'm the goat"; And Wattle never paid up on the nail; "young pullets make thin soup"; Canto 10: *"anno messo a saccho el Signor Sigismundo";* Carlo Gonzaga sitting like a mud-frog / in Orbetello; their best bear's-greased latinity; that kid-slapping fanatic; Pio lost his pustulous temper; Canto 11: Little fat squab "Formosus." (The closest Pound comes to the epic simile in these cantos is "like a hen in a coop" and "like a mud-frog.")

19. *Ab uno disce omnes:*

>   And they had a bow-shot at Borso
>   As he was going down the Grand Canal in his gondola
>   (the nice kind with 26 barbs on it).
>   (10.46.30–32)

20. From Canto 8: Slut; Bitch; Slanging; chucked away; an excellent hiding; the pest; To patch up some sort of treaty; Canto 9: bitched us; wangle; wiggling; waggled; Feddy; joy-ride; Wattle-wattle; Sidg; swindling; grnnh! rrnnh, pthg; vacation; the old brick heap of Pesaro; *m'l'ha calata*; lost his job; muck; Georgio Rambottom; his boss; no end of fuss and botheration; Canto 10: Siggy, darlint; Trachulo's damn'd epistle; couldn't be bothered; lunch; all right; gang; *la budella; la corata*; that pot-scraping little runt; bunkum; s. o. b.; pewk; the whole lump lot; old Pills; buttocks; we dragged in the Angevins; Canto 11: busted; dey got de mos' bloody rottenes' peace on us; Novvy; his big beam; giggled; the kids; the Mo'ammeds; pep; Damn pity; Fatty; joke; ornry. So much for epic *gravitas* or the elevated style.

21. A few examples: sindic; attainder; baldachino; *concret Allgemeine*; viels; *Casus est talis*; commendatary; defalcation; bol; spingard.

22. The poet Porcelio de' Pandoni, "the anti-Hellene" whom Basinio defeated in debate (9.34.18–21), wrote a *Feltria* on the deeds of Federigo d'Urbino and a *Vita militaris Jacobi Piccinini* on "Count Giacomo"—"the one that fell out of the window," "three days after his death." Basinio himself wrote a *Hesperis* in praise of Sigismondo, consisting of thirteen books of Latin hexameters that sing of Malatesta's victories against the Aragonese at Piombino and Vada. This work makes use of Odyssean motifs and also incorporates phrases translated from the *Iliad*. (Cf. 104/740: "Bassinio left greek tags in his margins / moulding the cadence.") His *Isottaeus*, three books of Latin elegiacs modeled on the *Heroides*, and which Pound praised as containing "fine poetry" (*SR*, p. 240), consists of letters feigned to have been exchanged between Sigismondo, Isotta, and Basinio, and between Isotta and her father, while Malatesta is away at war.

Might not this poem have provided at least a partial inspiration for the post-bag section? (Kenner's adducing of Henry James's "A Bundle of Letters" is unconvincing: *Pound Era*, p. 376). See Vittorio Rossi, *Storia letteraria d'Italia: Il Quattrocento* (Milan: Francesco Vallardi, 1973; 1933), pp. 230–32.

23. Surette, *A Light from Eleusis*, p. 106. This "siding" with the hero violates another epic canon—that of the objectivity of the poet in recounting his story. But compare Wayne Booth's remarks in *The Rhetoric of Fiction* (Chicago: Univ. of Chicago Press, 1961):

> When we come to Odysseus' enemies, the poet . . . does not hesitate . . . to speak in his own person. . . . Penelope's suitors must look bad to us; Telemachus must be admired. . . . Homer . . . lays on his own direct judgments with bright colors. The "insolent," "swaggering," and "ruffianly" suitors are contrasted to the "wise" . . . Telemachus and the "good" Mentor. . . . We seldom encounter the suitors without some explicit attack by the poet. . . .
>
> The result of all this direct guidance . . . is to leave us . . . perfectly clear about what we should hope for and what fear; we are unambiguously sympathetic toward the heroes and contemptuous of the suitors. (p. 6).

24. In which there is a parodic resemblance to the Homeric stock epithets. Compare *Magnifice ac potens domine, mi singularissime*; *Magnifico exso*. Signor Mio; MAGNIFICENT LORD WITH DUE REVERENCE; *Magnifice ac potens*; Magnificent and Exalted Lord and Father; and *Magnifice ac potens domine, domine mi singularissime* (all from the post-bag section) with the oft-repeated Homeric phrases "Zeus of the wide brows," "long-suffering brilliant Odysseus," "tall Hektor of the shining helm," "Menelaos of the great war cry," etc. (Examples drawn from the "Introduction" to Richmond Lattimore's translation of the *Iliad* [Univ. of Chicago Press, 1951], pp. 39–40.)

25. See Pound's remark, "Modern civilisation comes out of Italy, out of renaissance Italy, the first nation which broke away from Aquinian dogmatism, and proclaimed the individual; respected the personality," in *Selected Prose of Ezra Pound, 1909–1965*, ed., William Cookson (New York: New Directions, 1973), p. 199. (Hereafter cited as *SP*.)

26. See Clark Emery, *Ideas into Action: A Study of Pound's Cantos* (Coral Gables, Fla.: Univ. of Miami Press, 1958), p. 40.

27. Perloff, "Pound and Rimbaud," p. 109.

28. Walter Benjamin, *Illuminations*, ed. Hannah Arendt (New York: Schocken, 1969), p. 79.

29. Indeed, Pius II's full name, "Aeneas Silvius Piccolomini" (10.44.16), epitomizes this essential antinomy: the epic connotations of the names Aeneas and Silvius are "deflated" by the cognomen "Piccolomini" ("little men").

30. Unpublished letter to James Sibley Watson, Jr., Jan. 4, 1923, pp. 1–2.(Copy furnished by Dr. Watson.) Though Pound is referring to the Watson Typescript, his remarks are equally pertinent to the Malatesta Cantos in their final form.

31. Unpublished letter to James Sibley Watson, Jr., Jan. 4, 1923, p. 2. See Bernstein's remark in *The Tale of the Tribe*: "The seemingly unobtrusive moment in Canto VIII, when the first series of historical letters is introduced into *The Cantos* . . . , represents one of the decisive turning-points in modern poetics, opening for verse the capacity to include domains of experience long since considered alien territory" (p. 40).

32. George Dekker, *Sailing After Knowledge: The Cantos of Ezra Pound* (London: Routledge and Kegan Paul, 1963), p. 31.

33. This is the view of Michael F. Harper in "Truth and Calliope: Ezra Pound's Malatesta," *PMLA*, 96 (Jan. 1981), 86–103.

34. *Poetics* XXIII.1, in S. H. Butcher, *Aristotle's Theory of Poetry and Fine Art* (New York: Dover, 1951), p. 89.

35. Cf. *Purgatorio* III.107: "biondo era e bello e di gentile aspetto."

36. Because Alessandro was Negroid in appearance, his contemporaries suspected him of being the bastard son of Pope Clement VII and a Moorish slave. See Ferdinand Schevill, *The Medici* (New York: Harper and Row, 1949), pp. 203–4.

37. Discussed above, p. 25.

38. Yriarte gives 1430 as the year of Malatesta's first public acts—the military events mentioned at the end of Canto 8 (*Un condottiere*, p. 86).

39. Quoted above, p. 22.

40. Cf. the similar process in Pound's "Papyrus," in which a time-ravaged poem by Sappho yields: "Spring . . . . . / Too long . . . . . / Gongula . . . . ." (*PERSONAE*, p. 112).

41. It is interesting to note that the first spoken word in *The Divine Comedy* is in Latin ("*Miserere*," *Inf.* I.65), as is the first word spoken in Joyce's *Ulysses* ("*Introibo*"), as is Malatesta's first utterance in Cantos 8–11 ("*Frater tamquam . . .*").

42. See above, p. xix.

43. Pound's source for this letter is Yriarte, *Un condottiere*, p. 381.

44. Cf. Yriarte, pp. 382–83.

45. Troy had to be *destroyed* before it became "a heap of smouldering boundary stones" (4/13).

46. "Destroyer of ships, destroyer of cities, destroyer of men" (*Agamemnon*, line 689).

47. "Formosus" also calls to mind the opening of Virgil's second eclogue, with its theme of homosexuality: "Formosum pastor Corydon ardebat Alexim."

48. The only exception is the comparison of the Malatesta family with the House of Atreus (8.32.31–32).

49. Cf. Pound's quip in the *Pisan Cantos:*
>I knew but one Achilles in my time
>and he ended up in the Vatican.
>(80/502)

(Pound had met Achille Ratti, the future Pius XI, when the latter was still librarian of Milan's Ambrosiana.)

50. The phrase ("concrete universal") is associated with Plethon in Fritz Schultze's *Geschichte der Philosophie der Renaissance* (Jena, 1874):
> Denn Plethon ist durchaus Platonischer Realist im Sinne des Mittelalters. Das Allgemeine ist ihm das wahrhaft Wirkliche. Dies Allgemeine ist aber nicht ein abstract Allgemeines, sowie es die Nominalisten fassen, sondern das concret Allgemeine, welches alle Besondern in sich enthält . . . (p. 159).

(On pp. 155–58, Schultze discusses the role of Poseidon in Plethon's allegorical pantheon: "Poseidon ist die Ideenwelt in ihrer Gesammtheit" [p. 157].)

In the *Pisan Cantos*, Pound posits a relationship between Plethon's notions about

Poseidon and the many sculpted aquatic scenes in the Tempio:
> Gemisto stemmed all from Neptune
> hence the Rimini bas reliefs.
> (83/528)

(See Carroll F. Terrell, *A Companion to the Cantos of Ezra Pound* [Berkeley: Univ. of California Press, 1980], p. 40.)

51. In associating Sforza's shifts with different times of the year—as if the mere passage of time determined his allegiances—Pound may have been remembering (and expanding) Dante's charge against Florence in *Purgatorio* VI.143–4: ". . . a mezzo novembre / non giugne quel che tu d'ottobre fili" (" . . . what you spin in October does not last to mid-November").

52. Various forms of this phrase resound through the pages of *Rock-Drill* and *Thrones*. (See Appendix D.)

53. It seems that the "Truth" behind the Pesaro affair (attested to by Broglio's account here) is indeed a "Bitch." (See 8.28.2.)

54. Pound's own identification with Sigismondo is curiously revealed in a remark made in *Guide to Kulchur*, where, in speaking of the various artists employed by Malatesta, he says: "Federigo Urbino was his Amy Lowell, Federigo with more wealth got the seconds" (p. 159). (The reference is to the "*Amy*gists" [*SL*, p. 212], who, under the ample aegis of Lowell, kept on producing one *Imagist Anthology* after another—long after Pound had lost interest in the movement he had inaugurated.)

55. The story of Paolo and Francesca Malatesta is told in *Inferno* V; Pound conjures up the atmosphere of their punishment in Hell in the lines,

> And the wind is still for a little
> And the dusk rolled
> to one side a little.

Parisina Malatesta, Sigismondo's cousin and the mother of his first wife, Ginevra, was executed in 1425 by command of her husband, Niccolò d'Este, who suspected her of incestuous relations with his illegitimate son, Ugo, who was also sentenced to death. (See 20/90–91 and 24/112–13.) The Malatesta clan is compared with the House of Atreus (8.32.32) because of these motifs of incest and violent death.

56. This note of futility echoes unobtrusively through Canto 9: "for whatever that was worth afterward" (9.35.23); "for all the good that did" (9.38.17); "for all the good that does" (9.39.3); "for all the good that does" (9.39.4–5).

57. See above, p. 8.

58. Like a slightly awkward Beowulf, Malatesta "floundered about in the marsh / and came in after three days"—the second "epic descent" in the sequence.

59. Erich Auerbach, *Mimesis: The Representation of Reality in Western Literature*, trans. Willard R. Trask (Princeton Univ. Press, 1953), p. 243.

60. Cf. an autobiographical passage in Pound's "Indiscretions," in which polysyndeton and the mock-chronicle style are used for humorous effect: pp. 42–43 of the reprint available in *Pavannes and Divagations* (New York: New Directions, 1958), pp. 3–51. (See also *LE*, pp. 109–13, where Pound imitates the polysyndeton of the Provençal *razo*.)

61. "Taker of cities."

62. For an ampler discussion of the post-bag letters, see above, pp. 41–43, 50–51.

63. "And he was madly in love with Isotta degli Atti, and she was worthy of it." Yriarte provides a French version of the sentence on p. 155. The next four lines of Pound's text, Latin phrases in honor of Isotta, derive from two sources: *"Italiaeque decus"* is an adaptation of a phrase ("ITALIE DECORI") that appears on a medallion of Isotta struck in 1446 by Matteo da Pasti (see Yriarte, p. 142, fig. 71); the rest of the Latin passage is from a 15th-century Riminese chronicle (relevant excerpt provided by Yriarte, p. 155).

64. Pound here adapts the first words of "To Ianthe" by Walter Savage Landor: "Past ruin'd Ilion Helen lives." He reproduces the first stanza of the lyric in *Confucius to Cummings: An Anthology of Poetry*, eds. Pound and Marcella Spann (New Directions, 1964), p. 200, and he reprints the poem in its entirety (three stanzas) in *ABC*, p. 184.

65. Cf. the cultural overlaying in Canto 1, which constitutes a translation into "medieval English" (Anglo-Saxon rhythms) of an ancient Greek text via the Renaissance Latin translation of Andreas Divus.

66. From his untitled review of Adrian Stokes's *Stones of Rimini* in the *Criterion*, 13 (April 1934), 495–97.

67. Cf. the line from the Watson Typescript: "The empires slide to nothing here in the marsh-drift" (#56, p. 25).

68. See 8.31.18–25 and *GK*: "Sigismundo brought back Gemisto's coffin. . . ."; "And the Malatesta had his high sense of justice, for I think Gemisto wd. be even more forgotten without Sigismundo's piety" (frontispiece; p. 160). See Kenner, *Pound Era*, p. 341, for photos of the sarcophagi by San Vitale and of those cut into the walls of the Tempio.

69. Michael F. Harper, in "Truth and Calliope: Ezra Pound's Malatesta," makes the following observation: "The Malatesta sequence is a critical *reading* of some of the chief primary sources for any understanding of Sigismundo; Pound does not just present his results, he invites us to repeat the process by which he arrived at them: to study and weigh the styles—and hence, Pound believed, the essences, *les hommes mêmes*—of Malatesta and his chief accuser" (p. 99).

70. Note the studied anticlimax of the last two lines: "traitor, rapist, incestuous, arsonist, and / concubine-keeper."

71. The "kid-slapping fanatic" was actually the renowned theologian, Nicholas of Cusa.

72. The line "And what he said was all right there in Mantua" is an example of the "formulaic repeats" in these cantos—this particular one echoing "And what he said was all right in Mantua" in 10.43.8. Other instances:

>   Down here in the marsh they trapped him
>   in one year . . . (9.34.4–5)
>   And they trapped him down here in the marsh land,
>   in '46 that was. (11.50.23–24)

>   And the poor devils were dying of cold. (9.37.25)
>   And the poor devils dying of cold, outside Sorano. (10.42.1)
>   And the poor devils dying of cold, that was Rocca Sorano.
>   (11.50.25)

>   And Piccinino was out of a job. (10.43.6)
>   And Piccinino, out of a job. (10.46.16)

And he fell out of a window, Count Giacomo . . . (10.43.24)
(Piccinino, the one that fell out of the window). (10.47.3)

> *E gradment li antichi cavaler romanj*
>   *davano fed a quisti annutii* (10.47.7–8)
> (Repeated verbatim in 11.48.1–2.)

73. This last line may be an ironic glance at the many "well-made" artifacts in the Homeric poems.

74. The main narrator here "identifies" himself as one of Sigismondo's men: "And he put us under the chiefs" (11.48.3).

75. "Gay bird" is a deliberately humorous rendering of the Italian "gagliardo" ("valiant"), via an archaic meaning of the English noun "galliard"—"a gay fellow; a man of fashion" *(O.E.D.)*.

76. The meaning is that Malatesta, crazed by the plague and his defeat, "seems to be out of this (Sigis) world."

77. Pound's line, it should be remembered, is associated in the Watson Typescript (see Appendix C) with the mausoleum of Galla Placidia at Ravenna, as it is in 21/98.

78. See Appendix B for the source of this curious document.

79. This line resonates ironically against "And all of it down on paper" (11.51.12), with reference to the papal curtailment of Sigismondo's men: "64 and no more, and he not to try to get any more" (11.51.11)—the Pope's repressive document set off against Malatesta's good-humored one.

80. In addition, Canto 11 begins with two lines of Italian which, in the midst of war, hark back to the ancient Romans, whereas it ends with two lines of Latin which, as part of a joke, ratify a contract between two Italians.

81. Quoted by D. W. Robertson, Jr., *A Preface to Chaucer: Studies in Medieval Perspectives* (Princeton Univ. Press, 1962), p. 360.

Chapter 4

1. Ezra Pound, "Love-Song to Eunoë," lines 4–7, *Collected Early Poems of Ezra Pound*, ed. Michael King (New York: New Directions, 1976), p. 285. (Hereafter cited as *CEP*).

2. Ezra Pound, "Gaudier: A Postscript 1934," *Gaudier-Brzeska: A Memoir* (New York: New Directions, 1970; 1916), p. 141.

3. Noel Stock, for example, claims that "in the Malatesta cantos, there is no proper coverage of the less savoury aspects of Sigismundo's life" (*Reading the Cantos* [London: Routledge, 1967], p. 28).

4. "Villonaud for This Yule," *A Lume Spento and Other Early Poems* (New York: New Directions, 1965), p. 24. (Hereafter cited as *ALS*.)

5. Letter to William Carlos Williams, Oct. 21, 1908, *SL*, p. 3. This letter contains Pound's remarks on many of the poems in *ALS*.

6. "Histrion," *ALS*, p. 108. As the title suggests, Pound here sets forth his early notions of the poetic mask. See also "Masks" and "On His Own Face in a Glass" in *ALS*.

7. See also the later treatment of Piere Vidal and "how he ran mad, as a wolf" in "Piere Vidal Old" and in Canto 4.

8. This poem contains an interesting adumbration of the *Cantos*:
   And I see my greater soul-self bending
   Sibylwise with that great forty-year epic
   That you know of, yet unwrit
   But as some child's toy 'tween my fingers.
   (*ALS*, p. 38)
   (Lomax, it seems, is Pound's invention and not a historical personage.)

9. The affirmative thrust of Pound's first volume is emphasized by the exhortation appended to *ALS*: "Make strong old dreams lest this our world lose heart." At about the time that Pound was beginning work on the Malatesta material, he wrote to Felix E. Schelling:

   . . . There are things I quite definitely want to destroy, and which I think will have to [be] annihilated before civilization can exist. . . . I mean all that is left is exiled, driven in catacombs, exists in the isolated individual. . . . If the poets don't make certain horrors appear horrible who will? All values ultimately come from our judicial sentences. (This arrogance is not mine but Shelley's, and it is absolutely true. Humanity is malleable mud, and the arts set the moulds it is later cast into. Until the cells of humanity recognize certain things as excrement, they will stay in [the] human colon and poison it. . . .)
   (*SL*, p. 181)

10. For a discussion of Pound's gradual retreat from Swinburnianism, see Louis L. Martz, "Introduction," *CEP*, pp. vii-xxii.

11. "Revolt: Against the Crepuscular Spirit in Modern Poetry," *CEP*, p. 96.

12. *SR*, pp. 67, 73. (See also *SR*, p. 68, for Pound's delight in the Cid's tricking of Raquel and Vidas, an incident to which he returns in Canto 3.)

13. "The headless trunk which Dante meets in Malebolge is not more arresting to the attention than the fierce words of the chastelan of Aultaforte—'lover of strife for strife's sake'—who sang of his Lady Battle. . . .
    . . . It is not . . . for his love songs that he is most remembered, but for the goad of his tongue, and for his scorn of sloth, peace, cowardice, and the barons of Provence" (*SR*, pp. 44-45).

    Pound's self-identification with Bertran seems to have been especially strong. In a letter to William Carlos Williams (Dec. 19, 1913), Pound says of Henri Gaudier: "He is the only person with whom I can really be 'Altaforte'" (*SL*, p. 27). In "Near Perigord," Pound creates a Bertran after his own image: ". . . a lean man? Bilious? / With a red straggling beard? / And the green cat's-eye . . ." (*PERSONAE*, p. 154).

    Two full-length studies of the role of Provençal poetry in Pound's work are: Stuart Y. McDougal, *Ezra Pound and the Troubadour Tradition* (Princeton Univ. Press, 1972), and Peter Makin, *Provence and Pound* (Berkeley: Univ. of California Press, 1978).

14. "Na Audiart," "Sestina: Altaforte," "Planh for the Young English King," "Dompna Pois de me No'us Cal," and "Near Perigord."

15. Pound had probably begun working on the *Cantos* in September 1915.

16. ". . . S.P. is tying blue ribbon in the tails of Virgil and Horace . . ." (*SL*, p. 178).

17. An example of such a tradition would be the Eleusinian strand in Western poetry, which Pound traced from Greece to Rome (mainly via Ovid), and then on to Provence and Tuscany, where it finally culminated in Cavalcanti and Dante. See Leon Surette, *A Light from Eleusis* (Oxford: Clarendon, 1979). Cf. also Pound's early remark: "There was no abrupt humanistic revolt. Boccaccio and the rest but carry on a paganism which had never expired" (*SR*, p. 167).

18. Stock emphasizes Douglas's contribution to Pound's thought by entitling the chapter of his biography dealing with the years 1918–21, "Major C. H. Douglas." Besides sketching briefly Douglas's ideas, this chapter describes Pound's growing enmeshment in social, political, and economic issues. A clear, interesting exposition of Douglas's notions, and their implications for Pound, may be found in Kenner's *The Pound Era*, pp. 301–17.

19. Not counting the unnumbered "Envoi," which in several ways dissociates itself from the previous twelve sections. (Two books useful for their comments on *Mauberley* are John Espey's *Ezra Pound's Mauberley* and K. K. Ruthven's *A Guide to Ezra Pound's "Personae."*)

20. "Vent'anni fa, quindici anni fa, gli americani uscivano da America, venivano a Europa con idea di studiare, di rubare cultura europea e *poi tornare far una civiltà* . . . nel America" (letter to Carlo Linati, June 6, 1925, *Paige*, #747, p. 2).

21. "Don't be descriptive; remember that the painter can describe a landscape much better than you can, and that he has to know a deal more about it" (*LE*, p. 6).

22. See Pound's "Murder by Capital" (July 1933) for a later formulation of his views on this issue:
    I have blood lust because of what I have seen done to, and attempted against, the arts in my time (*SP*, p. 229).
    The unemployment problem that I have been faced with, for a quarter of a century, is not or has not been the unemployment of nine million or five million . . . , it has been the problem of the unemployment of Gaudier-Brzeska, T. S. Eliot, Wyndham Lewis the painter, E.P. the present writer, and of twenty or thirty musicians, and fifty or more other makers in stone, in paint, in verbal composition.
    If there was (and I admit that there was) a time when I thought this problem could be solved without regard to the common man, humanity in general, the man in the street, the average citizen, etc., I retract, I sing palinode, I apologise (*SP*, p. 230).
    Whatever economic passions I now have, began *ab initio* from having crimes against living art thrust under my perceptions (*SP*, pp. 230–31.)
    . . . C. H. Douglas is the first economist to include creative art and writing in an economic scheme, and the first to give the painter or sculptor or poet a definite reason for being interested in economics; namely, that a better economic system would release more energy for invention and design (*SP*, p. 232).

23. Daniel D. Pearlman, *The Barb of Time: On the Unity of Ezra Pound's "Cantos"* (New York: Oxford Univ. Press, 1969), p. 40.

24. Cf. the similar rationalizations ("What gain with Odysseus, / They that died in the whirlpool") of the Lotophagoi in 20/93–94.

25. "You were not made to live as brute beasts, but to pursue virtue and knowledge" (*Inferno* XXVI.119–20). This is Ulysses exhorting his crew to follow him on what proved to be his disastrous last voyage. Pound alludes to the incident in the *Pisan Cantos*: "You who have passed the pillars and outward from Herakles" (74/425).

26. "The Cid has been exiled on the false charge of malversation of booty taken at a siege . . ." (*SR*, p. 68).

27. Pound begins his new book of cantos by applying Malatesta's personal motto to Jefferson. (An adaptation of Ecclesiastes 3:7, it is carved on Isotta's tomb in the Tempio.) Toward the end of his life, Pound quoted the words at a concert in Rimini, upon being asked to speak (*Pound Era*, p. 560). (See also 9.36.29, where Malatesta is considered "a bit too POLUMETIS.")

28. "... from the time of Tiberius the Italian intelligentzia has been *talking* about draining the swamps" (*J/M*, p. 23).

29. See 81/519:
    George Santayana . . .
    . . . kept to the end of his life that faint *thethear*
    of the Spaniard
    as a grace quasi imperceptible
    as did Muss the *v* for *u* of Romagna.

30. "The secret of the Duce is possibly the capacity to pick out the element of immediate and major importance in any tangle; or, in the case of a man, to go straight to the centre, for the fellow's major interest. 'Why do you want to put your ideas in order?'" (*J/M*, p. 66). Pound was to make much of this other snippet from Mussolini's talk with him. In *GK*, he quotes the words in Italian—"'*Perchè vuol mettere le sue idee in ordine?*'"—as an example of the leader's carrying his thought "unhesitant to the root" (p. 105), and he memorializes the question in 87/569, 89/601, and in 93/626—where he also records his own answer on the occasion: "'Pel mio poema.'" (See Stock, *Life*, pp. 399–401.)

31. See *J/M*, pp. 26–27.

32. Letter to John Drummond, Feb. 18, 1932, *SL*, p. 239.

33. From an article first published in July 1933. (Pound's last sentence continues: "since Cosimo, since what's-his-name, the Elector of Hanover or wherever it was, who was friendly with Leibnitz?")

34. See Stock, *Life*, p. 521, and Barbara C. Eastman, "The Gap in *The Cantos*: 72 and 73," *Paideuma*, 8, (Winter 1979), 415–27. The two cantos were first published in *Marina Repubblicana*, an Italian Navy newspaper, early in 1945. They were republished in 1973, in a pamphlet edition of 25 copies, which were distributed to a number of American and Canadian libraries. (I have examined the copy housed at Yale's Beinecke Library.)

35. The "Torquato" of 74/446. (The *Annotated Index* guesses "Tasso.")

36. *Inferno* XII. 109–10. Ezzelino was the brother of the Cunizza (*Paradiso* IX) who ran off with Sordello. (See 6/22–23, 29/141–42, and *Pisan Cantos, passim*.)

37. Translated from Giovanni Villani's *Cronica* (VI, 73) in Charles S. Singleton, trans., *Inferno* (Princeton Univ. Press, 1970), pt. 2, p. 199.

38. "The Tempio was partly destroyed in the Allied bombing raids of December 28, 1943, and January 29, 1944" (Terrell, *A Companion to the Cantos*, p. 41).

39. In effect, Ezzelino is here doing to Mussato's version of his life what Pound had already done to Pius's assessment of Malatesta.

40. "This poem is exceptional among all of Pound's *Cantos* as the only one to condone violence and to glorify it as 'heroism' in whatever 'cause'" (Eastman, "The Gap in *The Cantos*," p. 424).

41. At the time of composition, Pound evidently believed that the Tempio had been totally destroyed.

42. "This notion of the failed hero . . . is fundamental to the *Cantos*, and is most clearly exemplified in the Malatesta cantos. . . . Indeed, the whole enterprise of the *Cantos* has a dimension of Quixotic pathos which becomes apparent only in the *Pisan Cantos*, where Pound himself emerges as a failed hero, as the 'idealist vanquished'" (Surette, *A Light from Eleusis*, p. 35).

43. "Profile 'to carve Achaia'" (74/444) and " . . . cheek bone, by verbal manifestation" (74/446). (See *PERSONAE*, pp. 198, 200.)

44. A reversal of Eurylochus's words: "nec ivi in harum / Nec in harum ingressus sum" (39/194). (Pound's source is a Latin version of the *Odyssey* by "Samuelis Clarkius" and "Jo. Augustus Ernestus," published in Glasgow in 1814. See *LE*, pp. 265–67, and Terrell, *A Companion to the Cantos*, p. 161.)

45. Pound gave the name "Taishan" (a sacred mountain in China, where sages went to pray) to one of the peaks visible from the cage at Pisa. He thus may be alluding to the death of Dante's Ulysses, who is drowned upon approaching another holy mountain—Mt. Purgatory (*Inferno* XXVI.130–42).

46. Toward the end of *Rock-Drill*, Pound continues the episode by depicting the intervention of the sea-goddess, Leucothoe (95/645, 647), who gives Odysseus her charmed veil ("Then Leucothea had pity"; " 'My bikini is worth yr/ raft'"). He begins *Thrones* with the word for her veil ("Κρήδεμνον") and with her disappearance beneath the waves (96/651), and goes on to record Odysseus's grateful returning of the veil to her (100/716–17)—the entire tale serving as an instance of the outsider being saved by love and beauty.

47. On why he fell in North Carolina, and why it is Dante's Lucifer that is meant, see my "Canto 74: New Light on Lucifer," *Paideuma*, 10 (Fall 1981), 297–301.

48. See also 78/480 and 79/487.

49. Clark Emery, *Ideas Into Action*, p. 159.

50. Ouan Jin, who "spoke and thereby created the named / thereby making clutter," a type of the muzzled poet, "whose mouth was removed by his father" (74/426–27); Philomel, a similar case (82/525); the Villon of "Ballade des Pendus" (74/427); the "Seafarer" poet, whose words Pound uses to record "the companions" he had lost (among them, Yeats, Joyce, and Ford), as predicted by Tiresias in Canto 1 (74/432–33); the mad Ophelia (74/435); the crucified Christ (74/436); the Albigensians massacred at Montségur (76/452); Cassandra (77/475; 78/477); Ixion (80/503); Bertran de Born (80/516; 84/537); Whitman, who, when Pound was in college, was "exotic, still suspect" (82/526); and the other prisoners in the camp (*passim*).

51. In "Pound and Rimbaud," Marjorie G. Perloff says of the style of Cantos 74–84: ". . . the Pisan sequence . . . carries on the mode of the Malatesta Cantos and, indeed, brings that mode to its logical conclusion. Sharply-etched literal images composing flat surfaces, multi-linguistic perspective, syntactic and verbal dislocation—all these features recur in the Pisan Cantos, but now the fragmentation . . . becomes more and more extreme; the basic unit is no longer the verse paragraph or group of lines as in Canto 9, but often the individual line, word group, or even the single ideogram" (p. 112).

52. See Mary de Rachewiltz, *Ezra Pound, Father and Teacher: Discretions* (New York: New Directions, 1971), p. 22.

53. This phrase of dispossession recurs in 80/501 and 83/529.

54. The *Annotated Index* (p. 119) translates "la vecchia sotto S. Pantaleone" ("the old road beneath . . .") as "the old lady under ST. PANTALEONE"!

Pound also remembers the threats exchanged between Sigismondo and Federigo d'Urbino (81/518), and he laments on several occasions the damage done to the Tempio (76/453, 76/459, 80/497).

55. It is ironic that John Adams, the factive personality of Cantos 62–71, has been metamorphosed into Canto 74's prisoner of the American army.

56. Michael Alexander, *The Poetic Achievement of Ezra Pound* (London: Faber, 1979), p. 191.

57. Massimo Bacigalupo, *The Formèd Trace: The Later Poetry of Ezra Pound* (New York: Columbia Univ. Press, 1980), p. 39.

Notes for Appendix A

1. *The Criterion*, 1, 4 (July 1923), 363–84.
2. *A Draft of XVI Cantos* (Paris: Three Mountains Press, 1925).
3. *A Draft of XXX Cantos* (Paris: Hours Press, 1930).
4. *A Draft of XXX Cantos* (New York: Farrar and Rinehart, 1933).
5. *The Cantos* (London: Faber, 1954).

Notes for Appendix B

1. François Villon, *Oeuvres*, ed. Louis Thuasne (Paris: Auguste Picard, 1923), 3 vols., I, p. 191.
2. I found this issue of *Arte e Storia* among Pound's Malatesta papers at Yale's Beinecke Library.

Note for Appendix C

1. After a long return to the deeds of Sigismondo, the scene continues with "And / We sit here . . ."

Selected Bibliography

Pound's Major Sources for the Malatesta Cantos

Banchi, Luciano. "La guerra de' Senesi col Conte di Pitigliano." *Archivio Storico Italiano*, 4, 3 (1879), 184–97.
Battaglini, Angelo. "Della corte letteraria di Sigismondo Pandolfo Malatesta." *Basini Parmensis poetae opera praestantiora*. Rimini, 1794. Vol. 2, pp. 43–255.
Battaglini, Francesco Gaetano. "Della vita e de' fatti di Sigismondo Pandolfo Malatesta." *Basini Parmensis poetae opera praestantiora*. Rimini, 1794. Vol. 2, pp. 259–698.
Broglio, Gaspare. *Cronaca universale*. Unpublished MS, Gambalunga Library, Rimini; photocopy of pp. 148–303r at Beinecke Library, Yale University.
Clementini, Cesare. *Raccolto istorico della fondazione di Rimino e dell' origine e vite de' Malatesti*. Rimini, 1617.
Grigioni, Carlo. "Documenti inediti intorno a Sigismondo Malatesta." *La Romagna* 7 (Aug.-Sept. 1910), 367–83.
―――. "Un capriccio di Sigismondo Malatesta." *Arte e Storia* (Florence) (Mar. 1908), 40–41.
Pius II. *Commentarii*. Frankfurt, 1614.
―――. *Epistolae*. Milan, 1487.
Schultze, Fritz. *Geschichte der Philosophie der Renaissance*. Jena, 1874.
Soranzo, Giovanni. *Pio II e la politica italiana nella lotta contro i Malatesti (1457–1463)*. Padua: Drucker, 1911.
―――. "Un'invettiva della Curia Romana contro Sigismondo Malatesta." *La Romagna* 7 (Nov.-Dec. 1910), 462–89; 8 (Mar.-Apr. 1911), 150–75; 8 (May-June 1911), 241–84.
Tonini, Luigi. *Rimini nella signoria de' Malatesti*. Rimini, 1880.
―――. *Storia civile e sacra di Rimini*. Rimini, 1882.
Yriarte, Charles. *Un condottiere au XVe siècle*. Paris: J. Rothschild, 1882.

Other Works on Sigismondo Malatesta and the Tempio

D'Annunzio, Gabriele. "Commiato" to *Francesca da Rimini. Tragedie sogni e misteri*. Milan: A. Mondadori, 1939. Vol. 1, pp. 708–12.
Hutton, Edward. *Sigismondo Pandolfo Malatesta, Lord of Rimini: A Study of a XV Century Italian Despot*. London: Dent, 1906.
Jones, P. J. *The Malatesta of Rimini and the Papal State: A Political History*. London: Cambridge Univ. Press, 1974.
Ricci, Corrado. *Il tempio malatestiano*. Milan: Bestetti, n.d. [1925].
Stokes, Adrian. *Stones of Rimini*. London: Faber, 1934.

Works by Pound in Editions Cited in the Text

ABC of Reading. New York: New Directions, 1960.
A Lume Spento and Other Early Poems. New York: New Directions, 1965.
Cantos. London: Faber, 1954.
Cantos. New York: New Directions, 1972.
Cantos LXXII and LXXIII. Washington, D. C., 1973. (Copy at Beinecke Library, Yale University.)
Collected Early Poems, ed. Michael King. New York: New Directions, 1976.
Confucius to Cummings: An Anthology of Poetry, ed. with Marcella Spann. New York: New Directions, 1964.
A Draft of XVI Cantos. Paris: Three Mountains Press, 1925.
A Draft of XXX Cantos. Paris: Hours Press, 1930.
A Draft of XXX Cantos. New York: Farrar and Rinehart, 1933.
Gaudier-Brzeska: A Memoir. New York: New Directions, 1970.
Guide to Kulchur. New York: New Directions, 1970.
Jefferson and/or Mussolini. New York: Liveright, 1970.
Literary Essays, ed. T. S. Eliot. New York: New Directions, 1968.
"Malatesta Cantos: Cantos IX to XII of a Long Poem." *Criterion* 1 (July 1923), 363–84.
Pavannes and Divagations. New York: New Directions, 1958.
Personae: The Collected Shorter Poems, rev. ed. New York: New Directions, 1971.
Pound/Joyce: The Letters of Ezra Pound to James Joyce, with Pound's Essays on Joyce, ed. Forrest Read. New York: New Directions, 1967.
Selected Letters, 1907–1941, ed. D. D. Paige. New York: New Directions, 1971.
Selected Prose, 1909–1965, ed. William Cookson. New York: New Directions, 1973.
The Spirit of Romance. New York: New Directions, 1968.
Unpublished letters. Yale University, Beinecke Library. Paige Collection, 601–773.
Unpublished letters to James Sibley Watson, Jr., Jan. 4–5, Mar. 26, May 29, June 27, and Aug. 4, 1923. (Copies furnished by Dr. Watson.)
Unpublished notes and drafts for the Malatesta Cantos. Yale University, Beinecke Rare Book and Manuscript Library, Pound Archive. *Cantos* Folders, 40–70.
Untitled review of *Stones of Rimini* by Adrian Stokes. *Criterion* 13 (April 1934), 495–97.

Works on Ezra Pound and on the Malatesta Cantos

Alexander, Michael. *The Poetic Achievement of Ezra Pound.* London: Faber, 1979.
Bacigalupo, Massimo. *The Formèd Trace: The Later Poetry of Ezra Pound.* New York: Columbia Univ. Press, 1980.
Bernstein, Michael André. *The Tale of the Tribe: Ezra Pound and the Modern Verse Epic.* Princeton Univ. Press, 1980.
Blackmur, R. P. "Masks of Ezra Pound." *Form and Value in Modern Poetry.* Garden City, N. Y.: Doubleday, 1957, pp. 79–112.
Bornstein, Daniel. "The Poet as Historian: Researching the Malatesta Cantos." *Paideuma* 10 (Fall 1981), 283–91.
Bush, Ronald. *The Genesis of Ezra Pound's Cantos.* Princeton Univ. Press, 1976.
Davidson, Peter. "HERACLES & m'la calata." *Paideuma* 8 (Winter 1979), 413–14.
Davie, Donald. *Ezra Pound: Poet as Sculptor.* London: Routledge and Kegan Paul, 1965.
Dekker, George. *Sailing After Knowledge: The Cantos of Ezra Pound.* London: Routledge and Kegan Paul, 1963.
de Rachewiltz, Mary. *Ezra Pound, Father and Teacher: Discretions.* New York: New Directions, 1971.

Drummond, John. "The Italian Background to *The Cantos.*" *An Examination of Ezra Pound,* ed. Peter Russell. Norfolk, Conn.: New Directions, n.d., pp. 100–18.
Eastman, Barbara C. "The Gap in *The Cantos*: 72 and 73." *Paideuma* 8 (Winter 1979), 415–27.
Edwards, John Hamilton, and William W. Vasse. *Annotated Index to the Cantos of Ezra Pound.* Berkeley: Univ. of California Press, 1957.
Emery, Clark. *Ideas into Action: A Study of Pound's Cantos.* Coral Gables, Fla.: Univ. of Miami Press, 1958.
Espey, John. *Ezra Pound's "Mauberley."* Berkeley: Univ. of California Press, 1955.
Flory, Wendy Stallard. *Ezra Pound and "The Cantos": A Record of Struggle.* New Haven: Yale Univ. Press, 1980.
Gallup, Donald. *A Bibliography of Ezra Pound.* London: Rupert Hart-Davis, 1963.
Harper, Michael F. "Truth and Calliope: Ezra Pound's Malatesta." *PMLA* 96 (Jan. 1981), 86–103.
Hesse, Eva. "Books Behind *The Cantos* (Part One: Cantos I-XXX)." *Paideuma* 1 (Winter 1972), 137–51.
Jackson, Thomas H. "The Adventures of Messire Wrong-Head." *ELH* 32 (1965), 238–55.
Kenner, Hugh. *The Poetry of Ezra Pound.* Norfolk, Conn.: New Directions, 1951.
_____. *The Pound Era.* Berkeley: Univ. of California Press, 1971.
Kimpel, Ben D., and T. C. Duncan Eaves. "Pound's Research for the Malatesta Cantos." *Paideuma* 11 (Winter 1982), 406–19.
Libera, Sharon Mayer. "Casting His Gods Back into the NOUS: Two Neoplatonists and *The Cantos* of Ezra Pound." *Paideuma* 2 (Winter 1973), 355–77.
McDougal, Stuart Y. *Ezra Pound and the Troubadour Tradition.* Princeton Univ. Press, 1972.
Makin, Peter. *Provence and Pound.* Berkeley: Univ. of California Press, 1978.
Moramarco, Fred. "The Malatesta Cantos." *Mosaic* 12 (Fall 1978), 107–18.
Norman, Charles. *Ezra Pound.* New York: Funk and Wagnalls, 1969.
Northwestern University, Dept. of English. *The Analyst.* Nos. 5, 7, and 13 by Robert Mayo; No. 11 by Anthony Manganaris-Decavalles.
Pearlman, Daniel D. *The Barb of Time: On the Unity of Ezra Pound's "Cantos."* New York: Oxford Univ. Press, 1969.
Peck, John. "Arras and Painted Arras." *Paideuma* 3 (Spring 1974), 61–66.
Perloff, Marjorie G. "Pound and Rimbaud: The Retreat from Symbolism." *Iowa Review* 6 (Winter 1975), 91–117.
Ruthven, K. K. *A Guide to Ezra Pound's "Personae."* Berkeley: Univ. of California Press, 1969.
Slatin, Myles. "A History of Pound's *Cantos* I-XVI, 1915–1925." *American Literature* 35 (May 1963), 183–95.
Stock, Noel. *The Life of Ezra Pound.* New York: Avon, 1970.
_____. *Reading the Cantos: A Study of Meaning in Ezra Pound.* London: Routledge and Kegan Paul, 1967.
Surette, Leon. *A Light from Eleusis: A Study of Ezra Pound's "Cantos."* Oxford: Clarendon Press, 1979.
Terrell, Carroll F. *A Companion to the Cantos of Ezra Pound.* Berkeley: Univ. of California Press, 1980.
Wilhelm, James J. *Dante and Pound: The Epic of Judgement.* Orono, Maine: Univ. of Maine Press, 1974.

Index

Adams, John, 100, 104, 150 n. 55
Adams, John Quincy, 104
Aeneas, 62
Aeneid (Virgil), 62
Aeschylus, 72
Alberti, Leon Battista, xviii, xix, 2, 12, 13, 15, 28, 61
Aldington, Richard, 6, 7, 57
Alexander IV, 106
Alfonso V of Aragon, xvii, xx, 9, 10, 30, 37, 41, 49, 51, 73, 75, 80, 119
A Lume Spento, 85-87, 145 nn. 5, 6, 146 n. 9
Anjou, René d', xx
Aquabello, Enricho de, 53, 83, 121-22
Aristotle, 33, 69
Arnheim, Rudolf, 138 n. 24
Arnold, Matthew, 68
Atti, Isotta degli, xiv, xviii, xx, xxii, 6, 13, 15, 16, 22, 26, 28, 29, 30, 34, 42, 43, 61, 63, 72, 75, 77, 106, 107, 110, 140 n. 22, 144 n. 63

Badoglio, Pietro, 106
Baker, Carlos, 134 n. 12
Basinio Basini, xviii, xix, 76, 132 n. 13, 140 n. 22
Battaglini, Francesco Gaetano, 3
Beinecke Library (New Haven), xv, xxiii, 7, 134 n. 16
Bellini, Giovanni, xix, xxii, 102
Benjamin, Walter, 67
Benzi, Andreas, xx, 9, 38, 39, 52, 78
Beowulf, 143 n. 58
Bernstein, Michael André, 14, 141 n. 31
Bird, William, 5, 6, 7, 57-58
Blackmur, R.P., xv
Boccaccio, Giovanni, 146 n. 17
Booth, Wayne, 141 n. 23
Borgia, Cesare, xxii
Born, Bertran de, 23, 62, 63, 86-87, 88-90, 113, 138 n. 2, 139 nn. 3, 6, 8, 146 n. 13
Broglio, Gaspare, 3, 4, 10, 14, 19, 52-53, 54, 75, 81, 104, 132 n. 26, 134 n. 16, 137 n. 6, 140 n. 15, 143 n. 53

Browning, Robert, 86, 87, 89, 102
Burckhardt, Jacob, xiii-xiv, 62
Burke, Kenneth, 5

Caesar, Julius, 12, 16
Calixtus III, xx, 119
Cantos LII-LXXI, 127
Capaneus, 109
Carmagnola, Francesco Bussone da, 44
Cathay, 62, 67, 90
Cavalcanti, Guido, 18, 106, 107, 146 n. 17
Cervia, xxi, 11
Cesena, xxi, xxiii, 4, 7, 46, 55, 106
Cid, The, 53, 62, 63, 88, 99, 101-2, 146 n. 12, 147 n. 26
Circe, 100-101, 109
Clementini, Cesare, 3, 9
Commentaries (Pius II), xiv, 3, 35, 78
Conti, Giusto de', xviii, xix
Criterion, The, 5, 6, 7, 52, 57, 135 n. 27
Cronaca universale (Broglio), 3, 4, 10, 53, 54, 104, 134 n. 16, 140 n. 15
Cunard, Nancy, 58
Cunizza da Romano, 148 n. 36

Daniel, Arnaut, 23
D'Annunzio, Gabriele, xiv, 2-3, 56, 61-62, 68, 131 n. 7, 133 n. 6
Dante, xiv, 23, 29, 50, 70, 75, 85, 86, 94, 101, 106, 107, 109, 131 n. 8, 143 n. 51, 146 nn. 13, 17, 149 nn. 45, 47
Davie, Donald, xxii
Dazzi, Manlio Torquato, 4, 7, 106, 148 n. 35
Dekker, George, xxii
de Rachewiltz, Mary, xxiii
De vulgari eloquentia (Dante), 137 n. 55
Dial, The, 1, 2, 3, 4, 5, 31, 33, 135 n. 26
Dionysius of Syracuse, 50, 78
Discipula veritatis (Pius II), xx, 79
Divine Comedy (Dante), 142 n. 41
Divus, Andreas, 135 n. 18, 144 n. 65
Douglas, C.H., 93, 147 nn. 18, 22

Index

Draft of XVI Cantos, xiii, 5, 6-7, 57, 83
Draft of XXX Cantos, xxii, 58, 104, 125-26
Drafts and Fragments, 129
Duccio, Agostino di, xviii, 12, 15

Eccerinis (Mussato), 106
Eleven New Cantos, 103, 126
Eliot, T.S., xix, 5, 6, 21, 23, 25, 27, 47, 48-49, 57, 59, 69, 112, 123-24, 136 n. 53, 137 nn. 54, 55, 60
Emery, Clark, 110
Este, Borso d', 30, 36, 55, 80
Este, Ginevra d', xiv, xvi, 22, 29, 36, 61, 76, 137 n. 7
Este, Niccolò d', xvi, 143 n. 55
Eugenius IV, xvii
"Exile's Letter," 95-96
Ezzelino da Romano, 106-7, 148 nn. 36, 39

Fano, xvi, xxi, xxii, 5, 9, 46, 50, 64, 82, 110
Ferdinand I of Naples, xx, 17, 80, 132 n. 12
Ficino, Marsilio, 83
Fiesole, Mino da, xix, 2
Fifth Decad of Cantos, 126-27
Foscari, Francesco, 4, 38, 53, 63
Francesca da Rimini, 22, 29, 35, 50, 109, 143 n. 55
Francesca da Rimini (D'Annunzio), xiv, 61-62
Francesca, Piero della, xviii, xix, xxii, 2, 12, 26, 28, 102, 137 n. 57
Frederick II, 85

Galla Placidia, 23, 24, 25, 48, 123
Gambalunga Library (Rimini), 3, 4
Gaudier-Brzeska, Henri, 93, 146 n. 13
Gemisthus Plethon, xxi, 15, 20, 28, 29, 35, 49-50, 73, 78, 106, 137 nn. 4, 59, 142-43 n. 50, 144 n. 68
Gonzaga, Carlo, 51
Guide to Kulchur, 11, 103
Guillaume Poictiers, 18, 22, 28, 34

Hannibal, 16, 43
Harper, Michael F., 144 n. 69
Hartman, Geoffrey, 139 n. 8
Helen of Troy, 72
Hemingway, Ernest, 3-4
Heroides (Ovid), 140 n. 22
Hesperis (Basinio), xviii, 140 n. 22
Homage to Sextus Propertius, 62, 90-93, 96, 98, 113, 146 n. 16
Homer, 95, 141 nn. 23, 24, 145 n. 73
Horace, 25, 91, 146 n. 16
Hugh Selwyn Mauberley, 23, 62, 92-95, 96-99, 107
Hulme, T.E., 87, 93
Hutton, Edward, xv, 19
Huysmans, Joris-Karl, 98

Iliad (Homer), 95, 135 n. 18, 140 n. 22, 141 n. 24
"Indiscretions," 143 n. 60
Inferno (Dante), xiv, 23, 29, 88, 89, 109, 131 n. 8, 143 n. 55, 147 n. 25, 149 n. 45
Isottaeus (Basinio), 132 n. 13, 140 n. 22

Jackson, Thomas H., 63
Jefferson, Thomas, 6, 100, 103-4
Jones, P.J., xiv, xvi, xvii, xx, xxii

Kenner, Hugh, xv, 48, 58, 83, 93, 141 n. 22, 147 n. 18

Landor, Walter Savage, 144 n. 64
Lodi, Treaty of, xix
Lowell, Amy, 143 n. 54
Lucifer, 109, 149 n. 47
Lustra, 90

Machiavelli, Niccolò, xxii-xxiii
Malatesta, Carlo, xv
Malatesta da Verrucchio, xv, 22, 29
Malatesta, Domenico (Malatesta Novello), xv, xx, xxi, 4, 11, 18-19, 30, 37, 40, 41, 50, 55, 58, 64
Malatesta, Galeazzo, xvi, 13, 30, 36, 37, 53, 72, 74
Malatesta, Galeotto Roberto, xv, xvi
Malatesta, Gianciotto, 22, 29
Malatesta, Paolo, 22, 29, 35, 50, 109, 143 n. 55
Malatesta, Parisina, xvi, 29, 143 n. 55
Malatesta, Roberto, xvi, xxi, 82, 121
Malatesta, Sallustio, xxii, 11, 16, 42
Malatesta, Sigismondo Pandolfo, xiii-xxii, 2, 8-9, 12-14, 16-17, 20, 22, 34, 38-39, 44, 52, 85, 92, 94, 95, 99, 102-3, 105, 106, 107, 108, 110, 111, 112-13, 120-22, 132 nn. 12, 14, 23, 143 n. 54
"Malatesta Cantos," xiii, xxii, xxiii, 63-83, 102-3, 105, 112-13; allusions to in *Cantos,* 125-29; censorship of, 7; early versions of, 12-31, 58-59; late versions of, 52-56, 59, 135 n. 19; publication of, 5-6, 57-58; reading notes for, 7-11; research for, xiv-xv, 1-4; sources for, 119-22; textual variants of, 115-17; "Watson Typescript," 3, 16, 31, 33-51, 123-24
Malatestine Library (Cesena), 4, 7, 106
Manetti, Gianozzo, xvii
Manfred, 70, 85
Manfredi, Astorre, 50, 75
Mantua, Congress of, xx, 12, 80
Marinetti, Filippo Tommaso, 106
Martin V, xv
Martz, Louis L., 146 n. 10
Medici, Alessandro de', 70, 142 n. 36
Medici, Cosimo de', 17, 26, 30
Medici, Giovanni de', 25, 26, 35, 49

Medici, Lorenzo de', 49
Medici, Pier Francesco de', 120
Metaphysics (Aristotle), 33
Milton, John, 107
Montefeltro, Guido da, 109
"Murder by Capital," 147 n. 22
Mussato, Albertino, 106
Mussolini, Benito, 100, 104-5, 106, 107, 108, 112, 148 nn. 29, 30

"Near Perigord," 88-89, 146 n. 13
Nicholas of Cusa, xx, 144 n. 71
Nuti, Matteo, 41

Odysseus, 53, 54, 62, 72, 94, 95, 99, 100-101, 102, 103, 108-9, 112, 141 n. 23, 149 n. 46
Odyssey (Homer), 99-100, 109, 141 n. 23, 149 n. 44
Ovid, 146 n. 17

Pandoni, Porcelio de', 76, 140 n. 22
Panofsky, Erwin, xxii
Paradiso (Dante), 148 n. 36
Pasti, Matteo da, xviii, 15, 41, 80, 144 n. 63
Paul II, xiv, xxi, xxii, 2, 4, 20, 30, 45, 46, 52, 55, 56, 73, 74, 82, 132 n. 28
Peri Bathous (Pope), 66
Perloff, Marjorie, 67, 149 n. 51
Pesaro, xvi-xvii, xviii, xxii, 4, 5, 13, 29, 30, 36, 37, 38, 53, 54, 64, 72, 74, 75
Petrarch, xxii
Piccinino, Giacomo, xx, 17, 26, 45, 55, 80, 140 n. 22
Pisan Cantos, 84, 99, 107-12, 127-28, 142-43 n. 50, 149 n. 51
Pisanello, xix, xxii, 2, 12, 15
Pitigliano, Count of, xix, 39, 43-44, 51, 78
Pius II (Aeneas Silvius Piccolomini), xiv, xvi, xvii, xviii, xx, xxi, xxiii, 3, 6, 9, 12, 13, 19, 22, 29, 30, 35, 36, 38, 39, 45, 50, 51, 54, 63, 68, 73, 74, 77, 78-80, 112, 132 nn. 12, 23, 135 n. 31, 141 n. 29
Pius XI, 142 n. 49
Platina, xxi, 2, 73, 82
Plato, 50, 78, 83
Plutarch, 8
Pope, Alexander, 66
Pope-Hennessy, John, 132 n. 16
Portrait of the Artist (Joyce), 93
Poseidon, 73, 100, 109, 142-43 n. 50
Pound, Dorothy, 3, 4, 23
Pound, Ezra: *A Lume Spento,* 85-87, 145 nn. 5, 6, 146 n. 9; *Cantos:* **1,** 100-101, 144 n. 65; **2,** 1, 6, 68, 72; **3,** 24, 63, 101-2; **7,** 57, 70, 72; **8-11,** xiii-xv, xxii-xxiii, 1-31, 33-59, 63-83, 102-3, 105, 112-13, 115-17, 119-22, 125-29, 135 n. 19; **12,** 1, 56, 133 n. 35; 1; **13,** 1; **14;** 1,
73; **21,** 103; **31,** 103-4; **41,** 104-5; **72,** 105-7, 127, 148 n. 34; **73,** 105-7, 127, 148 nn. 34, 40; **74,** 108-9; *Cantos LII-LXXI,* 127; *Cathay,* 62, 67, 90; "*Dial* Letter" (Feb. 1922), 1; "*Dial* Letter" (Nov. 1922), 2, 5; *Draft of XVI Cantos,* xiii, 5, 6-7, 57, 83; *Draft of XXX Cantos,* xxii, 58, 104, 125-26; *Drafts and Fragments,* 129; *Eleven New Cantos,* 103, 126; "Exile's Letter," 95-96; *Fifth Decad of Cantos,* 126-27; *Guide to Kulchur,* 11, 103; *Homage to Sextus Propertius,* 62, 90-93, 96, 98, 113, 146 n. 16; *Hugh Selwyn Mauberley,* 23, 62, 92-95, 96-99, 107; "Indiscretions," 143 n. 60; *Lustra,* 90; "Murder by Capital," 147 n. 22; "Near Perigord," 88-89, 146 n. 13; *Pisan Cantos,* 84, 99, 107-12, 127-28, 142-43 n. 50; 149 n. 51; *Rock-Drill,* 128, 149 n. 46; "Seafarer," 67, 88, 95-96, 100; "Sestina: Altaforte," 88-90; *Thrones,* 112, 128-29, 149 n. 46
Pre-Raphaelites, 87
Purgatorio (Dante), 85, 140 n. 17, 142 n. 35, 143 n. 51

Quinn, John, xix, 1, 2, 132 n. 18

Reinach, Salomon, 97, 98
Rime (Petrarch), xxii
Rimini, xvi, xviii, xxi, xxii, xxiii, 1, 2, 4, 11, 26, 102, 104, 107, 134 n. 16
Rock-Drill, 149 n. 46
Roman Academy, 73, 132 n. 28
Rossetti, Dante Gabriel, 86
Rudge, Olga, 110

S. Apollinare in Classe, xviii, 6, 22, 38, 41, 52, 53
Santayana, George, 148 n. 29
Sappho, 142 n. 40
Schultze, Fritz, 142 n. 50
Scipio, Publius Cornelius, 10, 136 n. 45
Scratton, Bride, 21, 23, 47, 49, 136 n. 53
"Seafarer, The," 67, 88, 95-96, 100
"Sestina: Altaforte," 88-90
Sforza, Alessandro, xvi, xviii, xx, 13-14, 36, 37, 38, 53, 74
Sforza, Drusiana, 17, 26
Sforza, Francesco, xvi, xvii, xviii, 4, 9, 10, 13-14, 17, 26, 30, 34, 36, 37, 38, 40, 52-53, 54, 68, 73, 74, 75, 80, 143 n. 51
Sforza, Polissena, xiv, xvi, xvii, 9-10, 22, 29, 36, 61, 137 n. 7
Shakespeare, William, 86, 98
Shapiro, Karl, xxiii
Shelley, Percy Bysshe, 146 n. 9
Sigismondo Pandolfo Malatesta (Hutton), xv
Slatin, Myles, 135 n. 30
Soncinus, Hieronymous, xxii
Sorano, xix, 43, 72, 76, 78

Soranzo, Giovanni, xxii, 3, 4, 9, 80, 119-20, 132 nn. 23, 26, 134 n. 10, 135 n. 31
Sordello, 148 n. 36
Sordello (Browning), 89
Stock, Noel, 134 n. 12, 138 n. 25, 147 n. 18
Strater, Henry, 5, 6
Strozzi, Filippo, 41, 44
Surette, Leon, 139 n. 14, 148 n. 42
Swinburne, Algernon Charles, 86, 146 n. 10
Symonds, John Addington, xiii, 62
Symons, Arthur, 97

Tempio Malatestiano (Rimini), xiii, xiv, xv, xviii, xxi, xxii, 13, 14, 15, 20, 21, 22, 24, 25, 28, 30, 34, 41-42, 43, 56, 58, 61, 63, 70, 75, 77-78, 102, 106, 107, 113, 132 nn. 14, 16, 134 n. 16, 143 n. 50, 144 n. 68, 147 n. 27, 148 nn. 38, 41, 149 n. 54
Thayer, Scofield, 5, 31
Thiy (Ti), 23, 25, 48, 123, 136 n. 53
Thrones, 112, 128-29, 149 n. 46
Tiresias, 100-101
Trachulo, 16-17, 42, 43, 51
Turner, J.M.W., 98

Uberti, Farinata degli, 109

Ugolino, Count, 109
Ulysses (Joyce), 142 n. 41
Urbino, Federigo d', xvi, xvii, xviii, xx, xxi, 9, 13, 19, 25, 30, 36, 38, 45, 52, 53, 68, 74, 78, 82, 120, 140 nn. 17, 22, 143 n. 54

Valturio, Roberto, xvii, xviii, 75
Van Buren, Martin, 104
Vatican Archives, 4
Vidal, Piere, 145 n. 7
Villon, François, 86, 88, 119
Virgil, 91, 92, 142 n. 47, 146 n. 16
Visconti, Bianca, 4, 10, 26, 28
Visconti, Filippo Maria, xvii

Waste Land, The (Eliot), 5, 21, 22, 23, 27, 33, 48, 69
Watson, James Sibley, Jr., 3, 4, 5, 31, 33, 57, 69, 133 n. 8, 135 n. 17
"Watson Typescript," 3, 16, 31, 33-51, 57, 123-24
Wharton, Edith, 5
Whitman, Walt, 88, 90
Wilde, Oscar, 98

Yeats, William Butler, 86, 134 n. 12
Yriarte, Charles, 3, 42, 49, 57, 78, 133-34 n. 9